Also by Charles Jennings

Up North: Travels Beyond the Watford Gap
People Like Us: A Season Among the Upper Classes
Greenwich: The Place Where Days Begin and End

Fathers' Race

A Book About Paternity

Charles Jennings

An *Abacus* Book

First published in Great Britain by
Little, Brown and Company in 1999
This edition published by Abacus in 2000

A CIP catalogue record for this book
is available from the British Library.

ISBN 0 349 11135 9

Typeset in Bembo by
Palimpsest Book Production Limited,
Polmont, Stirlingshire
Printed and bound in Great Britain by
Clays Ltd, St Ives plc.

Abacus
A Division of
Little, Brown and Company (UK)
Brettenham House
Lancaster Place
London WC2E 7EN

To my Mother and Father

PREFACE

Two photographs of me: one taken in the year before I became a father; the other taken a month ago. In the earlier one, apart from sporting a pair of remarkable Eighties adman-style big spectacles in tortoiseshell plastic and a red and grey striped T-shirt (those vivacious Eighties colours), I have a huge crown of dark umber hair, as big as a fun wig, and pale pinkish unblemished skin. We are in the back garden of my parents' old house on a pleasant midsummer day. Apart from a faint shadowing under the eyes, I seem to bear no marks of age or experience. Those same eyes, half-closed in the beginnings of a lazy smile, suggest that everything for me is just fine. Nothing can go wrong, for as far ahead as the imagination can project. I look about twelve.

The second picture shows a middle-aged man apparently about to pull a knife on the photographer, or at least hurl some kind of intensely personal abuse. Me again, but now seen in the living-room of our house in southwest London. The bouffant hair of eleven years earlier has been replaced with a spikey *maquis* of tufts, the umber now frosted around the temples with bristles of grey, the bent fleshy lobe of one ear poking out into the cold. My skin is blotched and sandpaper-coarse. I have two deep lines like callipers running down from my (hooked) nose to the corners of my mouth. A pair of leathery jowls are thinking about getting it together to transform the outline of my head from that of a neatly rounded triangle to that of an old overnight bag. The specs too are smaller, wire-rimmed, neurotic. But the eyes are the worst. Not only are they sunk into olive-grey pools whose margins run off somewhere by my cheekbones, they have cicatrices and score marks radiating out from them and a look of startled hostility deep in their centre. Part of this is a natural reaction I have to being photographed, but most of it is down to some inner derangement, some chronic personal suffering that I have yet to come to terms with and possibly never will. And I have a bow tie tied round my neck, made for me by my younger son Tim out of string and red foam rubber.

How could it have all gone so wrong? How could anyone let themselves go so badly? The answer is so commonplace, so quotidian, it's hardly worth giving: fatherhood.

And this is how it happened.

Eleven years ago, when Susie and I first embarked on the madcap adventure of pregnancy, test kits were a farce. Modern pregnancy test kits work by detecting the presence of the hormone HCG – human chorionic gonadotrophin – a product of the family of peptides associated with reproduction. Nowadays, the presence of HCG in the urine, and therefore the probable pregnancy of the tester, is indicated in test kits by means of, say, the appearance of a clear blue line against a white background – the entire assay apparatus contained in an easy-to-hold plastic stick or wand. The chemistry of such test kits is both accurate and reliable, and in many cases doesn't require the use of the first urine of the day. Test kits are easily managed, quick-acting and relatively robust. Pregnancy testing nowadays is a triumph of long-term research and development. But eleven years ago, determining your condition was as awkward and time-consuming as repairing a wristwatch.

We had this thing which not only required Susie to bottle her pee, but then to tip a tiny quantity of it into a test tube. The test tube had a sort of impacted powder at the bottom and was held in a miniature plastic gantry with a mirror just below the bottom of the tube, angled at forty-five degrees so that you could see whatever was at the very end of the tube without having to lift it to the height of your nose and squint into it.

This last point was important, because what Susie and I were looking for was a sediment which formed if you were pregnant. In fact, the diagram in the (dauntingly thick) instruction booklet showed a symbolism-rich bull's-eye: a dark, solid inner full stop, surrounded by an outer, lighter ring, surrounded by a final, dark ring. Like an Air Force roundel, but in ochre and saffron. This is what was reflected in the mirror at the bottom of the gantry. If you weren't pregnant, all you got was a cloudy yellow disc, no inner or outer ring. But then you could get the same effect as a negative test by unintentionally jiggling a positive test so that the darker shapes got mixed up in the lighter ring. It was critically important not to do so much as fart near the test kit in case you disturbed it and muddied the result. And it took half an hour to appear.

So Susie got up one morning, went off to the bathroom, peed, came back. I can remember lying painfully half-asleep, waiting for the performance to finish, my stomach in knots. It was early spring and quite light. We fell asleep again, and then jerked awake at eight, staring into the middle distance. The test was an intended test, it was part of a rationally instigated plan to start a family – but when the crunch came, all we could feel was a sense of the world tilting blearily on its axis, of some awful, reckless lurch into the void.

At that moment, we came up against the truths of life and death and biological purpose, while the suburban world went on as usual outside and our neighbour's gutter leaked into our wall. We were helpless, having placed ourselves in the presence of something more awesomely real than anything we had experienced before, more real than sex or drink or summer holidays or crashing the car or having a great time or Christmas or work or going to the cinema or losing your job or falling in love or being ill or buying a house or any of the interesting things we'd done up to then. We had pink frilly covers on the pillows in those days. God knows why. I fiddled with the frill to try and quell my fingers.

Eventually Susie couldn't stand it any more and went back into the bathroom. She screamed. I caught the mood and screamed as well and bolted out of bed to see what she had seen. And there it was: the Air Force roundel, ochres and saffron, winking at us from the little mirror. We had created life, but we were absolutely not to jump or hug each other or ourselves, in case we bumped into the phial of piss on the bathroom table. We left the bathroom to have a celebratory cup of coffee, then minced back in every five minutes to re-examine the roundel. Finally Brownian motion saw to it that it faded away. Looking back, I suppose I'm not unhappy that we had to do it this way. The whole performance had something of a sacramental drama about it, a ritual charged with significance, the little plastic gantry taking on an iconic meaning. All in all, maybe it was better than peeing over a stick. We felt pride, indignity, hysteria, a vacant heroism. We were obsessed with urine. In many ways, this made it a fair introduction to parenthood.

Why does anyone start a family? Why did we do it? Baroness Thatcher was to blame, as in so many things. One of the great features of the mid-1980s was the apparent endlessness of money.

We decided that because the rewards of the Lawson boom were flowing in and showed no signs of ever flowing out again, we were in a position to have a child. We'd just moved into a house large enough for more than two adults and I can remember capering around our shit-brown drawing-room (brown walls, toxic brown carpeting, brown Seventies shelf units, all left by the despairing previous owner) and suddenly being flooded with the sense that *now*, at the age of twenty-eight (seems so *young*, now), this thing, this most unimaginable of actions, was possible. There Susie was, there I was, there the money was. We knew that, fertility and accidents aside, the most important things about having a child were (a) the capacity to love it, and (b) the capacity to pay for it. And in those days, with the Stock Market going exponentially up and hordes of Tories baring their teeth at us in the newspapers and on TV, it seemed that whatever kind of society our child might be born into, we could at least afford to buy it shoes.

There were, of course, other compelling reasons to make it happen. Our friends, for instance, started to have children. I can remember the first time I saw – I mean, really *looked at* – one of these new homunculi, as opposed to merely passing one in the street or glimpsing one in the arms of a cousin (never an especially fertile family, at my generational level there was really only me and my brother, and he'd ruled it out). I was standing in a front room in Clapham when two people who, up to then, had been our friends, our coevals, pursuing a similar course through life, suddenly produced their very new baby daughter. I was both impressed and appalled. Laurie Lee catches the presence of a neonate pretty well when he describes his own baby in *I Can't Stay Long*: 'When awake, and not feeding, she snorts and gobbles, dryly, like a ruminative jackdaw, or strains and groans and waves her hands about as though casting invisible nets.' This baby, too, was wrinkled and groping and snuffling and not really human. There was something ju-ju about it, with its frizz of dark hair, its unearthly, fragile skin, its ET movements and gestures. I knew that I was meant to admire it and praise it to its dazed, weepy parents, but I couldn't even begin to think of what to say about it. I had no comparisons to draw on, no critical terms available. I was so far from knowing anything about babies that apart from stating the blindingly obvious ('She's very small'; 'She has all her fingers and toes') the best I could do was leer at it approvingly.

What's more, the mere presence of this thing seemed to have changed the nature of a room I used to feel relatively at home in. Instead of having beat-up yellowish walls and an almost indescribable, adult, human mess of newspapers, coffee mugs, fags, picture frames, paperbacks and tapes littering its surfaces (as if a poltergeist had just dropped by), it was now bathed in a kind of glow of sanctity, a solemnity, a sort of unkempt holiness.

Then the child started to turn red, the colour of infection, and I said, 'Why's she gone so red?'

'Well, when do *you* turn red?' quizzed the mother back at me.

I sat and thought for a moment. 'When I get angry?'

'When you want to do a *poo*,' she finally said.

'Oh, *right*,' I said. *Nursery speak*, I thought. *How shocking*.

Susie, on the other hand, understood what it was she was looking at. Somehow she could tell that this was a nice baby. She could read things into its minuscule fingers and flawless skin and big, alien, liquid eyes. Looking back, I can also see that it was in the first seconds of holding this child that she became broody. From then on, it wasn't a question of if but when. A light came into her eyes as she held the child, a kind of super-acquisitiveness I'd never seen before. I know that she'd been thinking – we'd both been thinking – about the prospect of children, but I suppose that must have been the point at which the idea became valid.

For me, it was much more part of an accumulation of sensations and ideas that finally pushed me over the edge. I wasn't much taken with the physical reality of the babies that started to appear at this time (once one couple started, in the space of a couple of months everyone was at it, like infectious vomiting in a crowd). But I was impressed by the aura they conferred on their parents. Babies made it appear that these people, my contemporaries, had leap-frogged into a new and superior state of being. They looked as if they'd added an interesting and maturing component to their lives, something which enhanced their grip on the world, something which completed the full set of adult characteristics and (I inferred from somewhere) made them better able to be in the world. Perhaps it was just the shock of hearing people the same age as me being referred to as *father*, or talking about *poo* which did it, that sudden vaulting of the generations. But however it was, they had become bigger people. There was something fundamentally socialising about children, and I envied it.

At the same time, I knew that it also had a lot to do with vanity. Bertrand Russell asserts that wanting to have children contains 'an egoistic element, which is very dangerous: the hope that one's children may succeed where one had failed, that they may carry on one's work when death or senility puts an end to one's own efforts, and in any case, that they will supply a biological escape from death, making one's own life part of the whole stream, and not a mere stagnant puddle without any overflow into the future'. As well as advertising to the world that you're a completely functional man with working testicles and incorporating you into the fold of fully-realised adults (those, that is, with children), kids contain this kinkily seductive notion of continuity, of packaging your genes up for a further generation. The reality, the here-and-now of children, brings out an atavistic side in most parents. But the *concept* of offspring goes beyond mere atavism and occasionally drifts into the kind of megalomaniac fantasy that prompts you to think of dynasties, heritage, the endlessly procreating bloodline. Babies in the flesh make you feel like a kind of jittery caveman, connecting you with some buried, barely understood proto-past. The idea of children connects you with the infinite potential of the future, makes you feel visionary, scheming. I've never been particularly fond of the surname *Jennings* (lacks incisiveness, too much like someone trying to speak with their mouth full of cheese) but I suddenly liked the idea of my child bearing this name as a monument to my remarkable past. Indeed, at moments when my guard has slipped, I've found myself rampantly and tastelessly declaring to others that my boys are *the best things I've ever done*.

So we started. And what do you know but, after a couple of months of activity, there we were, staring at the little brown Air Force roundel, wondering whether this meant that we were at last grown-up.

Several weeks later we were in a hospital, trapped in a sort of Luis Buñuel scenario – surreal, slightly perverse – as this middle-aged man, dressed in a dark blue chalkstripe suit and wearing the hospital consultant's habitual foppish affectation of a spotted bow tie, bore down on Susie. She had been required to remove all her lower garments and lie down on a rubber-sheeted bed. I was sitting on a chair, about halfway down the length of the bed, feeling useless and emasculated. He pulled on a transparent plastic glove, stuck his hand up my wife and started to talk to me about fishing.

This is what happens. Pregnancy is a long-drawn-out emergency,

and in an emergency, society sanctions aberrant behaviour. Strangers
– in this case, an obstetrician in a London hospital, doing one of
his routine checks – come and interfere fundamentally with your
wife *and there is nothing you can do about it.*

'You much of a one for fishing?' He jerked his head my way. I
let my mouth fall open and managed to say that, no, I wasn't.

'I do it as often as I can,' he went on, momentarily frowning
with concentration. 'I go with my son. Fly-fishing. You're not a
fly-fisherman, then?'

I could feel Susie's reaction going on just behind me, silently. I
didn't even have to turn my head. She was irradiating me. I started
to try and piece together a form of words by which I might suggest
to the doctor that he should address some thoughts to his patient
– *not* patient, that word was proscribed, part of the corrupting
medicalisation of childbirth – to his *client*, and ask her how she
felt and was she quite happy to go along with this treatment? Or
was it something she found both humiliating and ludicrous? But he
read my shameful passivity correctly and was already ahead of me.

'Trouble is, you have to get up so early in the morning. We
like to go down to the Test. It's a super river. Do you know
Hampshire at all?'

He had at least partly drawn the curtains round the bed, so that
not every passing rubbernecker could take a peek. But there was
still daylight flooding from one corner.

'Just stay like that for a second, will you? Caught a four-pounder
last week.'

'Is everything okay?' said Susie, miles away at the other end of
the bed.

'Yes, yes. Nothing to worry about,' said the consultant, *winking*
at her: one of those staggering infelicities which male doctors
– what? Learn by rote at medical school? Have some genetic

predisposition towards – the same gene which prompts them to become doctors? It's one of those actions which is simultaneously patronising, uninformative, anxiety-provoking and stupid. I mean, this person was an obstetrician – he spent his working life with his hands up women, inside women, delivering their babies. You'd think he'd have found a way of putting things that wasn't quite so off-hand, so insulting.

But then, it's also part of his job to put women into a position where any sort of intelligent exchange is impossible. You'd have to be lacking in self-consciousness to an almost pathological degree – at the level of, say, Salvador Dali or Jerry Lewis – to be able to have a serious conversation while your hips are in the air and a stranger is prodding your uterus with his fingers and making little humming noises to himself and talking to your partner about fly-fishing. And I guess that most consultants simply don't want to take the risk of exploring your psychopathology in this way. The male equivalent of having a pregnancy check-up would (I imagine) involve making a visit to a fantastically casual proctologist: one who busied himself up your problematical arse in front of a roomful of other patients while chatting with your wife about the best way to cook aubergines, or visa requirements for visiting the States. It is a human interaction in which you do your best to remove the element of humanity.

And in all this, I was no more use than a paperclip. Trapped between Susie's wordless incandescence and the consultant's hotel-bar logorrhoea I just opened and closed my mouth in a succession of non-committal *moues*. But then this made me part of a male complicity with the obstetrician: witnessing and raising no objection. Thus I mutely tolerated that male approach to doctoring which gave us all the horrible things that enrage childbirth experts like Sheila Kitzinger – enemas, shaving, deliberate starvation (a practice popular in the late 1940s, until it was finally recognised that starved babies died more than fed ones), deliberate refrigeration of newborn babies (popular in the 1950s, until it too, was recognised to be fatal), scientific formula milk, oxytocin abuse. My silence was a tacit involvement in this scheme of things and I don't know whether Susie has ever quite forgiven me. I do know, however, that in a recent newspaper interview a woman called Prunella Briance recalled how, when three months pregnant, she was told that she was going to be internally examined by a group of *thirteen* medical students: 'When I objected, the matron said, "This is the National Health Service and you do as you are told"'. This took place during the 1950s, and Ms Briance was so outraged by this crassness that she went off and founded what subsequently became the National Childbirth Trust. Thirty years on and something qualitatively similar was going on with me, Susie and the doctor.

Towards the end, the obstetrician paused and turned to me thoughtfully.

'Tell me,' he said, 'where do you get your car serviced?'

But we'd gone to this hospital because Sheila Kitzinger had told us to. At least, she'd recommended the place in her book *The New Good Birth Guide*, and when Kitzinger passes any kind of value judgment, it's not so much an opinion, more an imperative.

She is a terrifying and vital force. Indeed, Kitzinger is one of the twin lodestars of pregnant middle-class couples (the other is Penelope Leach: I tend to muddle the two up in my nightmares, in which they fuse into a single, intensely robust, competitively clever grandma academic with spectacles and frown lines arcing across her face; although, in fairness, Kitzinger at least looks more grandmotherly in her photos than Leach does). Not as universally famed as the late Benjamin Spock with his *Common Sense Book of Baby and Child Care*, Kitzinger is nonetheless regarded in Britain, at least, as a touchstone in matters of obstetrics, pediatrics and the general health of families. This means that, working from a basis of social anthropology (her formal degree at Oxford), she now encompasses breastfeeding, comparative motherhood, medical culture (one of her books recently drew this comment: 'Kitzinger's fire . . . is erratic and wild . . . she hates male, Western doctors so much she cannot admit that there is any beneficial side to their work'), birth at home, birth over thirty, and the condition of grandmotherhood (for *Becoming A Grandmother*, on the other hand: 'Buoyantly user-friendly guide' ran the review, from 'a delighted and involved grandmother'). Her reach is phenomenal.

And Kitzinger was the one with the *Birth Guide*, the immediately relevant one, the one that told you about which hospital in your local health authority area to opt for and, yes, the palpable terribleness of the medical profession ('Modern obstetrics treats a woman's body as a machine which is constantly going wrong and the workings of which only the doctor can understand'). We stared at this book for hours, trying to second-guess the best hospital for us to check into. Penelope Leach was, at this time, no more than a minatory shape on the bookshelves, as was *The Modern Book Of Babies' Names*. But Sheila loomed over us – as she looms over thousands of families.

The *Birth Guide* was basically a review, like *The Good Food Guide* or *What Hi-Fi?*, only hospitals were its obsession and there were no pictures. It worked through all the big institutions in the UK, awarding two stars for somewhere good and no stars for somewhere that had made Kitzinger draw her breath in sharply. We read this thing and re-read it, trying to conjure the hospitals and their staff off the pages, trying to connect mystically with them through the dry textual sense of Kitzinger's prose, trying to come to terms with a style which tries to be both consoling and supportive to the expectant mother, and balefully no-nonsense when dealing with clinical procedures.

There is, frankly, nothing emollient in Kitzinger's voice. Empowerment, for her, is all about being blunt: 'rectal', 'uterine', 'demand', 'dominating', 'flailing', and 'barrage' pepper her text like gunshots. By speaking without euphemism, she accustoms her readers to the truth of childbirth at the same time as she spooks them into greater agitation than they felt at the outset. This has the result that they – we – then consult her even more strenuously, searching for reassurance. The book turned into a kind of sacred text; something the Christian Gnostics might have wrestled with. And whenever we thought we'd reached some kind of balance, some kind of responsible level-headedness about what we were embarking on, we'd come across these terrible anecdotes about episiotomies and enemas ('A woman told me recently that when she said that she would prefer not to have one, her obstetrician exclaimed: "Not have an enema? There will be shit on the walls, shit in me boots, shit everywhere!"') and would lapse into spirals of depression.

Pregnancy for a man is a phoney war, in which – you hope – all the little alarms and unpleasantnesses (like visiting the consultant) are subsumed into a slow, dithering preparation for an event you can't properly anticipate or imagine. Studying Kitzinger was about as intense and emotionally racking as it got. Otherwise, life went on as before. Susie went on running her research business and I sat at home, turning out pieces for the *Daily Telegraph*, *Times*, *Evening Standard* – anyone who rang my phone, basically – and felt simultaneously nervous and complacent. My friends were pleasantly upbeat about the prospect of my being about to become a father: some out of a genuine sense of approval, others because they were just beginning to toy with the same idea and wanted to see what happened to me before they committed themselves, and a third group – those who were already fathers – welcoming the support I brought by swelling their numbers. Only one person sounded downbeat (a woman friend, oddly), warning me not to 'people the earth with Calibans'. I still don't know what she meant by that.

Occasionally in this pleasant afternoon-time existence we moved up a gear and went out to buy a cot, or some feeding bottles. This meant strange hours at Mothercare, light-headedly inspecting the goods as if they were imported from another planet, guessing at how they might work, how one would feel with these colourful, plasticky things in one's adult house of glass and wood. But the rest of the time we just did what couples do. We went out, heedlessly. We stayed in bed all day if we wanted to. We went abroad and we went for walks. We spontaneously listened to records, read books, went to the movies. We thought as much about the tenor of our lives as we did about the weather. I don't think we once stopped to consider that these were the last days in which we would ever be able to do these things again.

Eventually we found the entry in the *Birth Guide* for the West London Hospital, in the Hammersmith Road. 'Decrepit, antiquated, off-putting building,' it began, but immediately brightened up after that. 'Labour,' it announced: 'No shave/enema.' Anaesthetist was a 'tower of strength.' Partner 'can attend.'

The West London was small (all it had, in fact, was antenatal and, well, natal – apart, portentously enough, from a ward full of dying geriatrics; like something out of Goya) and its walls were mottled with damp attacks and the outside of the building was littered with huge, damaged gas bottles and was held together with chicken netting. Its antenatal reception area had precisely that NHS-makes-do quality – expressed through a wasteground of soiled plastic toys and defective indoor children's-slides – that makes you wonder why you don't simply piss off and live in Germany. Someone had gone round with a revolver ten years earlier and shot all the corners off the doorways. After dark, the hospital name in wobbly red neon made it look like a Soviet bloc hotel.

It was also under a permanent closure threat from the local health authority because of its size. Being small (a mere forty or so beds) and surrounded by other, bigger institutions (Queen Charlotte's Hospital, the Charing Cross, St Mary's, Paddington), the West London looked dangerously redundant. It did about two thousand deliveries a year, half as many as Queen Charlotte's (which had, nonetheless, three times as many beds) and doubtless at greater overall expense than somewhere which could guarantee economies of scale. Despite its reputation for good, modern, caring birth practices (duck-egg-blue birthing rooms, some with ominous specially shaped black rubber labour mattresses, like something from a bondage dungeon) it was on the way out. But we chose it, and we chose it because the people were nice, the atmosphere was relaxed – not quite to the point of recumbancy – and with its ruinous paintwork and defiled furniture it reminded us of home.

The last time I saw it, the axe had finally fallen, the windows were boarded up, the marks and stains on the walls outside were epically large and the chances were that it was going to be turned into offices. It looked as if the rooms where my beautiful children had taken their first breaths and seen their first daylight were going to be filled with Roladexes and grouchy young men wearing ties and short-sleeved shirts.

Every Wednesday evening we went along to its antenatal classes.

These were run by the hospital itself, rather than the National Childbirth Trust. There was a homogeneous mix of white, middle-class
couples and I think one black middle-class couple. And one pregnant
Frenchwoman. A midwife explained, with the help of a collapsing
rubber womb – built in sections, so that she could fit and re-fit the
components of birth together by way of demonstration – what was
happening, to answer questions of pregnancy management and to
show us what best to do.

The problem with the rubber womb was that it kept collapsing
when it wasn't meant to. The baby kept thudding out onto the floor,
followed by the plastic umbilicus and the placenta. The midwife
would scoop these up with a brittle laugh and cram them back
in place, before making the mistake of removing the baby again
(to display the positioning of the head relative to the cervix, say)
at which point all the stuff would crash back onto the carpeting.

The would-be parents, meanwhile, spread themselves around her,
their backs pressed against the wall, smirks of unease on the men's
faces. According to Richard Seel, author of *The Uncertain Father*,
'Many men are reluctant to attend antenatal classes simply because
they feel that the classes will not be relevant to them. And they
are often correct.' Many of us must have been there as a kind of
atonement for being male, for not actually having to go through the
toil of pregnancy. In my case, I also wanted to define a difference
in manhood between myself and the obstetrician who talked about
fishing with his hand up my wife. I was prepared to put up with
the boredom of antenatal lessons as a token of my sympathetic
modernity. As with most things to do with childbirth, antenatal
classes – although in theory a matter of simple education and
practicality – are freighted with emotional baggage. Of the twelve
or so who went to the West London (the numbers varied from
week to week) none of us, I would guess, went simply to learn

about childbearing. We all had agendas – multiple agendas, some of us – points to score, issues to settle, declarations to make.

To its credit, the West London made a point of trying to justify our grudging male presences by finding things for us to do, including: making a birth plan; helping with the contractions; doing the housework; helping get the hospital bag ready (a kind of overnight bag without anything to wear during the day); assisting with the birth where possible; helping to choose non-chemical relaxants; practising the breathing exercises. We would help our pregnant partners to sit up, then curl our arms round them, suck in, push, exhale, go red in the face, try not to crap. A bit would drop out of the rubber womb with a *clack* and everyone would look round guiltily in case they were somehow responsible. The pregnant Frenchwoman worried a lot about whether she would still be able to have a glass of wine in the evenings. The midwife said she thought that was fine, in the ambivalent, disingenuous way that medical people do when faced with questions about food or drink.

We learned about pain relief. As well as the old favourites of pethedine, gas and air and epidurals, there was something called TENS. TENS – Transcutaneous Electronic Nerve Stimulator – was pretty new at the time. It was a primitive New-Age device in which two pads were attached to the labouring woman's back, there to administer a gentle electric current. This current stimulated the nerves in a way analogous to acupuncture, it was claimed, causing the release of naturally generated pain-inhibitors – endorphins and enkephalins – so limiting the pain of labour. Given that the crowd there was already predisposed to an alternative view of life (by opting for the West London, we had joined a very slightly progressive club), we all fell on TENS with nervous excitement.

It didn't inspire. There were a couple of saucer-shaped pads, some straps, a tangle of wires and a kind of generator box at the other end.

Everyone had a chance to manhandle the thing and one or two of us even switched it on and tried it out, just to see whether it felt like the electrified fence round a field of sheep, but it didn't do anything obvious, like make our hair stand up or cause sparks to jump across our spectacle frames. Susie was, all the same, impressed by it. I actually spotted that it was not going to work and tried to talk her out of it, but she insisted and so I meekly kept quiet and started counting off the days until I could say *I told you so*. How could I be so sure? I just knew that in comparison with large painkilling drug dosages, this simple nerve stimulator was not going to be enough. I was also free to hold on to my conviction because I knew I wasn't the one who was going to have to suffer the large drug dosages and so could afford not to have any qualms about them.

And then there was the relaxation session at the end. We had to learn how to relax in order to stimulate a healthy mental environment during pregnancy, and, more practically, as an aid during the pain of contractions. So, at the end of each session, the midwife would close the curtains, dim the lighting and put on a tape of relaxation music. This was the sort that sounds like a synthesiser playing modally in the background, while, foreground, someone's stomach digests a large meal. 'All right,' the midwife would say, 'I want you to lie back, close your eyes, let your muscles go limp, try and think of something *nice* – a bit of seashore you know well, at sunset, maybe . . .'

Well, after the pushing and gasping and breathing and bending of the first part of the class, we were all pretty well inflated. And the moment we all lay down in the dark and listened to the provocative stomach noises of the tape, we entered into an orgy of farting. It was terrible. Masked by the New-Age music, everyone parped and quacked uninhibitedly and after three minutes, a blanket of gas lay over the floor. So then someone (quite often one of the mothers-to-be) would rip out an especially loud and dangerous fart and someone else would start to have an attack of poorly suppressed hysterics, which would spread in the dark round the class, until everyone was lying in this awful, suffocating fog, farting and sniggering instead of breathing deeply and thinking of Big Sur. One guy came out and said to his wife, 'I'm taking a snorkel next time.' I believe that at NCT antenatal classes they're prone to lighting scented candles. When I first heard this, I dismissed it as a hippyish affectation. I now realise that it's no more than a precaution against the closing ten minutes of the session.

How did *you* get on with sex in pregnancy, by the way? I hope you don't mind my asking, but it seems to be the orthodoxy these days that sex in pregnancy is a hoot, a riot, a whirligig of outlandish pleasures. You can do it as often as you like, without fear of an unintended pregnancy; and you will find yourself doing it in exotic, slatternly positions, to accommodate your pregnancy bulge. It will be liberating and highly erotic, or, as Sean Callery puts it in his *First-Time Father*, 'There is no reason why you should not both get a lot of enjoyment out of this experimentation.' It's a belief that even creeps into works of fiction, as a denominator of the author's wholesome frankness. I stumbled across it the other day in John Irving's *The Cider House Rules* (admittedly, a book all about conception, parenthood and society): 'There was a freedom about their lovemaking, now that Candy was already pregnant.' There it is again, I thought. *Have sex in pregnancy*. It's a challenge!

Well, okay. But I do wonder how liberating it is, when one of you is hot, knackered, prone to vomiting and physically tender; and the other is in a cauldron of anxiety, lest he rupture some essential membrane, or wake the unborn baby up, or induce a premature birth. Sex and pregnancy have an uneasy relationship. Without the one, you wouldn't have the other; but once you are pregnant, the whole business of sexuality is compromised. It's not that you can't do it (and the discovery that you can, technically, is empowering, I suppose). But the aura of nervous sanctity with which the Victorians veiled all aspects of Motherhood still lingers. Even now, even in London, even among the most cynical and progressive metropolitans. And although the pregnant female form is often praised for its beauty, its luscious ripeness, its lustre – is it *sexy*? Does it turn you on, as opposed to being movingly lovely? The male libido is unreliable and erratic enough under normal conditions: why should it get a kick out of bulges and distortions, however adorable, however natural? I suppose we're meant to celebrate aspects of our sexuality and fertility in a way that our hung-up parents could never have done. Well, it didn't do it for me. It was like pretending to enjoy fried seaweed, or Philip Glass. Something you only really did because you'd read about it.

Sex aside, the paradox of this time is that nothing much happened; and yet I remember it as a period which was weirdly alive and intense, a period when the living was good and full of an unhinged kind of excitement. And one of the things that made it so weird was the way we found ourselves, as I said, poring over these textbooks like Christian hermetics, looking for signs and portents, news of the future. Something awesome and frightening was going to happen to us, and it was all there in black and white – if only we could connect with the sense beyond the words and *know* what it was. And because we didn't have (at least *I* didn't have) an awful lot to do, conning the books became so obsessively important.

As well as Kitzinger's *The New Good Birth Guide*, we had Penelope Leach's *Baby & Child From Birth To Age Five*; Gordon Bourne's *Pregnant*; Peter Mayle's *How To Be A Pregnant Father*; Michel

Odent's *Entering The World*; and a couple of anomalous entries – *What Every Pregnant Woman Should Know (The Truth About Diet And Drugs In Pregnancy)* by Gail Sforza Brewer, and *The Modern Book Of Babies' Names*.

With the possible exception of *Entering The World*, these were uniformly unsettling reads. Kitzinger was necessarily but grimly frank; Leach was dealing with a world (post-partum) which we dared not even imagine; Odent ('At the moment I am listening to Rimsky-Korsakov's *Hymn to the Sun*, but it could equally well be a Hindu chant') was too good to be true; Sforza Brewer was plainly from another universe. And Dr Gordon Bourne's book drove Susie into prodigies of rage with statements like, 'Even the most highly competent and efficient woman may find that her judgment is impaired' and 'The nervous system is more sensitive during pregnancy, making women sometimes seem almost unreasonable and occasionally they will not even respond to logical argument'. He managed to strike a tone which was both comprehensive and patronising; highly technical and entirely unsympathetic. As a result, we never got beyond page 21 of what is a 542-page book.

Of course, Dr Bourne suffered unusually from the problem of being a man (an Englishman, specifically – Michel Odent, being French, was beyond the constraints of gender) writing about something that only women can experience, for an audience of women. So to add to his crimes, he was guilty of presumption. But then, he was nowhere in comparison with *How To Be A Pregnant Father* (and nor was *The Pregnant Father's Cookbook*, by Len Deighton, yes, author of *The Ipcress File*). This was a truly fantastical book, lent to us by one of our first friends to give birth, and was evidently an object which had been passed totemically from couple to couple for years. It bore a massively out-of-date stamp page from a library in Wandsworth: it had been taken out about five years previously and never returned. And it was by Peter Mayle, the *Year In Provence* author, written in the mid-1970s, long before he'd become famous. It made a deep impression on both of us. Why? At random:

'You'll discover that it's quite normal for a pregnant woman to have cramps and cravings, to feel occasional nausea and irritability ... Give her flowers, buy her perfume, notice her hair – treat her, in other words, like the woman she is ... These gastronomic adventures are called cravings ... What harm can a few extra pounds do? Quite a lot, as your doctor will tell you ... Your wife's doctor will almost certainly give her a diet designed to give her and the baby the necessary nutrition without excess weight gain ... Some men have been known to faint in the delivery room. And maybe because of that, many hospitals don't allow the father in until it's time for him to meet the baby ... you're certainly going to need something to sustain you through those hours in the waiting room ... treat your wife to a new outfit when she gets back to her old size ... the basic incentive of wanting to be attractive is built in to every woman ...'

So the women's movement in Britain had been going seriously since when? Say, since 1970, when *The Female Eunuch* came out? Since 1971, when Marsha Rowe and Rosie Boycott produced *Spare Rib*? Well, Peter Mayle used to be in advertising, not a progressively-minded profession; come 1976 when he was getting *How To Be A Pregnant Father* together, the Slits were barely going, let alone Chrissie Hynde. You couldn't reasonably expect him to be anywhere near the cutting edge of sexual politics. You have to see these things in context. Still. By the second half of the 1980s, when we stumbled across it, it was like something from the Black Lagoon, a dinosaur of a book (despite being only a few pages long), astoundingly retrogressive, an amazing assertion of man's implicit right to be culturally and socially dominant ('You might also need your secretary's home number in case she has to cancel a few meetings'), a book so embarrassing, it was good.

It didn't cross our minds, of course, that even as we yowled and pointed and spat at Mayle, we were only surrendering to whatever ideology was available at the time. We thought we were doing the right thing, because there was nothing to suggest we weren't. But even as we bought Kitzinger wholesale and scorned Mayle wholesale, it never occurred to us (why should it?) that we could have been floundering around a couple of generations earlier, and buying – say – Truby King wholesale.

New Zealander Truby King is now just a footnote, unknown to most modern parents, but when he brought out his bestselling *Feeding and Care of Baby* (1913) and *The Expectant Mother and Baby's First Month* (1924), he was hugely influential. King was the original feed-and-sleep-according-to-a-timetable proponent, the chief propagator of the idea that babies should be trained to fit in with an adult schedule, rather than be allowed to create their own rules. Children were to be regulated in their demands, whatever suffering this may have caused them or their parents. Before the War, he was known as a saviour of babies and mothers. One posthumous verdict was that 'his teaching was based upon respect for the laws of nature, and the rules of common sense'. Today he's remembered as being, at best, misguided; at worst, insanely authoritarian. But for years he ruled the roost. His ideology was *the* ideology. So where is he now? Where are the mothers and fathers ready to keep his name alive?

Where, for that matter, are the friends of Grantly Dick-Read, and his *Natural Childbirth* (1933)? Deeply controversial at the time, Dick-Read rejected anaesthetics during childbirth and insisted instead on prenatal relaxation exercises to relieve pain and ease the process of birth. Would anyone buy this nowadays? Frankly, the answer is probably *yes*, but only for a marginal handful. And yet, without him, there would have been no National Childbirth Trust. When Prunella Briance started the NCT she put an ad in *The Times* which read: 'A natural childbirth association is to be formed for the promotion and better understanding of the Dick-Read system'; and indeed, the NCT actually began life as the Natural Childbirth Association, after Dick-Read's teachings.

Or, coming back up-to-date, we could have hit upon Jean Liedloff, author of *Continuum Concept* (1977). This is a book which advocates the *continuous holding* of the child and comes as the result of Liedloff's studies of the Yequana Indians of South America. Since coming to prominence with this work, she has privately acknowledged the impossibility of translating her ideas into practice in Western society, but at the time of writing is still happy to give personal consultations on her houseboat in Sausalito.

Or Spock? His *Common Sense Book of Baby and Child Care* came out in 1946 and throughout the Fifties and Sixties outsold everything except the Bible. 'What good mothers and fathers instinctively feel like doing for their babies,' the late Doctor said, 'is the best after all.' When he died, early in 1998, it was said of him (among other things), 'When the rollcall of the men and women who shaped the 20th century is read, Benjamin Spock will be way up the list.' Spock was the first great modern guru, an advocate of love; and yet his name has been traduced, too. He's been accused not only of creating the permissive society, but of emotionally denying his own children. In turn, he once accused modern children of having 'toxic values'. So no unequivocal vote for him either. And now, post-Spock, the Thirties have caught up with us again in the form of a pediatrician called Christopher Green, who has written a childcare manual containing a chapter entitled 'Smacking used correctly'; and in the form of a pair of US Christian Fundamentalists (of course) who have gone on record as arguing that it's God's will to leave your child to cry indefinitely, whatever the provocation. There is, in other words, no fixed centre to this ideological universe. We could have tried any of these people and trusted in them and believed their wisdom. But we believed in Kitzinger and Leach, and we still have no idea if we were right, or wrong, or helpless victims of the times, just as we would have been if Truby King or Spock had been the current arbiters of good practice.

Why didn't we get this into some kind of perspective by asking our parents or other relatives for insights into managing gestation? Well, they never encouraged us to, and anyway, they seemed to be separated from us in time and experience by such a vast gap (having borne us into a lost and fantastical post-war world of Vauxhall Veloxes, Players Please, Burt Lancaster) that it would have been like quizzing an Edwardian dowager on aspects of her Confinement to ask my mother about *her* pregnancy. Mum did, when I pressed her, claim that she'd done it without the aid of books ('Apart,' she disingenuously noted, 'from a pamphlet on breast-feeding from the doctor's') but that was as far as it went.

I found this incredible. How could anyone try anything as complex as bringing up a child without a book of instructions? Didn't she feel that she had to make a *success* of her child? How could she have been so careless? For a while, I bore a grievance over this. There would have been a time (I told myself) when she would have been clapping her hands together in a prematurely grandmotherly fashion and laying in supplies of comfrey and witch hazel and other sovereign remedies, and readying a Moses basket for the child. She would have brought out a large, age-blackened book and quoted from it. She would at least have sworn by something. Pregnancy is a protracted crisis, as I said, and we need external reassurances to see us through.

But I now accept that the generational and cultural gap was probably too great for her to bridge. I also suspect that her reticence might have been because she knew that an Alexandrian Library of how-to parenting books will not ensure satisfaction for parents and child. Striving for *success* in these matters is no more than symptomatic of an age with hopelessly distorted priorities. Or it may have been because mothers simply do not share these confidences with their sons, any more than fathers share confidences with their daughters about nose-picking and getting drunk. Or it may have been because she simply wanted to be unhelpful. I gave up asking.

We did quiz our contemporaries for advice, that was true. But that was also a lost cause. Other people's circumstances were always somehow obscurely different from ours even though they themselves were exactly like us in so many ways. When it came to their pregnancies, they seemed to have complaints which put the whole enterprise on a different footing. They had quaintly old-fashioned views about the procedures involved. They had attached themselves to hospitals which were either in the wrong end of town or else lost in the countryside. Or they appeared (surprisingly often) to have signed themselves up to astonishingly rapacious and cynical private obstetricians who never actually made it to the birth.

More importantly, whatever circumstances attended them, they always had a terrible time. No one experienced anything but the most harrowing pain and indignity. From the moment of conception (throwing up every hour for three months) to later in the pregnancy (permanent bed rest/depression/high blood pressure) to the actual birth, it always seemed to have been an elemental disaster.

A typical re-visiting of a friend's labour and parturition would run along these lines: 'There was blood everywhere. And I was exhausted by this time, and the midwife just kept telling me to *push* and I'd been on that sodding bed for *eight hours* and the pethedine didn't work and I got a *tear* and it was *ghastly* . . .' Susie's face would blanch as she listened to these depravities, while the fathers of the new infants ('*He* just wasn't *there*! Just sat in a corner, reading a John le Carré') stared at their hands and allowed their eyebrows to rise and fall in sympathy with the story. I feigned an interest in the carpeting.

We stopped asking, after a while, and went back to our source books. And then, a week early by the hospital's calculations, the world of theory turned into a world of inescapable fact.

ONE

The thing about babies in the first half-hour of life outside the womb is that they give the impression of knowing much more than you do. When I held my son Alistair for the first time, apart from being small, light, alien, incredibly beautiful, he had this expression in his eyes that I guess must come from having recently taken part in the deepest processes of time and creation. We, of course, had just been through a drama rooted in the primally immediate and were in a condition to be impressed. But even allowing for that, he did seem unusually thoughtful.

Everybody's first child is a drama, though. For what it's worth, this is what happened with ours:

At around four in the morning, Susie's waters break, all over the bed. There is no ambiguity. It's like a burst bath overflow. *Christ*, I say. Although ahead of schedule, we are ready for it and have our bag packed. Kitzinger writes that, in her experience, women often want 'something beautiful to focus on during contractions. Occasionally they took bunches of flowers into the hospital and kept them with them during labour'. We stumble round the house, looking for something, anything, beautiful. There isn't anything apart from a plant in a pot – a Kalanchoe – a little shrub-like thing with clusters of small red flowers. The nearest thing to a bunch. We take it. The overnight bag is in our hands and we hurry out to the car. The mood is a little like that when we first found that we were going to have a baby – awed, overtaken by immense events. The difference is that then we could be overwhelmed and then procrastinate more or less lazily for nine months. Now, we have to take part in it, act and react. We can't stop it. I feel intensely nervous, my freewheeling, semi-hysterical thoughts only partly calmed by the fact that I'm still half asleep; and by my obligation to fulfil my part of the contract with Susie, which is to be coping, supportive, functionally useful. We drive to the hospital. I am hunched psychotically over the wheel, hauling at the gear lever, chewing the inside of my cheek, my hair standing up and my eyes bulging like John Turturro in *Barton Fink*. We check in (*I think we're having a baby!*), carefully import the Kalanchoe, the Thing of Beauty, and the nurses admire it. Susie is having contractions and paces angrily around. I get into her hospital bed and fall asleep. I dream about being in a hotel room.

I am awoken at seven by a terrific, stout nurse who shouts at me: 'You havin' your wife's baby for her, darlin'?' She gives me a cup of tea which I drink in bed. After a bit, Susie's contractions decrease, she gets into the bed which I have vacated and I read *The Tin Men* to her, crouching and confessional. This lasts most of the day. It gets dark. Susie's contractions start again. The doctor in charge decides to move us all to a delivery room. We form a train, with Susie processing in the middle, me behind her with the bag and the book and a nurse in front, bearing the Kalanchoe, like something out of Rubens' *Roman Triumph*. In the delivery room, the Thing of Beauty goes on a far windowsill as there is nowhere closer to put it. But Susie has taken out her contact lenses to make herself more comfortable and can't see the Thing of Beauty. So she goes through the whole of labour with the Thing of Beauty no more than a fuzz of red and green on the far side of the room.

The contractions start to get more severe. Susie asks for the TENS machine. It arrives on a trolley and someone plugs it in. She presses the pads to her back and trusts to science. But it doesn't work, as I knew it wouldn't. I allow myself an infinitely small smirk about this. Even in childbirth, we can nurture disagreements and score minor victories over each other. With TENS out of the way, Susie goes for the full epidural, administered by an eerily calm anaesthetist. Susie drifts into a half-doze after the excitements of her earlier contractions and, not having eaten for ten? twelve? hours, I go to the nearest McDonald's for a Big Mac. I bring it back to the delivery room and chew it in the quiet and the half-light. It's a bit like the start of a long and potentially interesting railway journey: the uneasy feeling of being entirely in someone else's hands; the tremors of adrenaline flitting up and down my arms.

Then, in the early hours, everything starts to happen. Susie is fully dilated. We have a truly beautiful midwife with us, called Loretta. She looks like one of The Supremes and has an aura about her which makes me want to tell her all my hopes and anxieties. She is the word made flesh, the embodiment of all the drily cautious wisdoms of the textbooks, the translation of thought into being, anxiety and hope brought forth in the shape of one of The Supremes in a white coat, and she makes an almost unbelievably comforting sight. She is so wonderful that I even write a piece about her later on for the *Evening Standard*, run with the weepily grateful title *A man, a baby – and a hospital*. Together we form a sweaty trinity (I tell a lie: I was sweaty, Susie was hot, Loretta was pleasantly temperate) and gather round for the moment of final revelation.

Exhaustion – I've been awake for nineteen hours, after four hours' sleep – has left me pretty composed by now. I may be bristling with nerves, but am too tired to tell. This is a moment – and they hardly ever happen, in the general bourgeois scheme of things – when you are obliged to surrender to the moment, a moment in which, frankly, destiny has you in a cruel existential clinch. I rather like it, at the time. I also rather like the fact that now there's almost nothing I can *do*: I can breathe heavily along with Susie and hold up her shoulders and mutter *yes* and *good*, but essentially I am background material. I could be almost any sympathetic friend. And being naturally rather a lazy and disengaged person, this suits me fine.

There is a moment's crisis when Loretta tells Susie to *push* and we discover that in all the shambles of the antenatal classes, we haven't learned the *correct* way to *push*. We improvise. This is, of course, the moment for which cruel obstetricians insist on an enema beforehand: you push, you crap. But the West London is kind and low-intervention and Susie has not had to go through the humiliation of undergoing an enema. And anyway, we are a fairly retentive couple and the crap problem turns out not to be a problem at all – in merciful contrast to what happened to a friend of mine whose wife gave birth in a pool. He was told to equip himself with a net on a stick – the sort you use for pulling small fish out of rivers. Why? he asked. So that he could fish the buoyant turds from the water (all released during the *push*) in order not to have the baby born straight into a load of sewage. And he did, apparently: an image with which I have trouble, even now.

Anyway, this last-minute confusion is, in the event, a good thing as it distracts us from the sheer terror of what's happening and has us concentrating on a useful diversion. I feel stupidly pleased with myself for not feeling squeamish, despite my Big Mac.

And then, suddenly, a baby's head appears. Then the rest of the baby comes out, the skinned rabbit, the slosh of liquids. This is the point at which fathers are supposed to weep, but I don't weep. I feel lightheaded with release and say *There he is!* as if there was any chance of his being somewhere else. I read in *She* magazine, years ago, that the placenta is delicious fried with onions, and I find myself thinking that it *does* look tasty. I force this idea out of my head as Susie rests Alistair (as he has been known, in the event of his being male, for a while) on her breast and Alistair looks around with these big, clear, wise eyes. I am allowed to hold him for a bit, which I do, like a piece of Meissen, my elbows poking out at angles, while Susie takes a photograph of me doing this. In the picture, I look tramp-like and bewildered. Then she takes him and I take a fuzzy, uncertain photo of her. Then I take a photo of Loretta (who by this time is doing some paperwork in her office) and then I lurch home at dawn, sniggering to myself with tiredness and relief. I ring up the grandparents and interested friends (we were supposed to be having dinner with someone; never told them we were busy. They took it well) and shout *He's a peach!* down the phone. This mood of almost hallucinatory elation stays with me for a whole week, and only really returns when our second son is born. I would say that it is still the happiest time of my life. There you go: a few things are unforgettable.

But then, would I have felt any less elated if I hadn't been in on the birth? If I had been like one of the cartoon old-style men in Peter Mayle's book, my mouth a concertina of cig butts, a trench worn in the floor of the waiting-room, a second-time-around father dozing moronically in the corner with yesterday's paper spread across his lap? If I'd seen nothing of my wife for four hours, and then only been able to view my son through a window, in a heated dormitory full of other children? Would I have known what I was missing?

The expectation which has grown up over the last ten or twenty years – of *being there* – is partly an ideological construct, partly an answer to a real need, like any other aspect of fatherhood. But that need is contingent, not necessary. The language alone suggests a schism. When a man *fathers* a child, he fertilises the egg and then stops to see the process through, or, on occasion, bunks off completely. When a woman *mothers* a child, she's there, wholly involved, a full-time and central participant. For men, this is a recent option. Think back: how many iconic representations are there of men holding newborn children, Madonna men? St Joseph is an obvious candidate, but he's frequently relegated to the margins, depicted as old and fatuous (as in Brueghel's *The Adoration of the Magi*, in the National Gallery, where Joseph is not only past it, but plainly on the way to drunken senility) and, above all, cuckolded by God.

Indeed, any kind of depiction of men with their small children is a potentially dangerous or plausibility-defying act. Between the sixteenth and nineteenth centuries, there was a trade in maternal man images which showed *the world turned upside down*: i.e. with the father depicted as looking after his own children and, as a consequence of this anarchic reversal of the roles, being beaten by them. Warnings were sometimes attached. Rocking a cradle was said to have a weakening effect on a man, while seventeenth-century French fathers were presented with pictures of a mentally enfeebled dad nursing a baby, while elsewhere in the frame, the wife dressed herself up to go out on the town and cheat on him.

In this century, large-scale Socialist Realist painters might depict, say, a burly Russian stoker from the Novorossiysk region holding up a very small child to glimpse the future under scientific Socialism (and, of course, Stalin was always keen to be portrayed in the presence of children). Or, on a more intimate, domestic scale, they might produce something like Vladimir Favorsky's somewhat uninflected 1961 linocut *We Will Achieve Disarmament*, in which a man in a suit holds out his arms to receive a (recklessly nappyless) baby, while his wife in a long gingham frock zooms in to interpose her body before he can actually lay hands on the child. Or, latterly, you might get a Richard Avedon-esque art photograph of, say, a large black man cradling a white baby in *Vogue*. A recent ad for Lanvin fragrance for men went down this road by depicting a handsome model in a dark business suit, cradling a naked baby (sheer madness: crap, puke, piss – all over his wool mixture) and looking emotionally engaged. Indeed, one of the most popular Athena wall posters of the 1980s was an art photograph of a guy and a baby – as commonplace, in its way, as the girl tennis-player scratching her backside was in the Seventies – but bought by whom? Women college undergraduates who found this as potent an embodiment of their dreams as the men found pictures of Sam Fox?

But generally these iconic representations are laboured and always slightly controversial, *making a point* somehow – rather as the Saatchis did when they produced a picture of a pregnant man for a 1970 campaign on contraception. What there is, is a shortage of bold, commonplace depictions of the man as Madonna, the man as witness and participant in the holy birth. There is not enough straight up-and-down visual confirmation that this is a positive, manly thing to do. Being men, we thrive on bold affirming images and we feel uneasy in their absence. We feel uneasy having to rely too much on abstractions and ideological positions. Insofar as being in on the birth is the product of ideology and belief – the outcome of dangerous and possibly foreign intellection – it strikes us as a purely abstract goal made real, an action poised somewhere between answering a psychological demand and fitting the bill of the *Zeitgeist*. Even now, it's still quite a defining thing to do – less radical than twenty-five years ago, but still something which identifies you as a particular kind of person, a modern person, a man who at the very least has given some thought to the idea of sharing parenthood.

Would this make it all right not to bother? I'm not arguing that we should throw contemporary practice out of the window and follow the example of, say, Lenny Bruce, who went and screwed one of the nurses while his wife was in labour; but, as with the ideologies of Kitzinger and Leach, it's sometimes surprising to see how an orthodoxy gets entrenched. I did a flying survey among the fathers I knew of my age, to see how they felt about being there at the birth. Three quarters (of an admittedly minuscule sample group) said that while it was nice to be present, they didn't see themselves as *indispensable*. A sister or the mother, or a close friend of either sex, they tended to say, might have done as well. One guy missed the birth of his second son altogether because he had to rush out and move the car off a double yellow, leaving his wife uniquely in the hands of the midwife. Just about everyone said that they felt awkward and guilty at all the bother (mess, pain, indecorousness, turmoil) that they'd been responsible for. *I felt bad at having caused it*, said one; *my wife an exhausted wreck, fluids all over the place*. Those who had only had one kid – only attended one birth – felt more strongly that it was worth their while being there than the ones who'd done two or more, for whom the novelty had worn off almost entirely. And for sure, while I can remember an awful lot about the process of Alistair's birth, I can remember almost nothing about Tim's (which was, predictably, much quicker) except from the point at which he appeared. Only then do the pictures become clear. Susie, I might point out, was adamant when I quizzed her as to whether or not I should have been there. For her, there was no question about it, and she argued that almost all other mothers in relationships would have said the same thing: *of course I should have been there*. Who else has more right? she went on. Who else has a greater obligation? Who else's genes are more frankly involved in the baby being born? Who else could be closer (assuming a fairly okay partnership) to the mother? It was not even worth querying.

And all the men agreed that if you intentionally don't turn up for the birth then you mark yourself out at best as stuck in the same ideological generation as your own father; at worst as a reactionary, woman-hating primitive. In fact, you start to look a bit like, say, Nicholas Soames, who, when asked in a recent interview about Isabella, his new baby daughter, announced that 'We are *not* going to talk about nappies.' He added that he never went to antenatal classes, either – 'Of course not, it wasn't convenient' – and that 'I'm never left alone with Isabella. I have a wonderful wife.' The Soames way: and if that is what happens to you if you go the conservative route, then there really is no arguable escape from modern practices, nor should there be.

In the closing months before birth, we had gone through Obadiah, Lawson, Ellard, Van, Cadmus, Zelotes, Adelbert, Knut, Pedro, Schuyler. Alistair could have been any one of these (still could, if he wants to badly enough), since all these are in our copy of *The Modern Book Of Babies' Names*, the received wisdom which took over about two thirds of the way through pregnancy. Touchingly, I see that we earmarked Sophia and Emily in the event of a daughter – although now I remember that I had a problem with Emily Jennings, reminding me with its dactyl/spondee tie-up of *Eleanor Rigby* or, more generally, *See Emily Play*, and I didn't want my kid to sound like a Sixties pop hit. This in fact was typical of the whole process of naming. The irrational, unsuitable or plainly mad names (above) ruled themselves out at once; and the handful of plausibles sorted themselves out slowly, arbitrarily and reductively.

According to *The Times*, the most popular boy's name at the moment – the name most commonly given to baby boys – is Jack, and has been for the last three years; while Chloe, Emily (there you go again) and Sophie are the most popular girls' names, in descending order of popularity. Well, *Jack*, okay, I could buy that, except for the fact that it would end up in the singsong clinch of *Jack Jennings*. There's also the problem – as I now know – that there are so many Jacks and Bens and Wills at school that you have to suffix the name with a clarifying initial. This would lead to *Jack J*: Live at the Las Vegas Hilton. But *Chloe*? There's a mystery to names like Chloe (also, Danielle, Natalie, Gabrielle) which must have something to do with simple class prejudice (is it smart or council estate?) and the fact that it's a foreign name and so doubly unfathomable in its overtones. But then, all girls' names are unfathomable to me now. I'm too far into the boys' world to think about Lucys and Dees and Catherines and Karens. I can't read the significance properly. I'm told that for boys, old-fashioned working men's names are creeping back – not just Harry and Jack, but Albert and George and maybe even Eric: names which the middle classes now appropriate for their children as a clear line of demarcation between themselves and their own suburban parents, who in their day went for Michael, Robert, Christopher. Giving your kid one of those retro homespun Merchant Ivory names treads the finest line between earthy self-consciousness and jumpy urban fashionability – somewhere between putting a miner's lamp on your mantelpiece and liking Portishead. I couldn't have done it.

We went for Alistair for no.1 son, Tim for no.2 son – both by a process of laborious elimination which left us with almost no names to choose from. They had to be names which weren't effeminate (Julian, Crispin), pointlessly ethnic (Douglas, Hamish, Owen), were incapable of being abbreviated to something stupid (Wally, Nige), aspirational-sounding without being too swinging (Damien, Max) or too snotty (Henry, Rupert). On top of that, they had to be neutral when written down in initial form (Jennings, starting with a J, made that fairly easy – no Timothy William Alexander Thompsons or George Ian Thewlisses for us) and they had to obey a fantastically pretentious Jennings family rule, which stated that a male child's middle name always had to be Augustus. To be honest, my father was the last Jennings to be lumbered with that burden, as my mother put her foot down and said that my brother and I could have middle names which began with A, but not Augustus (we got Andrew and Anthony). By the time we got to my sons' generation, I had modified this to a new (but equally pointless) rule that at least one name had to begin with A, but not necessarily in the middle. So Alistair got Alistair and Tim got an Alexander in the second rank. There was a moment when we wondered about calling Tim Adam, but this got axed partly because it sounded poncey; partly because I had a panic about what the forces of bureaucracy would do with two sons whose first names both began with A. Various other names ruled themselves out, not because there was anything wrong with them, but simply because they reminded us of people we didn't like.

In the end, the short list was so short it was barely a list at all – which put the Gaspar/Sol/Alaric permutations of *The Modern Book Of Babies' Names* in an odd light. Clearly, Gaspar/Sol/Alaric weren't included because they were serious possibilities – of course they weren't; they were never intended as such. They were only there to give the impression that you could call your child an almost limitless number of things. In reality, the name – the thing which a child drags through his early years like a ball on a string – chooses itself through a process of strict and bitter elimination. You rule out as best you can the possibilities for humiliation, awkwardness, unreasonableness and error in later life, only arriving at something positive and affirming after all the nastiest contingencies have been confronted and dealt with. I mean, I *like* Alistair and Tim as names, and I don't care what anyone says about them. But the procedure which brought them about looks pretty niggardly ten years on.

Having chosen a name, though, we went ahead and had a christening. At the last christening we organised, I found myself opening the door to two of my closest friends and shouting, 'Where the fuck have *you* been, you fucking bastards?'

'We went to get some ice cream. There's some really good stuff—'

'You *fucking bastards*! You're three quarters of an hour *late*!'

That was our second christening: Tim's. They'd turned up at the church all right, but had then gone off to an Italian ice-cream parlour, miles away from our house, and had finally got back for the booze-up forty-five minutes after everyone else. For Alistair's christening, our groovy priest (slubbed silk tie, fine arts leanings) had taken the godparents to one side before the event and said, so I was later told, 'When you want to remember this christening, and you want to buy Alistair a present of some sort, buy him something . . . *nubbly*. That would be a nice thing to do.' They all nodded, apart from my own godmother, who was there to span the generations and whose claim to fame was that she was like *that* with Desmond Tutu. She thought that our man was a heretic, and was a bit deaf anyway. Every now and then I get a phone call from someone saying, 'I wanted to buy something, but what exactly is . . . *nubbly*?'

What *were* we thinking of?

I'd better own up here, and admit that at the time I was still in the hangover phase of a party I'd had with High Church Anglicanism (the music, the words, the incense – it was a time when I needed drama) but, even so, was more or less cured by this stage. Still, I had a residual Manichaean/eschatological anxiety about good, bad and death, and, being an anxious middle-class parent, I wanted the best start for my boy even if it had no useful or logical basis. A death unto sin and a new birth into righteousness is fine with me, rather like paying off all your credit card bills in one go. Susie, an unthinking atheist, went along with it as well. Probably to humour me. By the time we got to christening Tim, I'd decided that the whole thing was ridiculous, but we went and did it to him as well as Alistair so as to avoid sibling quarrels about baptism later on. My children will thank me, on the other hand, for never becoming a Jehovah's Witness, Seventh-Day Adventist or straight Baptist, requiring full immersion in a plastic tank at the age of thirty. It was all culturally acceptable.

And then we acquired all these godparents, two of whom were standing in my doorway while I called them bastards.

'We thought it was on the way.'

'Of course it fucking wasn't on the way. *Jesus*.'

So I pushed them roughly indoors, spitting with anger and remembering that my parents were in the next room and wondering, had they heard the bad language? Then we all had to stand around and force bits of food into our mouths while I failed to work my way round the room with a couple of bottles of fake champagne. I don't know why I can't manage this simple task of refilling people's glasses. I ought to relish it, since it gets me off the hook of having to think of things to say to my guests, but for some reason I always seem to begin an intensely involving and important conversation – usually with someone I barely know – the moment I have the bottles in my hands, and it seems rude to break it up and plough away to the far end of the room. So I just stand there with the wine warming silently in my boiling palms and a moustache of sweat growing on my upper lip, until one of the more action-minded men at the far end gets so sick of waiting that he dispossesses me of the drink and goes off to help himself and the other parched guests. That's what happened here. The grandparents made small talk and admired the baby, while the godparents and their friends and relations peered morosely into their glasses and tried not to look at their watches too obviously.

Other christenings I've been to have followed slightly different patterns and certainly the piss-ups afterwards have been better organised. But even if they haven't had the same mixture of terminal sloth and ground-breakingly inappropriate mania as ours, they have shared the same sense of puzzlement. If you asked most of the people there *why* they were there, they wouldn't have been able to give you a cogent reason. (One where I was actually fingered to be a godfather, we reached ten minutes after the ceremony should have started. I damn nearly lost my job to a stranger in the crowd, but then I still don't know why the parents picked me in the first place. Maybe my lateness was an expression of my inner ambivalence.) Why are godparents godparents? Why would anyone make *me* a godparent? I like to think that, all in all, I'm a nice enough guy. But I know I'm also self-absorbed, lazy and grumpy, irreligious and have no real spiritual wisdom to offer other than that human nature is just one big puzzle. Why *me*? I would have asked at the time, but it seemed uncouth.

And when it came to us to choose, why didn't we seem to know any moral people who could guide our children through the rapids of life? Why did we only know drunks and social inadequates and hypocrites? What function could they possibly fulfil? 'As godmother to a number of children,' explains Anne Watson in *Godparents* (foreword by Lord Blanch of Bishopsthorpe), 'I have made myself available to their parents for advice and help whenever they want it. They have also given me permission to point out things to them which need adjusting and correcting. Godfathers too can fulfil such a role, and need to be encouraged to do so.' None of this, though, escaped into the atmosphere with us. Instead, what we had was a vaporous unease, a feeling of misplaced ritual, a reward, principally, to the parents' friends for being the parents' friends, plus a chance to show off the kid much in the manner of an ostentatious house-warming.

Of course, the mood shortly after the birth of a child is pretty strange anyway. The whole house resonates to a curious note somewhere between bliss and hysteria. When people call you up about work, you have this shattering intelligence to impart to them – that you have become a father – which then gives you the short-lived but powerful satisfaction of hearing them struggle to take it on board and re-adjust their perceptions of you (*God! I mean, well done!*). But on the other hand, you are tired, hyper-emotional, persistently aware of this other permanent presence in a house which was once uniquely your own, a presence which has taken away all the little treats and indulgences you used to take for granted, like the freedom to move independently around the world, and to sleep on in the mornings. Everything takes on the muddled, provisional quality of a badly organised and very demanding weekend stay with friends. At the same time, you try to get through your work just as you did before, wondering why it makes you feel so tired. You feel fulfilled but dangerously brittle. When Tim was born, I actually went mildly nuts. Hardly a kind of post-natal *couvade* (that psychological red herring, in which men supposedly ape the symptoms of their pregnant female partners); instead an expulsion of stress which, for a couple of days, had me banging my head on the wall, crying and refusing to see my in-laws.

So far as the christening was concerned, I like to think it was less a post-natal mental disorder and more some deep inner reaction to the teetering hypocrisy of the situation which made me start swearing at my closest friends. After all, if they couldn't be bothered to go through the motions of piety (I mean: stopping off at an ice-cream parlour), then I couldn't either. Admittedly, I was wound up by the event anyway, since I hate most social gatherings involving more than about eight people. I was also wound up because this was one of those official first displays of the child to the world, and that carries with it a kind of stagey sacredness, christening or no christening. And being middle-class, I was already clear that whatever else my children might have wanted, *I* wanted things to be – in some way meaningful only to me – *perfect*. So, with all this stupid, inappropriate lumber inside my head, I suppose it's possible that I might have put two and two together, about the time we were all standing in the church with candles in our hands, and realised that what we were doing was not really in anyone's best interests and was essentially a charade. In fact, I think I knew that before we even started; I just couldn't stop the ball rolling once it had begun.

I was still mad, though, two days later. I rang up the chief perpetrator of the ice-cream outrage, shouted at him some more down the phone and then hung up on him. Twenty minutes later, he rang me back, shouted down the phone at me.

'If I'd been *you*—' he yelped '—I wouldn't have treated *me* like that. *I'd* have just said, *fair enough*. You're so bloody *pompous*.'

Then *he* hung up. That's bourgeois convention for you.

The feeling of *being a father*, though: that was terrific. Away from any sort of social pressure or middle-class ritual – in fact, on my own, whenever possible, without even the distracting presence of the baby – it was a fantastic sensation. I had to restrain myself from grabbing passers-by in the street and shaking them and shouting in their faces,

I'm a father! Complete! Not firing blanks! My biological destiny fulfilled!
Obviously, part of this was relief that mother and child were okay
and that the ordeal prefigured by Kitzinger and the others was over.
But a lot of it was also late-developer exhilaration at having stepped
beyond what I was before and into that real world of children and
grown-ups and responsibility which I'd glimpsed a year earlier.

On the other hand, I got appalling mood swings – mood swings
which every father of my acquaintance has suffered from, even
though they haven't always chosen to use the phrase *mood swing*
with its attendant static crackle of female unreliability: the way your
feelings change from something moderated by the adult world to
something ungovernable, unknowable, violently self-contradictory.

Nappies epitomise this contradictory state in the first year. Indeed,
they provide a nice physical correlative for the whole new-baby
period. There is a whole nappy culture out there. I know this
because, working at home, there is no way I could escape the
burden of nappy-changing. And the first time you deal with a
nappy full of impacted crap (a bit like ten-week-old *tapenade*), it
is a life-altering encounter. Your emotions when you come face
to face with it are something you could never anticipate, unless
you work in a hospital or on a pig farm. The whole thing is so
powerfully real, so much in the present, that it borders on Zen. I
can still remember the first time I changed a nappy. I was bubbling
with a mixture of dread at what I might do to my newborn son by
mistake and at what I might find inside the nappy when I undid it.
The sun was shining and the room was overheated and there was an
unfamiliar smell of medication from all the ointments and lotions we
had lying around, just in case. Although I'd been acting out the caring
man bit quite keenly up to now, I'd ruthlessly avoided nappies, using
a system of weak excuses and outright refusals. So Susie had had to
strong-arm me into it the first time, lots of threats and grievance. I

held my breath, leaned forward and gripped the tabs. It can't have been anything but completely depressing for Alistair, trapped on the table with this scowling, grimacing face bearing down on him, one of his beloved parents looking as if he was peering into a road accident. And then I gripped a bit tighter. And I made one of those decisions which freezes time, in which you can hear the blood roar in your ears in the moment before you act. I thought – I don't know what I thought. I thought that something was going to explode across the ceiling and the walls. That I was going to be calcified in crap like one of those objects people leave in limestone stalactite caves to be turned into stone. I pulled. And then it turned out to be a false alarm – I mean, it was just pee rather than anything worse. God, I was relieved. 'Well *that's* all right!' I shouted at the little chap. '*That* I can deal with!' He must have thought I was mad.

Some of the images I keep with me from my nappy-changing years will live forever in my mind, precisely because of the way they symbolise the contrariness of early fatherhood. You have, for instance, the unnatural loveliness of the baby's bottom, clagged up with the kind of stuff you normally wipe from the sole of your shoe, in a nexus of beauty and squalor; you have the desire to purify and care for your child, warring with an equal desire to forget the whole thing, or even wander away somewhere and puke; you have your paternal joy at seeing how fit and strong your kid is, fighting with your rage at the little bastard's refusal to lie still and *just get changed*.

So why doesn't this get written about more often? Why doesn't it get used? As conventional prose climactics, you get birth, death, sex, love, food, violence; but no nappies. Why not? The only really acute nappy passage that I can summon to mind is in a book called *The Big Picture*, by Douglas Kennedy. In what is one of the setpieces of the tale, the protagonist tries to change his small son's diaper (American author) and finds himself at once in a scene of horror: 'I pulled back the lower part of his suit, ripped off the plastic fasteners on his Pamper and stared straight into a diaper from hell: gooey diarrhoea which covered Josh's bottom and stomach so completely that I couldn't see his belly button. I shut my eyes in disgust – but not for long, as Josh started thrashing his legs, slamming them into his dirty diaper. Now the stuff was smeared across his feet and imbedded between his toes.'

On this cardinal moment ('the soiled diaper slid off me and, with a soft *plop*, landed face down on the rug') hinge all kinds of consequences, including murder, dismemberment of a corpse, barratry, car theft, photography and interior decorating. The only pity is it comes so early on. The tumbling shit signals the fact that our hero's world is on the brink of an irreversible disorder, threatened from within by forces too grossly primal for him to defend himself against. Moreover, the fact that he deals with his son's crap is a dramatic index not only of his unconditional love for the child, but also of his susceptibility to victimisation, his deteriorating relationship with his wife, his stoicism and his lack of manual dexterity. And of course, the tension you always feel in the presence of randomly mobile shit makes it one of those moments in literature.

It makes us uneasy – and not just because it's dirty and dangerous and smelly and cloacal – *The horror, the horror*, as one acquaintance put it. It makes us uneasy because we use disposable nappies. Now, let no-one argue that disposable nappies are not wonderful things, even though they do end up clogging landfill sites with polyethylene and crap. First appearing in quantity around the start of the 1960s, they've gradually lost the two-piece core nappy and outer plastic shell (which had to be thrown away separately) as well as the pin fasteners, and acquired all-in-one construction, tape fasteners (in the 1970s) and slimline designs (1980s). One of the world's biggest manufacturers of the absorbent polymers which stuff a nappy is called Stockhausen Inc., of Greensboro, North Carolina; where I guess *Stimmung* is played constantly to soothe the workers' nerves. Disposables are terrific, and everyone in this age has their own disposable nappy of choice. We tended to veer towards Pampers, but Peaudouce and Huggies have their admirers. It's very personal, your response to the sticky tabs, the crackle of the unfolding clean nappy and the promise it brings of a fresh start, a new beginning. Some nappies thrill you, others leave you cold. But all disposables work, and that alone makes them worth the pain of bagging them up and hiding them deep in the garbage sacks so that the garbage men won't spot them and leave them behind.

But at the same time as men rejoice in not having to soak crap-laden towelling nappies for hours in zinc buckets (what *can* it have been like?), we have the feeling that this is one of those times when technology has generated social change not necessarily to our advantage. The Pill gave women the freedom to control their own fertility, and from that any number of tremendous upheavals have sprung. The disposable nappy has enabled men to do the job of nappy-changing (because we categorically *would not* do it if it involved towelling nappies, we just *wouldn't*) – a job which is an emancipation, but also another pointed reminder of where we stand in the scheme of things. Because we now do nappies, we have it made plain to us that we are at the garbage disposal end. In the great chain of existence, it puts us round about the level of the night-earth man or the pure-collector (a pitiable nineteenth-century struggler, whose job it was to go around collecting dogshit, to be used in treating leather). There is an alpha and an omega. The alpha is breast-feeding the infant, bathed in a sea of love and providing, the mother giving and receiving and feeling uniquely happy. The omega is clearing up the end-product with a wretched, nappy-rashed child treading in its own crap. I don't claim that there's any unfairness in this – women have spent generations putting up with it, there are no good reasons why we shouldn't do it as well – I merely point it out.

Nappies aside, there's a natural tendency in the first six months or so to see your kid as a trophy baby and not much more. After all, while the mother's bonding, the father as often as not finds himself scraping around the house doing the washing-up and painting the kid's bedroom. At least, this is what I found. I wasn't an immediate participant in the psychodrama going on between mother and child. I was a more-or-less willing chamberlain of the house. This, I guess, is what paternity leave is supposed to facilitate. It's not something you take in order to make friends with your baby (who can barely recognise you anyway; and certainly can't smile or show appreciation or talk to you or laugh at your jokes); but to help generate some sense of domestic order in the first few weeks after the birth. Especially if there's already another child in the house who needs looking after.

At the time of writing, Swedish fathers can claim paternity leave for several months at a stretch, shortening or extending this time as their needs change before they go back to work. As a consequence of this progressive liberalism, take-up of paternity leave (or just *parental* leave as it's sometimes known) involves as many as fifty per cent of Sweden's working men. In the UK, where there's no legal framework for paternity leave, the take-up is about three per cent. This of course invites the question, what exactly are the Swedes *doing*? Do they simply know what to do when there's a new baby in the household? Are they given help in understanding the requirements of what they do? Do *their* fathers tell them? Which in turn prompts the question, even if we were allowed the same kinds of benefits as the Swedes, how well would we use them? How good *are* British men at providing a domestic framework in the very early days of parenthood? Is it even worth granting them this privilege, or would it be frittered away in afternoons of TV, beercans, cigs, while the child howls in the background? Being at home for much of the time, I could practise my skills whenever the need arose. But even so, I was never much more than barely competent. I suppose I was there for moral support.

Didn't I feed? Didn't I get up in the night when the newborn baby cried? There's a whole mythology of feeding, which incorporates the beliefs that:

—bottle-feeding at night is something the father should really do because the mother will be exhausted from the day's labours.

—you get so deliriously exhausted after a month of broken nights that it's like a protracted, monstrous drug high and is worth it for that alone.

—babies can be gradually lured into a more sympathetic sleeping schedule.

—now is the time when you and your partner are most likely to murder each other and so you should do whatever you can to make this less likely.

All of which are true up to a point, but not essential verities. Did I feed? No, I didn't really; and so never got involved in the mythology. I don't know why Susie let me off this chore, except for the fact – maybe – that I was still trying to work during the day, whereas she had given herself a notional three months off. In reality, this meant that she snatched work moments and business phone calls in the times when she wasn't looking after the baby, while I limped about feeling dreary and weak before sitting down at my word processor.

What I was good at, was being the Big Ear, becoming that thing you turn into when there's a new baby sleeping within earshot. I became one vast six-foot-long ear, lying in bed, listening with radar concentration, even when I was asleep, for those little mutterings and snufflings that babies make when they're restless. I could pick up these scratchy little noises and be onto them and bristlingly awake in seconds, lying there with all my concentration, all my being, poured into my ear, becoming the Big Ear, waiting for the sounds either to die away and cease or turn into the nervous whimpering that meant the kid was hungry. At which point I would dig Susie in the ribs, tell her the baby was crying and drift back into a troubled sleep.

None of which does anything for sex, as anyone will tell you. So tired, so blearily foul-tempered. All the love in the household beaming in on the baby, none left for each other, the paradox that having done this most affirming thing, this thing that definitively signals the permanence and depth of your adult relationship with each other, you can't always bear to be in the same room as each other, let alone show affection. On one occasion we had some nonsensical fight, a real screamer about – what? Who threw out the nappy bags? What time we were supposed to eat our supper? At the end of which I barged out of the house, stumbled into my car and drove off towards the southwest. It was late at night, and I soon found myself cretinously swerving around Weybridge, trying to compose my thoughts. I drove around for hours; the pubs emptied, the traffic on the A317 to Addlestone grew more and more sparse, I kept parking the car in affluent cul-de-sacs for a think and then driving off again in a rage because I couldn't think: I was too tired and furious. By the small hours, I was crossing and re-crossing my own path, unable to get any further away than Esher in one direction and Bracknell in the other. I had no money to stay at a hotel but felt that it would look stupid to go home, get some money and then go out again. I parked under a tree on Ham Common, got out, walked angrily up and down, decided to start work on a separation the following day, drove home, went to bed and woke up the next morning only to find Susie carrying on as if nothing happened, as if my whole furious protest hadn't occurred. Which it hadn't for her, of course, because she'd mostly been asleep in bed. I furtively dropped the separation idea and merely went around being shitty. Then I dropped that, too. It was not a romantic or sensual time for either of us.

What new fathers do enjoy, and what I did take advantage of, are certain sanctioned times when we can be close to our new children: especially when we parade them around in public. It may not be entirely culturally okay to hold your newborn in the male Madonna pose, but it is feasible to push your child around in a buggy, in agreed contexts, advertising the power and fruitfulness of your loins and your genius in creating a baby so beautiful, strong, thoughtful, sweet-natured. These contexts are: supermarkets at weekends, public parks, parties where there are lots of other children, school gatherings. It can get very tribal in a turn-of-the-century way in such locations, with porky middle-aged men (and the process of having a child makes you middle-aged, whatever age you are) looking sheepish and rueful and withal obscurely proud and complacent. There is a way men have of expressing their feelings that really trades on this sheepishness/ruefulness axis. You catch each other's eyes at the supermarket/park/party and shrug your eyebrows and give a small, harassed grin and maybe roll your eyes to the sky. You can nod, too, the cheesy nod of complicity, and say, 'Total hell, isn't it?' Or, 'God, it's hell.' Or, 'God, I've had enough.' To which the other person might say, 'Ghastly, isn't it?' And you say, 'Hell.' Some more hapless shruggings, maybe a whistle between the teeth, and you separate and go back into your own worlds. There isn't much more to it than that, other than some covert male competitiveness about the size, intelligence, strength of the baby. *Careful! You nearly pulled that strap off, you virile little fellow! See? He nearly broke his own buggy! What a muscular, inquisitive scamp!*

Mothers will use chance contacts with other mothers to discuss whatever's relevant at the time: childcare arrangements, feeding, clothing, illnesses, schools, sibling rivalry, first teeth – anything that can be expressed in words. Fathers – I've done this, I know what I'm talking about – have to make some gesture of confederacy, indeed, feel a need to show that they're part of the brotherhood, that they're proud in their wacky, compromised way – but without getting bogged down in anything smutty like details or feelings. We push our buggies around and hoist our eyebrows up and down like busted roller blinds and look put-upon, while acknowledging our new status in society as full-blown men with an almost wordless smug coyness. A truly satisfying experience.

But I can recall how quickly – in the very early days with Alistair – this game of competitively based mutual admiration would collapse, once outside the conventional display contexts. There was a time when we were sharing a holiday cottage with another couple. One day, the women went off into town to bond, leaving me and the other guy alone in the house with our respective very small children. The moment the front door closed, all pretence of being modern fathers (to which we had been paying fulsome lip-service up to that point) went out of the window and we found ourselves broken down in front of the TV like a couple of mattresses thrown out onto the street, pouring brandy into our mugs of coffee to fend off the cold. The children were crawling around somewhere – possibly playing with the dangerous holiday-let bare wiring or cache of rusty tools – but all we did was cock one ear (the vestiges of the Big Ear) towards the open door to listen for screams, while with the rest of our bodies we decomposed into the battered armchairs. All I can remember saying, while the kids distantly butchered one another, was, 'Do you want another coffee?' While all my fellow deadbeat said was, 'Oh, kick the bloody *ball*.'

That was the extent of our real, practical involvement with our newborn children: listening out for disaster, while blindly trusting that that disaster would never happen. We didn't begin to bother to try to impress each other with our fatherhood skills. We were delinquent. Compare that with the way the mothers (when they returned) incorporated their relationship with each other into their relationships with their children: talking to each other half the time, the other half – quite spontaneously – talking to the kids and answering their needs, prompting them to play, or make some noise, so that the adult dialogue and the childlike play became part of a larger, harmonious whole. This whole business of posturing in front of others with your newborn child is predicated on the incredibly short emotional attention span of an average middle-aged man. It is not something we can do for very long, or very often.

And when we are doing it, it's on a knife-edge, of course, that knife-edge of early emotions in which the world is always threatening to dissolve in some way. The kid in the buggy can freak out/explode into its nappy/throw up/swallow something toxic and in an instant shatter the mood of incredulous self-admiration you've worked so hard to build up. Always better to deal with these events alone (a) because if the mother is present she'll snatch the baby away at the same time denouncing your ability to look after it and (b) because – provided you *can* deal with it – the sense of achievement you feel at getting a baby to shut up is a gift that only fatherhood can bring. It *is* more satisfying if you can do it in front of the mother, thus giving the lie to the slur that men are unable to intuit their way into a baby's emotions, but riskier. Better still if you can do it in front of other fathers (that arrant competitiveness) or strangers who might nonetheless hold an opinion. I can remember doing it once (one time out of *many*) in front of an admiring crowd in the car park at some flyblown West Country beach. Tim it was who disintegrated in rage and instead of ignoring him or venting my wrath by yelling back at him, I had one of those accesses of compassion which I very occasionally get. I picked him up and talked to him a bit and walked around with him on my shoulder. Quite often this had no effect at all; or maybe it would encourage him to puke down my back. But that day it did work, and he became calm and began to look enquiringly and attractively around him. I actually elicited an approving *Ah, that's better* from an old bag in a car-coat. The sun came out, the wind was full of sea freshness, Tim was pacified, I had the approval of someone I didn't even know and I was making a statement about the possibilities of modern fatherhood.

Of course if you can't do it, the world falls in. It's philosophically necessary, of course, that you should fail, in order for the successes to seem successful. But the failures, with very small kids who are completely unreasonable, unpredictable, and who can simply decide to make your life an indefinite hell, are often so appalling that you quickly wish there was no philosophical necessity for anything except a kind of persistent, bland mutual toleration. There is a condition known as *colic* or sometimes *evening colic* in which your very small child (I mean really small, a week old, say) just cries and screams and will not stop, no matter what you do. And there was one evening when Alistair – still no larger than a cat at the time – just howled and turned purple and would not stop. Up to this point he'd been a model of sobriety, eating well, sleeping, looking appealing. Simply

correct in every respect. And then he went crazy. We were terrified
and bewildered; even more so when we roamed through Penelope
Leach's *Baby & Child* for the answer, only to find that what he had
appeared to be this colic thing, a complaint which, for no reason,
makes your baby scream constantly until it is old enough to talk.
'Your helplessness,' Leach writes, despairingly, 'together with the
fact that the dreadful bouts of screaming occur at the time of day
when you are most tired . . . makes colic one of the most difficult
things for new parents to cope with.'

So we sat and watched Alistair turn from purple to blue and
considered this death sentence. There were two possibilities. Either
he would die. Or he would go on screaming until he killed us. And
then – no notice given, no gradual subsiding into peace – he stopped
and went to sleep and that was that. Never happened again. Turned
out it wasn't colic at all. But this kind of crisis – the anti-climactic
medical panic – is one of those recurring experiences, recurring
as long as you have young children. Later on, the crises would
involve persistent vomiting, or fever and hectic pallor, reducing
your beloved one to a waif in bed, so enfeebled and tragic, like
that awful Luke Fildes painting *The Doctor* (meningitis? bronchitis?
flu?). Out would come the pointless brow thermometer – the sort
which is printed on a strip of plastic and which indicates the patient's
temperature by means of a sequence of heat-sensitive coloured
windows. The greenest window, it advises, is the one with the
accurate temperature reading: no matter that the greenest window
always reads around 105 degrees, even when nothing's wrong, even
when the child is cool to the touch and smiling placidly. That is what
we parents use in these sickness crises – a gadget which increases the
agony; a means of reassurance which brings on a breakdown.

And it's experiences like that which affirm your strength, your
love, your capacity to withstand assault at precisely the same time

as they drive you closer to the psychiatrist's couch. Provided you get over them, of course, you can congratulate yourself on having fleshed out your identity with another intense, deepening encounter. After the colic nightmare, I congratulated myself on living at an altogether higher pitch, at the same time as I wondered whether my whole life as a father was going to be lived in a kind of threshing waste-disposal unit of emotion.

Did I tell any other fathers about this? No, I don't think I did. After all, I was not yet one year into fatherhood. I thought it was an isolated incident.

But, illness aside, by the end of the first year – oh, we were walking and talking by the end of the first year. We were wildly successful. We passed those first tests with flying colours. Of course, it's impossible to recall that first step now. In fact, I'm not even sure there was *a* step. There was a grey period, a transitional time when we couldn't be sure if our baby was seriously walking or just staggering in a more upright position. After a few days, though, we knew that he *was* walking, that the staggering was true erect locomotion forwards. And then we did all those things that parents do: clap their hands together, cry out in delight, grin like monkeys. After all, this was the first serious, learned skill – that and smiling voluntarily. Why can't we remember it more clearly?

Partly because of the talking. The walking and the talking happened so close together that I can't recall which came first, nor how exactly it happened, given that I was so distracted by having to look out for two great improvements more or less simultaneously. This wasn't like learning to tie shoelaces, or ride a bike; it wasn't a discrete activity. Again there was a spell when we couldn't tell what the baby vocables – the usual mix of *dah* and *mah* – were adding up to, but there must have been a point for both of my boys where they pointed at a drawing of a cat and said, in all probability, *Tat* – and we latched onto the subtext of this word and so verbal communications began. Soon after that, they started to pick up the conventional mishmash of significant toddler words, with the sort of eclecticism that toddlers enjoy. Among the standards (*drink*, *Daddy*, *shoe*) Alistair got the hots for satsumas, and would roll the word *satsuma* around his tongue; while Tim got a bang out of *handkerchief*. Other kids, apparently, have picked up on football players ('Vialli') and motorcars ('Primera'). But the strangest verbal acquisition that I know of involved a family friend who spent his first eighteen months of life not saying a damn thing. In fact, he was so silent that his parents were starting to panic, debating whether to get in a child psychologist and have his brain tested, when one day the kid – sitting in his buggy in the street – looked up, pointed and said 'Telegraph pole.' He was faultlessly accurate. It *was* a telegraph pole. After that, everyone apparently relaxed a little while the son got on with skills acquisition, eventually taking a double first at Cambridge and becoming a professor of mathematics at one of Britain's senior universities. Einstein was the same, you know, not talking until he was three. He also reputedly said, on first catching sight of his younger sister, 'Where are its wheels?'

So we didn't have that, we didn't have that cataclysmic arrival at speech. But we did have, in succession, two boys who could more or less walk and communicate – no longer apes, but hominids! Real humans! – by their first birthdays. And from then on we were fastidiously keen to let the rest of the world know this and to gloat over how clever our boys were. Especially in the presence of kids of the same age who hadn't yet got the basics down. Those were good days.

TWO

It still gives me a frisson of fear and hatred when I look at Penelope Leach's *Baby & Child*. I'm surprised the thing's still in one piece, the battering it's taken over the years. Even now, her words give me the jitters: '. . . If you try to override his feelings, ignoring his cries, prising off his clinging arms or shutting him in a playpen to stop him following, he will get more and more anxious . . . juggling feeding times so that you get more sleep . . . some babies are much more difficult to look after happily than others . . . waking in the night . . . your baby's "help" will certainly slow you up . . . protect a sore bottom . . .' Leach's book has, in various forms, sold some three million copies worldwide since it was published in 1977, and has been translated into twenty-nine languages. It has been turned into a TV series and has even made it as far as the United States. Why is this? It is because Leach makes you believe that there are reasonable *answers* to the problems of bringing up children aged somewhere between nought and two; answers which are as grounded in rationality as your child is frequently grounded in vindictive craziness.

Now this is very soothing to the middle-class new parent like myself, for two reasons. First, because it makes you feel, generally, that most situations/catastrophes/chronic problems are going to be curable in the long term, even if not immediately (her prose style has a lot to do with this, being measured, free of nervous jokes, pleasantly bossy). Second, because she makes you feel that there is a right way and a wrong way of doing things; that there is a way of success and a way of failure — an approach which over-literal middle-classers like me lap up. I know that some people have found Leach over-prescriptive and narrowly demanding, but she suited us just fine. Maybe this is because she did her first degree at Cambridge, and we've always liked being hectored by a bluestocking.

Indeed, she became so central to everything we did that after a while we stopped calling her Penelope Leach, or Leach. We called her Pleach, not just because this was a handily emphatic way of saying her name, but because it contained elements of other words, words which were resonant in some way. So it had a bit of *please* in it, a bit of *plead*, a bit of *peach* (as in, what a peach my baby boy is when he's not being an arsehole), some *leech* (as in, bloodsucking, financially and emotionally), *leach* (as in, to drain of colour, possibly through fright), *preach* and *bleach* (although I think I may be adding that one simply for the sake of tidiness). The fact that it also spelled the verb *to pleach* — in other words, to intertwine the branches of young trees to form a fence or trellis effect — was accidental. I suppose the idea of training a growing thing into a pleasing shape has a nice appositeness about it, but that wasn't really what was uppermost in our minds at the time. It was just the word: *pleach!* which came out as a choked cry whenever anything went bad.

When it came to playing, about the best it got in those early days, I think, was carrying the one-to-two-year-old Alistair on my shoulders across Wimbledon Common. He seemed to like it (he could lean over from one side of my head to the other, alternately boxing my ears, hurting the one he loved) and I got a walk, with the extra satisfaction that I was entertaining my son *and* carrying a heavy burden around to increase my cardiovascular activity levels, like St Christopher. For some reason, I'd started to put on a lot of weight after the birth of my first child, a conscious decision, really, inspired by an untraceable conceit that to be fatter was to be more fatherly. Something to do with Santa Claus? Oliver Hardy (who was childless)? Orson Welles? Whoever I was trying to emulate, it was also a reflection of the fact that I felt more confident about my condition as a man – father of a marvellous child, what more could anyone want? – and no longer needed to try and look thin and interesting to gain the world's approval. There was probably even an undertow of sexual resignation, of retiring from the arena of lively sexual activity with which I'd tried to keep in touch, up to that point, exhaustion permitting. I was instead going to be an old pussycat, offering an expanse of fat Buddha paunch for my children to play on (it was still there when Tim was born, three years later) and a lot of not especially sexually adventurous beef for Susie to snuggle up to in the winter evenings. It was a sign that I felt comfortable with the world, and it meant that I started to wear stretchy cardigans a lot, buttoned taut over my gut, and looser-fitting trousers for that *rus in urbe* look. I stopped weighing myself and lost sight of my feet altogether.

All of which gave me an extra solidity as I carried Alistair across Wimbledon Common. It made me feel that I had arrived, finally, and that he and I were a unit. What's more, we were both agreed that this was a good thing to do and even if he did change his mind, he couldn't alter his circumstances, stuck up there on my shoulders. There was none of that pointless contentiousness you get with small kids, that imbalance of interests which infests game-playing, where the father rushes into the eighteen-month-old child's life and claps his hands together and cries, '*Now* we're going to learn about Premier League football, you and I', and the kid just burps. Or where the child shambles onto the sleeping father's lap with a slimy mouthful of glove puppet and a need to be applauded. Nor was there too much of that mind-twisting patter you can find yourself stuck in with a very small child—

'Look at the geese!'

'Where geese?'

'Over there! Oh, they've flown off.'

'*Where* geese?'

'No, they've flown off.'

'*Where?*'

'I don't know. Somewhere else.'

'Where geese?'

'No, they've gone. You missed them. I expect we'll see some more soon.'

'Where?'

'Ah, God . . .'

We just walked.

But the fact is that until children are old enough to talk to – and then talk to about something intelligible (cars, the irrationality and unpredictability of mothers, favourite foods) play of any kind is something I look on – looked on – with feelings of great uncertainty. And I say this as the father of two preternaturally bright, charming, entertaining, gifted, life-enhancing sons. It's not personal: it's an aspect of the condition of fatherhood. In the 1930s, apparently, *Parents' Magazine* yelled at any fathers who were reading that once Dad got home from work, he should immediately play non-stop with the kids – 'In this part of the day Dad should *reign*' – on the grounds that this was what they weren't doing enough of at the time. This wasn't just a taunt to fathers, nor a simple piety spoken with the aim of enabling families to function amicably together, but something to encourage society as a whole (which had suffered from previous generations of alienated, despotic fathers turning their children into anarchs and rebels) to remain integrated, co-operative. But an injunction like that must have appalled any father reading it. *Reign* – how do you *reign*, when you come home from work? Where do you find the time or the energy? And even if you have the will to play, how can you bridge the gap between the uniquely parochial interests of a toddler and those of a grown man? *Let's build a tree house!*

The kinds of things that very small children like to do are running around waving their arms and screaming, sitting in pools of filth and sucking their fingers, being hurled into the air and caught, swung round and round by their arms, throwing bits of building block across the carpet, vomiting in cars. Many will eat dogshit, not so much for the gameplaying element, more for the experience. However you dress it up, it is a poor litany for a grown-up person to base any part of his life on. I can remember afternoons which seemed like prison sentences, watching my bright, charming, entertaining etc sons plough up and down the front room, gumming bits of Duplo or banging slabs of wood against each other. It felt as if my brains were liquefying. In fact, we even have a bit of video film (part of the small, random and pointless collection of footage we've made over the years; unenlargeable, too, since the camera got nicked) taken of Alistair at some time in his first year, in which crawling, grabbing hold of things and looking worried are the absolute summits of this clever child's playing skills. And this level of complexity would have lasted, with modifications, for at least another year or so.

And yet, fooling around is meant to be the thing men are good at, the thing we're predisposed towards. It goes with the whole broader concept of fatherhood – particularly if you've got sons – that dads come into their own with cricket bats and goofing around and building tree houses, and should therefore be good at fooling about with children of any age, no matter how immature. Mothers nurture, fathers go out and act like morons. And there are environments in which it's easy enough to do that thing – chasing around on the beach, leaping amusingly about in the waves, staggering around on heathland waving your arms and falling over and suffering an early aneurism. But generally, in the domestic/real world environment, when you're in that period where children are still aged in months rather than years (someone touchingly told me the other day that his son was *twenty-one months* – an age still measured by fleeting moments rather than the prison sentence of childhood) I defy any father to do anything more than dabble in a world so alien it might as well be from Saturn.

In the Jennings family, we had several distractions for the toddlers. We had a toy house made of cloth, supported on a framework of interconnected plastic tubes. The whole thing rocked and swayed in the style of a Californian sauna in the Big One. My job involved putting the thing together and then climbing inside (easier, yes, to have inserted it into me) and then peering out and mugging and gurning and pulling faces, like a bogeyman out of a Maurice Sendak illustration. Once, on account of being so fat, I actually couldn't get the thing off and had to wear it for a while, like a personal monotent, until Susie could take some of the tubing apart and free me. We also had a plastic slide, supported by another kind of playhouse – really a reinforced plastic cube with holes pierced in its sides – which took up an illimitable amount of space and was always coming apart. It spent a long time on the landing outside the kids' rooms, where they and their friends could tumble off it and then fall headlong down the stairs. It was too big for anywhere other than Castle Howard but too small to be really satisfying, especially if an older kid (say, an older brother) decided to get in or on it at the same time as the tinies and mash them with his flailing feet and legs. My role as play companion was to pull bodies out of the wreckage and try to get the slide to go back on and stay on. It was both boring and futile, like counting lorries in a traffic jam.

Then there was the trike, which had to be pushed along by Dad with the kid on it: a job of mediaeval severity for anyone over six feet tall. There was the wooden pushcart (gets them up and walking, it claimed) which did nothing but lodge itself in cracks in the ground or bark the shins of adults. There was the gross paddling pool, as wide as two parked cars. This took half a day to fill, by which time the sun had gone in or everyone had lost interest. But in which, if you did brave its depths, you found that it was unbelievably cold for something with only a foot and a half of water in it, and really slippery underfoot. The plastic base must have been made out of something self-lubricating, because as soon as you rested your weight on it, you fell over. Children just got into it and drowned. Either that or they slipped, fell over and clamped their teeth in the plastic sidewall so that I had to unplug them and get them to stop howling. Water, pain, mud.

All of these things obeyed the general rule that the size of a child's plaything is in inverse ratio to the child's age. As kids get bigger, their toys get smaller – until we reach the stage now where a birthday's worth of presents takes up no more than a third of the kitchen table. Previously it would have taken up the table, the floor and part of the next room. They also obeyed the rule that simple toys are difficult to use. As with the size/age inverse ratio, the more instantly graspable a toy, the more effort it takes to get anything interesting out of it. What can you *do* with a plastic spike on a rocker base, over which a sequence of gradually diminishing rainbow-coloured rings is fitted? There's nothing you can do, except take it apart and put it back together again. Which is what the kid's supposed to do, not you. I can't even imagine an ideal scenario in which the child would throw itself delightedly on the plastic spike and play with it. I can't visualise what the kid would do, other than lift off the rings and replace them – perhaps laughing and clapping his hands at the outrageous novelty of it all – before starting again and going on happily for, what? Half an hour? Forty-five minutes? How *can* you make this process interesting for yourself or anyone else? And what do you do if the kid doesn't want to do this one thing? You can't make the toy any more appealing or enigmatic than it already is. You either let the kid fiddle aimlessly with it (chewing, beating, throwing) or you turn to some other hopeless item in the museum of toys, huge unusable plastic follies, which you are collecting (thanks to the fond grandparents and all those puzzled godparents) in the hope that *this* will be the one the child wants to concentrate on, the toy that will somehow magically excite it, leaving you to watch the TV or drift into an anxious daydream or attempt ninety seconds of work.

We are not all childlike men, like those characters played by Robin Williams, forever in touch with the inner juvenile. We cannot enter the world of play when our minds are lodged in the quiet, persistent nightmare of middle-age. I mean, if we could let go, we would – if we could escape our particular human condition and act the fool. And we do, sometimes, among other adults. But there is a categorical difference between making a fool of yourself for adults and making a fool of yourself for children. With adults there is a measurable advantage – sometimes – in being an idiot. You can – sometimes – get some leverage out of making yourself look like a moron, either as a diversionary tactic, or as a way of misleading them from guessing your real intentions. With children, on the other hand, it usually means getting a few cheap laughs (in my experience) followed by a spiralling loss of control, culminating in someone falling over and hurting themselves and the whole episode ending in tears. And more than that, however much we may judge our maturity as adults by our ability to control and adapt our emotions to circumstances, we find it hard to control and adapt our emotions the way children might want us to. We can be moody, depressed, irritable but still – just – polite enough for adult company. But we cannot be moody, depressed, irritable and be good company for kids. We cannot put on a happy face *that* well. Just like them, in fact.

(Did my father ever play with me, though, when I was young? Did I even *have* toys? Well I did, I suppose, but the only thing I can recall from way back, from when I was a very small child indeed, was a Sooty glove puppet of which I was inordinately fond, but with which you could, let's be honest, do only one thing: be Harry Corbett. My father spent most of his time coming back from work during the week and falling asleep in front of the TV; or mowing the lawn at weekends and falling asleep wherever he sat. I would stick Sooty on my fist and jab it towards him – the slimy mouthful of glove puppet – and he would prise open an eyelid and say, 'Not now' and go back to sleep. I hate myself when I do the same thing to my kids, but it seems to go with the condition. You only have to feel marginally tired and you can find yourself being wholly, callously dismissive. The rest of the time, what did I do? I think I may have gone outside and scoured the back garden for trash. I pushed a plastic car across the carpet. I took out my father's record collection and then spread the highly scratchable LPs around like lily pads and walked on them. This whole thing of fathers playing with their children has always been a radical programme for the Jenningses.)

*   *   *

It comes back to this central paradox, that playing is what dads are supposed to be good at; and yet, at the moment of demand, we frequently fail. But if we can't do it, given the resources normally at hand, what good are we? Where is the toy that can help us when we are, frankly, useless? Well, there is only one toy that has ever managed to defeat the paradox and bridge the chasm between the expectations of a very small child and those of a large, disillusioned adult. This is Lego.

Lego is unimprovable. It dates back – ultimately – to 1934, when a Dane called Ole Kirk Christiansen, who was making kids' toys out of wood, named his company LEGO, in a portmanteau of LEg GOdt: *play well*. In 1942, the company burns to the ground, but undeterred, Ole carries on and by 1949 has acquired a plastic injection moulding machine and is making something called Automatic Binding Bricks. By 1953, these are being called Lego Bricks and by 1955, Lego as we know it is coming onto the market. By 1958, the company has worked out and patented the little studs you have to have on the upper surface of any Lego component, to keep everything tightly together. And that's it – especially since the wooden toy factory burned down again in 1960 and the company decided to drop wood altogether from the range. From this deftly brilliant concept springs Duplo (big Lego for tots, 1967), Legoland (Disney World for people who like largeish models made out of nubbly – that *word* – plastic bricks, 1968), LegoTechnic (really fancy Lego, with gears and levers and motors and tiny pneumatic systems and even computers, 1977) and the current range – at the time of writing – of 542 different sets and 1,964 different moulded items.

And there are several reasons why Lego is so beautiful. The first is that, in my experience, it always supplies the right pieces in the packet. I only mention this because I'm British, and grew up with the nagging fear that whenever I opened a new construction toy – Christmas present, birthday gift, pocket-money job – there would be a part missing, or a section which was broken or malformed in some way. It was just something to do with growing up and living with our nation's tenth-rate quality control standards. You learned to adopt a certain philosophical approach. But amazingly, this has never been an issue with Lego. We must have had scores of kits – big, small, wildly elaborate – and yet they have always had the parts as advertised, sufficient for the models pictured on the box and not misshapen or covered in swarf or little plastic warts left behind by the moulding machine. This alone makes it worth some kind of prize, especially if you've ever been in the position of having to calm a child because a toy has turned out to have dud components. *Look! We'll make it into something else! It could be a sort of aeroplane dishwasher!*

The second reason is that my children *play with the stuff* and have done so ever since they were big enough to manipulate any object smaller and harder than a nylon dinosaur. Yes, things were primitive at first. A favourite play activity with Duplo was to build a very tall tower, as tall as you could possibly build, of single bricks, and then watch the edifice keel over, jackknife in the middle and smash the length of the floor. But at least it was the kind of thing I could understand. You build, you destroy, there is pleasure. And as a bonus, I could even play with it myself, partly to pass the time, partly as a loving example to my kids. Indeed, there's a slender but real connection across the generations, and this connection adds all kinds of nostalgic resonances. I had Lego when I was small and although the product's become a thousand times more complex in the intervening years, I still recognise the little connecting buttons and the feel of the plastic (acrylonitrile butadiene styrene) and the mental leap you have to make in order to translate the incomplete,

Cubist interpretations of the world which Lego offers into the thing you really intend it to be.

Frankly, I don't know whether it's better or worse as a toy for not looking like anything wholly real. Back in the Sixties, the only things you could make with Lego were houses (which looked like authentic scale models of garages and public toilets) or wheeled vehicles (which looked like ineffably brutish dustcarts or the sort of things that the South African Army used to quell riots). I can remember a feeling of perpetual frustration with Lego when I was young that the number of things you could do with it was so limited, even if they were somehow true to the manufacturer's principles. What I wanted were curves, sports-car curves, or the elegant V of a 1950s nuclear strike bomber. Lego high-mindedly gave me buses shaped like bricks. Nowadays, on the other hand, you can make extremely close approximations of executive jets, manned space stations and smart, technically advanced dustcarts – into whose plasticky steps and ledges and nearly-curved surfaces and unexpected cavities you can either read your disappointment at the way life is never entirely what you want it to be, or your burning imaginative desire to transform what is into what should be.

But at least you can make these things, and at least I have always known what to do with Lego. I can make dumb zoos and funfairs with the Duplo. I can make a go-kart refreshment area with Lego the next size up (that is, the smaller, less nursery stuff), and I have even been drafted in to help with the Technic variety in the course of spaceship/computer-controlled dinosaur/automated pantechnicon construction. I have a purpose when I am near Lego and I am as grateful for that as for the fact that my kids have always been able to entertain themselves with it. I know that to some people Lego and its zealous Scandinavian commitment to self-improvement is tiresomely pious. But this is nothing in comparison with the relief it brings – made all the sweeter because it is a toy that comes *with instructions*. I know you *can* improvise with it, but instructions give the father something to do, a plan to follow, something which you know will fill a certain amount of time. And that alone leaves all other, self-expressive, spontaneous, regime-less toys in the dirt. Lego is both expressive and at the same time regimentedly anal: which is about ideal.

But then I always tend towards emotional repression and the rule of law. I know this, because I have an index of emotionalism against which to judge my repressiveness. I know what a stiff I can be, because I now know how mad I can get. And I know how mad I can get, because I have children. I can now get mad with my children and with my wife in a way that would have struck me as incredible when set against the slightly frigid torpor of my own upbringing, or against the aimless tolerance of my later youth. And I don't think I knew what real, impotent fury was until those early years, when I held my lovely baby in my arms and gazed at him in loathing because he would not stop threshing his beefy limbs about and just *shut up*. I can remember this happening at some time in the first year with Alistair, and feeling that the top of my head was lifting off and a great mushroom cloud of rage and insanity was shooting towards the ceiling. A terrible sensation, this trembling agitation, this loss of control starting to rush over me because I had done everything I was supposed to do, I had fed and watered and changed and amused this child and yet he would not *shut up*. And I know that when I thrust him down into his cot to yell, I did it more violently than I should have (*by God, that'll teach him a lesson*). But I also know that I was just competent enough to realise that what I needed to do was put him down and go away and go mad somewhere else and not actually damage him. Which I duly did, coming back after ten minutes, shaking with fright and remorse. Had I been someone not living in a comfortable middle-class house but in a midget flat, who gets severely depressed, or pilled up, or pissed, or psycho at inconvenient moments, it could have been catastrophic.

That must have set the ball rolling, because I then found that I could also get apoplectic with Susie, instead of pursuing my usual dog-in-the-manger low-key shittiness whenever she crossed me. On one occasion, arguing with her, I found that I was so furious that I had to smash something to register my rage. Up to that point I don't think I'd ever smashed anything before, so my technique (what to smash? how to smash it?) was poor. I had a plate in my hand, with a smoked salmon sandwich on it, which I had been just about to eat. I smashed it on the floor. Five minutes later I was on my hands and knees, trying to reconstitute the sandwich (we just don't have smoked salmon that often) and put it on a fresh, unbroken plate. It tasted okay, but crunchy with stoneware.

Susie got it too. As well as throwing those very large, black plums which come from California at my forehead (I was bruised for a week by one), she hurled a mug of coffee at me which I dodged and which broke against a framed poster we had over the fireplace. Years later, the mess has gone, but fading coffee fingers still reach across the lower edges of the picture. There was, bluntly, a release of feeling which unnerved us.

To some extent I cope with this anger mountain by being much gruffer with my children than she is and getting it out of my system on a rolling basis. She can, and does, contain her rage under a lid of pleasantness which abruptly bursts and leaves her screaming so loudly at the kids it's impossible that the neighbours shouldn't hear, and wonder what sort of monsters live next door. I, on the other hand, go around getting my retaliation in first and quickly, and being pleasantish after. The problem with this is that sometimes you can't be pleasant after, because some technical problem gets in the way. I can remember having a vicious fight with Alistair, after which he slammed himself in his bedroom and burst into tears and I staggered downstairs, put on a particularly sombre record (*Five Variants Of Dives And Lazarus*, the brilliantly sentimental Vaughan Williams number) and started weeping uncontrollably. Indeed, I *fell on my knees to the floor*, distraught that I'd been so horrible to my son. So I ran back upstairs to apologise and ask for forgiveness, only to find that the little swine had pre-empted me by falling asleep. I tried to raise the issue the next morning, but by then he'd forgotten: a permanent infliction of guilt.

And we both found that we could smack our children. I'm dragging us both in here, because I feel guilty about it and I want to spread the guilt around as much as I can. And of course, Susie has never done it as much as I have – indeed, has never smacked Tim at all. Smacking always provokes a special kind of shame. Even as I did it to one of my children (still do it, sometimes, to the younger one), I felt humiliated and witlessly apologetic. Sometimes I'd even blurt out the apologies as I smacked (on the back of the hand, this is, and I must have delivered a single smack on at least ten or fifteen occasions to each child over the past ten years) because I understood perfectly well at the precise moment of the downswing that this had no corrective use whatsoever, but was merely an expression of anger, and of an adult's ability to physically overwhelm a child a quarter of his or her size. What you get out of smacking is an instant short-term release and a fleeting moment of revenge for the ordeal your child has just been putting you through. And it has the function of bringing whatever stupidity you're bogged down in to an end, by making him or her cry – a brutal punctuation point, after which you can try and rebuild some sort of order. But that's about the best that can be said for it. Beyond that? I can't think that smacking has any moral usefulness or instructive value, other than to demonstrate that the world is full of people who whup you to make their point – and that if it's okay for Dad (who loves you) to hurt and humiliate you, then hurting and humiliating must be acceptable in all forms of society.

It's just a vicious expedient, bullying to order. If I'd told myself during the time of pregnancy that I was going to smack my kids once I'd become a father, I would have been incredulous. How could anyone be so depraved? And it is depraved. But it's something that's grown out of the general climate of rage and irrationality that sometimes seizes this family. 'Whatever you do to your child's body,' Leach intones, 'you are doing it to your child's mind, too.' She's right. But then, it goes with the whole sinister threat of brutality that underpins early childhood and which erupts in forms other than smacking – dragging, for instance. I've dragged in my time, as has a friend of mine who once found himself in the supermarket when his two-year-old son opted for a cyclonic tantrum around the cereals (those terrible twos! *Now* we can laugh). So instead of trying to calm him – you can't do it with twos – he decided to get out quick, yanked on the son's arm, found that the son wouldn't move. So he pulled harder; the son – sobbing and shouting now – fell down. He picked the son up. The son fell down again. A red mist descended and my mate found himself *dragging* his son along the floor like an industrial mop, bits of fluff and detritus collecting on his child's sweater and little boy's cord trousers, past the disgusted gaze of the other shoppers. He dragged him all the way to the check-out, before picking him up bodily (still screaming) and bundling him viciously out to the car park. A long moment of shaming violence. But as if this wasn't bad enough, what made it especially memorable, especially unbearable to recall, was the fact that it took place around the time of the Jamie Bulger case. The disgust on the other shoppers' faces was more than revulsion at his spasm of bullying: it was true, momentary fear and loathing. He was not just a bad-tempered dad: he was a murderer in disguise.

Nowadays, the main reason why I don't smack number one son any more is because he can hit me back just as hard if he wants to; and number two's not far off. Doesn't that make you despair of human nature?

A recent madness, the latest flowering of this particular derangement. Tim has taken it into his head that he must engrave his name on the back of his digital wristwatch. He wants a sharp, pointed implement from the toolbox to do it with. We point out that no tool is tough enough to make a dent on the watch's hardened steel back; and that even if there were such a tool, he's not having it, visions of our child sitting blood-boltered on the floor, stabbing at his own hand. There's a bit of a blur at this point. Somehow we get into one of those stand-offs – me and Susie versus Tim – in which he has some kind of bargaining chip and will not give in. The bargaining chip in this instance is that he has got to the stage where he is beyond reason and is either going to follow us all over the house, repeating his demand for ever, or is going to creep down later and steal any pointed tool from the toolbox and start stabbing away in his bedroom. To make it worse, he is raving and, within about a minute, so are we. We are raving so much, in fact, that I find myself clutching the watch and brandishing it in one hand while I brandish a hammer in the other, shouting that if Tim doesn't *shut up*, I will destroy the watch with that very hammer—

'*I don't want to do it!*' I hear myself yelling. '*Don't make me do it!*' It is pitiful. Tim takes a step towards the stairs. '*Right! The watch gets it!*'

I put the watch on the floor and wave the hammer over it.

'*Don't make me do this!*' Tim looks at me strangely. '*Don't worry! I'll buy you a new one when I've broken this!*'

I wave the hammer round a bit more.

'*Right! I can't do it! I can't bring myself to do it!*' I put the hammer down. I can't bring myself to do it. I can't bring myself to smash the watch I have bought for my son. Why am I even in the position of threatening to do so? Am I having a breakdown of some kind? Then Tim seizes the initiative and starts going on again about the watch and how he wants to engrave it with a very cruel and dangerous tool. His irrationality sparks off my irrationality again and I brandish the watch some more.

'*Now I really mean it—*'

I chicken out again. I have talked myself into a corner. The hammer hangs limply in my fingers.

'Oh, all right,' says Tim.

What am I *doing* here? Not only have I abdicated my responsibility to the principle that a parent should be more self-controlled than his children, I've allowed my irrationality to build on his irrationality, to the stage where we have created a completely closed dynamic system, whose structure is broken only by the child losing interest, rather than by the parent reasserting order: the exact reverse of what ought to be the case. How has this happened? How have I created this paradoxical inversion – the fruits of my own childish irresponsibility?

Taking a vaguely R.D. Laing/John Bradshaw line, it may – just – be a good thing. It may just be that Tim's childishness has triggered off a dormant childish aggression in me, something which I should have got out of my system years ago, and which I have been smothering beneath the musty worsted of adulthood, itself the product of my own dysfunctional childhood. This leads me to a paradox which argues that instead of fretting about losing my adult sense of self-control, I should be grateful for the fact that I have been liberated into a world of childish spontaneity. My loss is actually my gain if it means that I can get to my repressed inner child. At the same time as an encounter puts grey into my hair, it puts youth into my heart. This *may* be why it happens and why it's a good idea.

But while I'm happy enough (I suppose) to be correctively put in touch with my own feelings in this way, I can't help but be haunted by two thoughts. It's much more likely to be sheer, dreary, mundane parental stress and exhaustion which have worn out my mechanisms of self-control. And my parents would never, never have done such a thing to me. So far as I can recall, they never hit me, not even lightly, and certainly not with the flat of the hand. And they never got dragged into these anarchic family breakdowns. I don't see why I should be much more stressed than my own father (who was always, it has to be said, unusually lacking in emotional lability when bringing me up, even for someone who'd been in the War), yet I find myself staggering around and shouting like a character in an opera, or a Tennessee Williams play ('But tenderness, the violets in the mountains – can't break the rocks!'), and waving a hammer at my son's wristwatch.

Certainly there came a nasty point in year two of my fatherhood when it occurred to me that (a) I was never going to be free again; and (b) I was going to have to work my arse off to pay for my new imprisoning domestic arrangement. This is a realisation familiar to all parents, but shocking the first time it comes to you. And maybe that set in train a series of mental dislocations which have left me permanently unhinged.

Maybe it's no more than a product of general ageing, this discovery of more and more peculiar sides to a personality I previously believed to be completely sunny and well-balanced. Looking back, I think I was probably behaving a bit strangely with regard to everything – family, friends, work: at around this time, I was involved in writing for a costly TV series which paid a skipload of money but demanded endless lunatic re-writes in return. The upshot? In a twelve-month period I bought myself four cars (in succession, not to own simultaneously) as a way of letting off some kind of weird psychic steam; frittering my income away to appease some chronic mental irritation. Getting scorchingly angry with my family was – no doubt – another aspect of this.

So in a way I ought to be grateful for being inducted into a more emotionally responsive, dangerous universe, given that all knowledge, especially self-knowledge, is worth acquiring. As the mathematician E.C. Titchmarsh put it, 'If we can know, it surely would be intolerable not to know.'

Have I learnt anything other than that, though? Now, years on, am I better at managing my anger and the lunacy of my children? In a sense, yes, because patterns of rancour recur, grievance themes persist, you can tell when things are going wrong and, if alert and good-tempered enough yourself, you can often deal with the situation. But then, in a sense, no, I am not better at managing my anger and the lunacy of my children. Because as soon as you learn to deal with one kind of behaviour, your kids grow up and invent a whole new way to drive you mad. So you get a handle on that and they grow up some more and invent yet other behaviour patterns, and you are always going to be behind in the arms race, never managing to draw level. Is this really what I had in mind when I looked at my friends with their new, peculiar babies and wondered what my own might be like? I'd normally claim that I couldn't possibly have had a precognition of the kind of emotional fall-out that's resulted from the birth of my kids. But there are times when I do wonder if I had an intuition that there would be some of this. And that, after years of being an emotional stiff, this was the real, intensely feeling commodity I was after. Which must make me either smarter or madder than even I knew when I started this whole thing.

THREE

So Mr Skweezum the Clown (not his real name) is cramming his gear (PA system, magic tricks set, collapsing Punch and Judy booth) into a couple of flight cases. His make-up is still on his face. He once, apparently, had a small speaking part in *EastEnders*, but got written out. I say, 'Do you want a drink. Or something?'

'No thanks,' he answers, breathlessly kneeing the front door open and hurrying out into the rain, to where his car (a surprisingly new Peugeot) is parked. 'Got another gig in Camberley at six,' he goes on. 'Sorry.'

I help him lever his stuff into the back of the car, and peel off the seventy quid I owe him for our gig. You can get Mr Skweezum by the measure – half an hour, forty-five minutes, the full hour. We've bought forty-five minutes' worth. He counts the cash out, like Chuck Berry, and splits. 'Gotta run,' he calls over his shoulder. 'The little beasts.'

We've had Skweezum before. Alistair got him once and he was so good at diverting the rabble for an hour that we asked him back. Another date in Skweezum's endless world tour around the suburbs of south London. Today it is Tim's fourth birthday party and Skweezum has based half of his act around some sleight-of-hand and closework, the other half around Punch and Judy and a terrible lot of shouting. He has stuck a red clown's wig on Tim's head in front of twelve blood-hungry four-year-olds, which has *very nearly* reduced Tim to tears. But I proudly watch him fight the weeping back and pretend to enjoy the Birthday Boy attention. Skweezum has also produced some spongy red balls from people's ears, folded a balloon to music and beaten himself up with glove puppets. He wears the statutory Coco/Grock clown's make-up, behind which a young middle-aged face looks warily out, like a businessman expecting a call from the Customs and Excise. I have only ever managed to watch his act through a blizzard of embarrassment and apprehension; not because he is especially bad, but because the situation is always so fraught, so crackling with tension, that I cannot bring myself to take it in fully. Sometimes I have felt myself experiencing out-of-body sensations. He drives off quickly and erratically, leaving me to face the mob indoors.

As my mother has rarely tired of pointing out, I was disbarred from ever again having large-scale parties in my own house after my sixth birthday party, in the course of which every single guest fought with every single other guest and I was found in the fireplace (the fire wasn't lit) punching someone's head in. Violence and gatherings of small children, I would have pointed out at the time, had I been able, go together: the fascism of the young. So in that respect I know what to expect from a kids' party, almost by instinct. What's changed since my time are the material accessories to kids' parties; and the expectations of how much the father is supposed to do. Nowadays, at an average middle-class kids' bash, the presumption is that there will be at least one entertainer, some professionally catered food (even if this only means a cake from the nearest shop) and a selection of goodies to take home in a printed polythene bag. Our statutory requirements in the early years also included some little low tables and tiny chairs that I had to hire from a frighteningly robust and competent woman in Kew. She used to keep a big stash of party things in her house and bustle some of them out to my waiting car (usually in the rain for some reason) with a cry of *Marvellous! Have a good time!* And when I gruntingly brought them back again, she'd shout *Marvellous! See you next year!* Nowadays I would bet money that she offers not only the fairy chairs and tables for hire, but also flashing lights, an illuminated dance floor, professional pyrotechnic displays, bungee jumping. The ratcheting effect of money and technology on the young child's birthday party is scary.

What's more, here in the suburbs, things change fundamentally every twelve months, to keep up with the natural cycle of birth and growth. At first it was enough just to have these little tables with melamine tops and chairs to match. Then the size and plenitude of the party bags for the departing guests started to go up, to the extent that our kids were going home with nicer gifts in the party bags than they'd brought as presents to the party. And then we had to invite along adults other than family and friends to keep the tots happy: professionals. We were modest, getting Mr Skweezum. Other kids have had proper conjurors, discos and The Animal Men. We never made it as far as The Animal Men, but from all accounts they were exceptional. They would bring in a selection of tarantulas, constrictors, lizards, birds of prey, coati-mundis, whatever came to hand. The tinies would then handle these beasts and answer a quiz on them and sometimes run from the room sobbing. One child got pissed on by a bushbaby. Both my boys went to parties where The Animal Men were, and indeed, I have an idea that The Animal Men got to recognise my boys and avoided asking them too many questions, since it was clear that they'd already learnt the answers.

The Animal Men were in fact at the apogee of most party ambitions – until much later on, when go-karting became a viable option – but a quick look at my current *Yellow Pages* reveals a mass of current pretenders to their throne. There are some forty-two local kids' entertainers (including Mr McDonut, Billy Bonkers, Professor Fumble, Twizzle Entertainment and Custardo), a *tsunami* of funsters which would have been unbelievable twenty-five years ago and which, even now, has something of American excess about it.

I hate to sound very old, but when I went to kids' parties as a kid, we were forced – our parents were forced – to take part in things like Blind Man's Buff, Pass-the-Parcel, Musical Chairs and Make Yourself Look Stupid. This last involved blindfolding the contenders and sending them into a room which was supposedly full of obstacles and traps. Whoever had done the course immediately before you talked you through the maze like an airport control tower talking down a pilot in fog. So you'd wobble your way from one side to the other, doggedly following your instructions, teetering and swaying and crouching so as not to hit anything, and when you got to the other side and had the blindfold removed, what did you find but that the room was actually *empty*, and that you'd contorted yourself and struck endless ridiculous postures in front of your coevals, for no reason whatsoever! What a kill! God, we made sure to get some sadistic pleasure out of whoever was next to come into the room. We also spent the rest of the game assessing how favoured we were by the party-giver's affections. If you went first, or at least early, you were being spared the humiliation of doing it in front of lots of people and were therefore a special friend; if you went last, you were irredeemably the party scapegoat, someone who'd been invited solely to make up the numbers. Those were the days when we not only made our own entertainment, but acquired our own special complexes as well. And I have to say that I view the ubiquitous presence of the professional party entertainer with the same unease that I view the ubiquitous presence of the computer game and the video – symptoms of a generation of children addicted to a solipsistic gratification of the senses, and forever dependent on the labours of adults to provide a focus for their own imaginations; as well as being a generation of children sadly out of touch with serious ritual humiliation.

The nearest we got to trying to re-invent this hectic, do-it-yourself state was early on with Alistair, on *his* fourth birthday. Susie did all the senseless things my mother once did (cake plus decoration, finger foods, Pass-the-Parcel, Hunt-the-Goodies trail around the house – involving, socialising games – all that) while I made – an endless labour, practically a whole afternoon's work – a kind of Pin-the-Tail-on-the-Donkey game, where you had to pin a pirate's galleon (photocopied from a book) on a treasure island. I was sadly proud of this. The galleon in particular was beautiful, a little engraved vision of some barquentine of the South Seas with a mizzenmast, forecastle, poop and complex rigging. I constructed a map of the world, with some islands in odd places, and even coloured it in – golden sands, azure seas, grampus whales and red Maltese crosses. I looked at it again and again, trying to surprise myself with fresh aspects of its beauty. And since it was intrinsically boys' stuff, I, as the most responsible boy, was put in charge of it at the party. But children have no interest at that age in honest competition. They have no wish to *try*. Instead, once I had revealed my beautiful game and explained the rules, they chattered among themselves, squabbled, ate crisps, lost interest and wandered off.

'What's it for?' one of them asked.

'You stick the little boat on the map. Whoever's nearest to the treasure island wins the prize!'

'Why?'

One or two hung around long enough to stab at the board ('Is that it? Do I get the sweets now?'), but I was left on my own by the end, shouting and waving the victor's prize (packet of Smarties, inevitably) to the vacant air like a bad fairground shill. The winner (by default) had bunked off. I looked at my little ship and felt humiliated.

The fact that none of the other things – Pass-the-Parcel, Hunt-the-Goodies – went down any better made no difference to my disappointment. It was something about the way it slighted my fatherly endeavour to create fun – that job of being playmaster, the ludic dad who *reigns* – that really hurt. Because, to be honest, I must have foreseen myself triumphantly orchestrating a terrific game of Pin-the-Boat, a crowd of happy, excited youngsters pressing round, begging to be allowed to try their luck, so delighted and amused were they by my enthralling game, by my larger-than-life personality and my railleries. It would have been compensation for all those years – from adolescence onwards – of not being the life and soul of the party. It would have been a deferred payment on teenage failure to become instead the ideal party dad, toiling to build his little Pin-the-Boat entertainment and then bring it to life in his own inimitable way. I would have won the admiration of the mob and the adoration of my kids. It would have been perfect, for a half-hour: drawing on what I guess must animate those oddballs who go into kids' entertainment and perform for young audiences in theatres – the knowledge that when children laugh or applaud or are frightened or enraptured, they are entirely sincere in their responses, unable to mediate them through expectation or experience and thus giving the entertainer the unusual certainty that he or she has really achieved what he or she set out to achieve.

Why did *my* father never have to go through this? There was nothing to stop him. He could have cleared his desk for an afternoon and come home and put up with the ghastliness as I have had to do and he could have lurked around, the same lowering presence as me. He could have done a Pin-the-Boat game. He could have swatted children and tried to look delighted with something that frankly nauseated him. *And* he could have made glassy-eyed conversation with the other parents – usually mothers – as they came by to collect their kids, or even stay the duration; long, tormenting hours with a glass of warm white wine, chatting about holiday plans. But of course he didn't because he didn't have to. He was sanctioned by the social conventions of the time. He was the only breadwinner in the family and as such could hide in his office, merely coming home hours later to find the house looking like a field hospital struck by a stray shell and my mother busily inhaling her third gin of the night.

But then one of the unexpected by-products of these birthday events was the realisation that even if no one wanted to play my game, I was now truly part of the generation in charge. I was one of the breeders, as my parents had been thirty years before. I was becoming my father, even though he never went to one of my parties. I had, at least, made progress of some kind. And I knew this because I couldn't remember what it was like to be a baby, but I could remember what it was like to be a child at a children's party, and consequently could appreciate the difference between what I was then and what I was now. There was a sense of perspective which I hadn't experienced before. When we had our first kid and he was tiny and new, it was as if this had never happened in my life, to me or anyone else: no one had ever been a baby before; it was novel, a unique experience. But by the time my baby was punching his guests in time to Mr Skweezum's 'The Wheels On The Bus Go Round Round Round', there was a link with the past which put my present into focus. The disparities between parties as I remembered them and parties as they seemed to be now pointed up the fact that I had had parties and I had behaved appallingly, and I had been three, four years old and wasn't now, and that I was, incontrovertibly, a father, a dad, an old geezer in rotten trousers in the corner. *It happened in my life: now it's happening in yours*, as Morrissey almost sang. I could begin to measure the distance between me and them. It was like the Lego, in that there was an involving, informing connection; unlike the Lego in that parties were rotten then and rotten now.

The other by-product was that my kids started to have social lives. They have parties, they invite people, therefore these people must be friends, therefore they must have social lives. In fact they have been having a kind of ur-social life from the time they began to have proto-parties, in which the tiny tots are so small – say, one year old – that they can barely socialise with their mothers, let alone with other children. On these occasions, the haggard middle-class parents feel the need nonetheless to make some kind of display, so they bus in some sympathetic friends with toddlers about the same age and call it a party. You end up with a roomful of alienated nappy-wearers, all slobbering and gumming and pasting food over themselves and the furniture while the mums – and one dad, me – bare their teeth and try to make it look like Happytime. I have a photograph of our first ever proto-party. About five women and five children are spread out on the floor, squatting in corners and turning their backs defensively to the camera. Only one child is looking up, a sob trembling on her lip. Babyish debris – plastic blocks, balloons, wedges of cake, dummies, bottles, bootees, sweaters, biscuits, party squeakers, vast cardboard beginners' books (the ones with bold primary realisations of cups and spades inside, no plot, like early toys, impossible for a sane adult to infuse with life), plastic cups, paper plates, my guitar (we wrongly assumed that I could get them to sing 'Happy Birthday' or

'The Wheels On The Fucking Bus' if they had an accompaniment) – all lie like the pathetic remains of a plague village. Looking back, the proto-parties were probably, despite everything, better than the later parties, because less prone to hysteria. And their atmosphere of glum incomprehension was easier to deal with than the open warfare of subsequent years. But they felt like wakes at the time.

But now, aged four, they no longer had their mothers with them. They were individuated members of a society. They had begun the long descent into Mr Skweezum. And just as I was beginning to feel properly individuated from my child, so my child was staking a claim to be a separate person with friends, preferences, social choices. And at the same time as I felt a poignant moment of pride in my son's independence, I felt all the apprehension of someone who worries that a person dear to them is going to commit some kind of social catastrophe, or be rejected by others, or just be unhappy in some way. Of course, with an adult, you'd be watching out for misdemeanours like nose-picking, audible farting, gross verbal infelicities, tactlessness, humiliating body-language, open flies, stains, poor dress sense, protruding bogies, inappropriate facial hair, dullness, racist jokes, pomposity, exaggerated self-abasement, halitosis, inappropriate lasciviousness, shouting, spots, mental-patient haircut, wonky tie, depression. With a four-year-old, most of these things are tolerated and indeed inescapable. So the transgressions you look out for are much simpler, much more visceral. You look out for hysteria, extreme physical violence, food-throwing, vomiting, abject tearfulness, catatonia, complete breakdown resulting in the child hiding under the table/in the laundry basket/behind the fridge. You loiter helplessly on the fringes of your child's first steps into a world beyond your grasp, a world of independent and self-actualising existence.

The strain is almost invigoratingly terrible, even if nothing bad happens. If he just looks bored or gloomy or somehow unimpressed by his new, real friends, then you speculate as to why, and how you can change his personality so that he looks at least cheerfully outgoing. But of course you can't. It dawns on you that you help him to grow up reasonably big and strong. You keep him clean and educate him. You can even teach him manners. But you can't make him nice or outgoing or amiable if he doesn't want to be. And this is how it's going to be, for ever.

I was reading a book the other day. It was called *The Mask Of Motherhood* and it was by someone called Susan Maushart, a Senior Research Associate in the School of Social Sciences and Asian Languages at Curtin University, Perth. In it she writes, 'Truly egalitarian marriages are probably a lot rarer than we like to admit, but an increasing number are at least approaching the ideal of down-the-line, fifty-fifty sharing.

'Yet, when the first child comes along, most egalitarian couples will hit the wall at high speed. Just when they thought the dangers of gender-typing were dead and buried, they find them rising up like unquiet spirits from the wreckage. Suddenly, she is "Mum" and he is "Dad".'

Well, this is gender politics, here, and of course when you see your situation printed in black and white, in a book of unremitting pessimism ('The result is a deal in which everyone feels short-changed without ever quite understanding how they got that way') you sit up: which is the primary function of the book.

I like to think that I don't fit handily into that category of men who pay lip service to the principle of equality but who then become nauseating recidivists when their own children come along. I know that the dynamic of these things is that when the woman has a child, she's more likely to put her career on hold to be Mother, while the man goes out and earns the money. It's happened – it's still happening – to surprisingly large proportions of our educated, semi-liberal friends and acquaintances. To Susie's horror, the men are, predictably enough, apt to sod off as much as they can to the office, trailing the surprising intelligence behind them that with two or more mouths to feed, they must work harder than ever before, and, incidentally, garner all the privileges of perceived high status that being the principal money-earner brings; no matter what praise attaches to the woman who brings up the children. I know that.

But we have an entirely different dynamic, based to no small extent on the fact that, as a hack working from home (in the way of many writers), I am on the spot very often and cannot physically avoid my duties of childcare, picking up from school, cooking meals. Susie also works at home and we have a strict and pedantic division of childcare, involving many sessions with the diary to determine, on a legalistically equitable basis, who's in charge on any given day. To be honest, this is just the way it's turned out. Although I sign up, like any middle-class liberal, to the broad, emancipatory ideals of modern womanhood, like any middle-class man, I'd much rather I didn't have to do these boring things. And there are many duties that I will not get involved in. I will not organise the boys' social lives because that is still essentially a mother-to-mother transaction and when a father starts trying to fix these things he comes over as either a weirdo or as some guy just trying cynically to off-load his kids for the day. Also, I will not take the boys to the hairdresser. And I will not buy uniforms from the school second-hand clothes jumble. In fact, I occasionally wish I'd managed my life more ruthlessly and was one of those writers (I have met one or two) who are *so* ambitious, *so* industrious, that they're simply never there at all; forever legging it to Nepal or Wales or São Paolo. Actually, Paul Theroux should have fitted this latter category to a T, and yet he writes, touchingly, (in *My Other Life*) about making supper for the kids after school: 'While they sat at the table, saying little, I made the spaghetti sauce . . . Later, waiting for Alison to come home, I watched a television game show with Anton, who had finished his homework . . . This ordinariness was what I liked and needed. It had been a perfect day.' A clever evocation of a writer's domestic Arcadia, and apparently all of a piece with supreme professional ambition. I just don't believe him, that's all.

Frankly, I feel ambivalent about the whole thing, and have been feeling ambivalent since about this third or fourth year of fatherhood, the time at which the novelty of the new child has worn off and the realisation has dawned that you are in for an incredibly long haul – one so long and protracted that it's impossible even to guess at the end to which you're striving. On the one hand, I have had the unarguable privilege of seeing my children almost every day of their lives, growing up in front of my eyes and – apart from the fulfilment that brings in itself – developing a certain closeness, mutual understanding, affection. On a cash basis alone, this means that I am getting value for every pound I put into them. On the other hand, as Cyril Connolly notoriously observed, 'There is no more sombre enemy of good art than the pram in the hall.' Well, Connolly's pram has not just been in the hall, it's been in the office with me and its occupants have quite often physically got out and dragged me away from my work. What's more, I have even *turned work down* because I have not been able to re-jig the diary commitments, so toilingly engineered with my wife. There's one hot-air balloon trip over the vineyards of the Napa Valley that a magazine once asked me to do and I didn't – on account of domestic commitments – that still rankles. These are sacrifices I have hated making (although let's not kid ourselves here: had I had all the time in the world, I guarantee that I would have wasted at least half of it and spent a further quarter in what my accountant would have regarded as questionable pursuits), presumably because, as a short-sighted, status-fixated man, I equate time spent with my boys at the expense of my career or bank account as lost time.

Do I, though, take a pride in my achievement when I look at them and admire their cleverness and handsome looks and their many skills? Well, that's the thing. They are their own people, so plainly themselves, so obviously filling exactly the space in the universe that they should fill, that I can't tell where my efforts have had much effect. They would have been like that whether I'd been around or not, is the thought that weighs on my mind. And then when I stop and reconsider how different they would have been if I *hadn't* been around, I start to wonder how much of my influence has been good, how much bad, whether they've come out broadly in credit for knowing me, or worse off. And that, in turn, is the way to a special kind of madness – trying to glean a sense of your own worth by guessing at how well or badly you've shaped the personalities and intellects of your kids, how much difference your presence has made, speculating on what a different past would be like and guessing at the projected consequences of something that hasn't happened and can never happen.

In the modern world, there's no escaping the truth that if you *can* both split the childcare down the middle, you *should*. Piety, however, doesn't make you – doesn't make *me* – feel much better. As Ms Maushart puts it, 'Such "success story" families look good but feel bad.' Indeed, so exercised was I by this problem that I asked Tim whether he thought it was better to have an equal amount of looking-after by both mother and father, or whether he thought it would be better done by one person. He thought, on the whole, that it was better with two – fairer, because, as he put it, 'That way they share the suffering equally.'

★　　★　　★

And where was the fatherhood book at this time? Up to and including the moment of parturition, there were masses of texts, as there were for the first twenty or so months of life. But after that? Where was my father-centred resource text when I needed it, now that I had a child of four, rather than two? How *about* books for dads?

Had I been looking now, of course, I'd be rich with possibilities.

Examples: the actor Nigel Planer did a book about being a new father a few years ago, called *A Good Enough Dad*. More recently, news correspondent Fergal Keane wrote an open letter to his young son, Daniel (*Letter To Daniel*, aptly). Still more recently, a load of hacks (including Tony Parsons and Stephen Bayley) contributed to an anthology called *Fatherhood*, while an Australian called Steve Biddulph has made a whole profession out of writing books about the subject (*Raising Boys* being the most recent addition). And the American on-line virtual bookshop, Amazon.com, lists a staggering number of books on the subject, including, *inter alia*: *The Christian Dad's Answer Book*; *If I Were Starting My Family Again*; *She Calls Me Daddy — Seven Things Every Man Needs To Know About Building A Complete Daughter* (I am not inventing this); *Thanks, Dad*; *Velvet & Steel: A Practical Guide For Christian Fathers*; *Daddy's Home: Reflections Of A Family Man*; *I Thought Of It While Shaving: Ideas For Devoted Dads*; *Bill Cosby's Fatherhood*; *Procreative Man*; and *The Fatherhood Of God From Origin To Athanasius*. Even Waterstone's will find you between five and ten books on the subject at any given time. *Now*, I'd be spoiled for choice — with the possible proviso that such fatherhood books as I have come across since *How To Be A Pregnant Father* either treat the issue with grim seriousness (*The Uncertain Father*, by Richard Seel; *Fatherhood Reclaimed* by Adrienne Burgess) or, alternatively, a bleary, tremulous sweetness (*Dads: Quotations Selected By Helen Exley*).

Take this *Letter To Daniel*. BBC news correspondent Fergal Keane, in all other respects a model of his kind – industrious, fluent, clear-eyed without being unemotional – wrote this one short, moist-eyed, Celtic Twilight piece to his baby son and broadcast it on the BBC, only to find that it was the best-received thing he'd ever done (despite his years of sterling service in Rwanda, Eritrea, Angola, South Africa). As a result not only did it make its way, incongruously, into a book of spunky newshound reminiscences, it even gave the thing its title. Thus, *Letter To Daniel* is mainly blood-filled reflections on tribal conflict and the last months of apartheid, prefaced schismatically by an exercise about 'the last stars flickering towards the other side of the world', and how 'days have melted into night and back again and we are learning a new grammar, a long sentence whose punctuation marks are feeding and winding and nappy changing.' This culminates in a lachrymose, Joycean 'story from long ago' about memory, alcoholism and the compromised and inexplicable personal affections that constitute a family. On the one hand, the world in turmoil and violence; on the other, a couple of thousand words of sacramental emoting.

Why does this happen, when men write about their own children? Look at Laurie Lee in *I Can't Stay Long*. Yes, he comes out with that terrific, alienated stuff about his baby snorting and gobbling like a jackdaw, but this is prefaced by much more typical prosing about how his baby daughter's 'frail self-absorption is a commanding presence, her helplessness as strong as a rock, so that I find myself listening even to her silences as though some great engine was purring upstairs.' Why not come out with it and tell the truth? Say it's driving you mad? D.H. Lawrence (although childless) manages to get something of the right mood in *The Rainbow*, when he describes Tom Brangwen's response to his new baby's crying: 'His soul answered its madness. It filled him with terror, almost with frenzy.' This is exactly right, straight on the money. But then even Lawrence falls under the spell and unnecessarily redresses the balance on the next page, with what he calls 'the joy coming.' This is in the form of 'the lovely, creamy, cool little ear of the baby, a bit of dark hair rubbed to a bronze floss', and so on. Why does Nigel Planer say, when recounting a futile chat-up of some girls, that all he could do was pick on the one with a baby and ask '"Does he sleep through the night? Is he having trouble teething? Has he had colic? Oh look, he smiled. Can I smell his scalp?" (Babies' scalps. Mmmmm.) All this with an idiotic and beatific grin right across my face'? Why, when he describes his wife's labour, does he say that 'it was extraordinarily soothing to be in the grip of such a powerful rhythm. Like the tide coming in. She knelt against the bed, breathing slow and deep. So calm, and so concentrated'? Why does he pepper the text with cutely lumpy original line-drawings of him and his child (*Who's sleeping in my bed? I don't need a bath; Which end do I put the bottle in?*)?

There's evidently some special pleading going on here. Given that men, taken overall, can veer wildly from affectionate, selfless, tender, prudent and loveable, to emotionally careless, denying, imperfectly integrated, aggressive and self-centred, I can see that any man committing himself in print would want to go out of his way to emphasise that the second list of attributes does not necessarily depict *him*. That *he* can move beyond that rationale. But writing in this vein starts to sound unreally tender, a confection of emotions meant to impress the reader with the idea that this particular author is a creature of extra-refined sympathies. What's more, it not only advertises the hypothetical niceness of the writer, it clearly carries a propagandising message to its male readership, a covert injunction to lay off the stereotypical male alienation and get in touch with your softer, more nurturing feelings. Which is socially and ideologically fine: it just reads falsely. I've been around this issue for ten years now, and while you can (*I* can) get these chocolatey wellings-up of love and protectiveness, there are plenty of other moods around, barking for your attention. The truth is not uniformly melting and tender and books which exclude the dark side do no favours to anyone.

(Parenthetically, did I ever try any other resources? Glean tips from the movies? Investigate magazines such as *Practical Parenting* or *Parents*? So far as the former are concerned, films that spring to mind with anything realistic about child-rearing tend to be things like *Kramer v. Kramer*, *Look Who's Talking* and *Mrs Doubtfire*: only of the slimmest use. Those and, say, *ET*, in which the world of the child is so neatly conjured up that you might learn something about your subject in that interestingly haphazard way that children learn about dating and snogging from *Blind Date*. As for genre parenting magazines – well, *Practical Parenting* and *Parents* are clearly aimed at the traditional world of mothers and their very young tots, with their acid colour schemes of magenta and blue, and articles which begin, 'He was there at conception, so should he be there at the birth? Antenatal teacher Jane Chumbley explores the role of your partner at the birth.' Nothing *there* for the man. Added to this is the fact that even in today's culture, books have a gravity about them, a sense that what they say is somehow canonical. The mass of text and the permanence of even a paperback gives it an authority that you just don't find in a monthly magazine, even one like *Practical Parenting*, even with sales of 80,000 an issue.

Then again, if I'd read Henry Miller before starting a family, I'd never have bothered at all. He testifies to a reality so awful, it's prophylactic (although not, maybe, as bad as the one conjured up from the child's perspective by the notorious Sylvia Plath: 'Daddy, Daddy, you bastard', etc). Writing (in *My Life And Times*) about a time when he was stuck in Big Sur with his small children, he says, 'I fed them, changed their clothes, washed them, told them stories. I didn't do any writing. I couldn't. By noon every day I was exhausted!' Things weren't helped by the fact that they were all stuck in one room, *and* he had to drag the laundry six miles on foot to get it washed. 'Finally,' he confesses, without any attempt at self-justification, 'I had to ask my wife to take them . . . I realized what a tremendous job women have, married women, cooking meals, doing the laundry, cleaning house, taking care of children and all that. This is something no man can understand or cope with no matter how hard his work may be.'

You offer your congratulations to the antipuritanical author of *Tropic of Cancer* for his honesty, and for his insights into being a father at home, but it makes a lousy advertisement for the condition of fatherhood. Like Evelyn Waugh, come to think of it, who, after eating all the rationed post-War bananas meant for his kids (according to Auberon Waugh in *Will This Do?*, and with cream, too) managed at best to say that 'The more I see of other people's children the less I dislike my own,' but also, far more typically, 'I now dislike them all equally.'

Can you imagine Fergal Keane coming up with anything like that? It's part of Waugh's character as a sacred monster to be able to say these things – terrible improprieties, embarrassing verbal cruelties – but then, hasn't Keane felt anything similar? Won't he? My guess is the British public fell upon his *Letter to Daniel* precisely because it was an idealised moment in fatherhood, an impossibility – about as representative of that state as Coventry Patmore's *Husband and Wife* is of the state of marriage. Fergal is writing at the very onset of fatherhood, when he's swept up in the novelty, infatuation, transforming energy of it all. Another decade, and it'll all be horribly different.

Or am I merely being repressed again? It occurs to me sometimes that Keane and Planer and Lee are right to articulate the purely sentimental and I'm wrong to censure it; because it isn't an easy thing to do, and one needs a lead, occasionally. In fact, I sometimes think that my children mean so much to me that I can't say how much they mean to me, either because it's incommunicable, unless as a coded message between myself and other fathers; or because I fear that if I were to say how much I love them, I'd only tempt fate to do something terrible, or myself to do something stupid. That's how important they are: so important I can't even put it into words.

Unless you're a child out of Dickens, in which case your development as a young person tends to be both accelerated and dysfunctional (*Little Dorrit*, *Great Expectations*, *Oliver Twist*), there's usually some sort of gradation from living entirely in a world governed by your parents, to a world peopled by non-family members of all kinds and interests. Kids are brought out like debutantes over a long succession of months. You start with the parents and then move on, conventionally, to the grandparents and then by degrees through close friends to broader acquaintances to utter strangers, some of whom will be responsible for the future growth and happiness of your kid. To put it another way, you go from a secular suburban Holy Family, to the Adoration of the Magi (arrival of grandparents) to the Presentation of Christ in the Temple (arrival of everyone else) in one long, seamless move.

In our case, being wacky nonconformists, we didn't get our in-laws round to our house together in one gathering until after the first baby was born. Normally you'd expect them to have met at least at the wedding, but since we weren't married at that stage, there'd been no wedding and so no convenient moment for them to meet. What larks! We dragged them in straight after Christmas to celebrate Alistair's birth and the four of them beamed and chortled at each other in a frighteningly middle-class attempt to size each other up for genetic implications without actually insisting on a blood test. We shoved some extra chairs round the dining table, cooked up a load of turkey, stuffed paper hats on our heads. There was an ectoplasmic sensation of Mike Leigh in the room for a while, but then after fifteen minutes it looked as if both parties had decided not to kill each other and I produced a really stupidly old bottle of champagne (which nonetheless – emblematically – tasted okay) and we all ate a big meal.

'Well, Ray,' my mother kept saying to my father-in-law, as he was soon to become, 'this is a pleasure, meeting you at *last*,' and flicking her gaze at me in a microsecond of outrage. 'I'm sure you didn't think we were going to meet in quite these circum-stances.' Then volleys of we're-all-in-it-together-aren't-these-kids-too-much? laughter, while I drank myself single-mindedly under the table.

Fair's fair, though: they did the decent thing and hardly bitched on at us at all to get married once Alistair had arrived; and they certainly didn't bitch at each other. And this is important. If the grandparents *are* one of the first real integrations of the outside world into the new personality of your kid, you don't want them being evil. It's surprising, though, the number of times you come across that generation screwing it up either for their children or for the other side of the family. Off-hand I can think of at least seven families in which the grandparents either make things awkward for the other grandparents; or – more usually – for the children, and get at the other grandparents that way. I don't mean (I think) that they shamble about the house like Burl Ives as Big Daddy, growling *mendacity* all the time and saying that 'truth is pain and sweat and paying bills and making love to a woman that you don't love any more' (cf. Blake Morrison, *And When Did You Last See Your Father?*, 'The unending cycle of sex and parenthood, never enough time, never enough patience'). They just act quietly like bastards, playing stupid games of hierarchical seniority which revolve around who gets to see more of the kids and grandkids at Christmas; who gets invited away at Easter breaks; whose photographs are more prominently displayed (if displayed at all) in public places; who can give the more expensive presents. In one case I know of, this ferocious pettiness meant that the family with the kids had to enjoy two Christmas dinners – one at one grandparents' house, the other at the others', a sweaty car sprint in between, just to placate everyone's *amour-propre*. In another, it meant constant elaborate lying to each party about how much attention the other party was getting, in order to avoid rows and scenes and vendettas. This became more and more untenable as the children got older, more independent-minded and articulate – culminating in a whole six months' banishment from one grandparental house when the truth came out, courtesy of a five-year-old, that they'd taken the other grandparents away with them *on holiday*. In a third case – involving a particularly messy family break-up – one lot of grandparents simply denied the other lot access or visiting rights.

Outsiders usually only experience these corrosive disagreements at second-hand. As Heisenberg pointed out, the act of observing a phenomenon will change the nature of the phenomenon being observed. I've been at get-togethers where both sets of grandparents have been present, plus all possible children and grandchildren, and everything has gone just fine – largely because strangers like myself were present. A few weeks later, though, and we're with the party hosts, minus grandparents, and the line has been, 'So *your* mother couldn't wait till everyone had left before she started complaining about the way *my* mother had been allowed to spend the night with us while *they* had to stay in a hotel. She cornered me in the kitchen and started going on and on.'

'Yes, but at least *my* mother didn't try and upstage the whole event by producing that ridiculous cake thing and making us all eat a piece.'

'But then your *father* . . .'

Maybe this is just an index of what a viciously small-minded middle-class world I inhabit. Maybe it happens with everyone. The fact is, we've managed to avoid it *so far*, for which I am thankful.

But then, what are grandparents for? Mystical Connectedness about sums it up. Before kids, I tended to assume that grandparents just do what they do, and by virtue of being of *that* generation, what they do is axiomatically grandparental – whether it's romping in a fuddy-duddy way with their small grandchildren, or cooking large, old-fashioned Sunday lunches, or being foul to the other side of the family, or just slouching around smoking fags and reading the *Daily Mirror*. Why should uncles be avuncular? They just are. Why shouldn't grandparents be the same?

But once I found myself doing it for real, sandwiched by grand-parents on one side and children on the other, I started to appreciate that *all* oldsters – family or not – have a powerful iconic value, and that grandparents feed off that, becoming receptacles for our needs and dreams. If you think of the ways oldsters, grandparental, avuncular or just old, tend to be depicted or presented, you sense this residue of symbolic meaning, building up over the years. I mean, they crop up in all kinds of guises and with all sorts of character-istic inflections: Lord Emsworth, the P.G. Wodehouse character; Rembrandt's Margaretha de Geer; Marlon Brando lurching around the plum tomatoes as he gives chase to his little grandson in *The Godfather*; the old Captain Birds Eye; Mr Pastry; the Queen Mother;

Karl Marx; Antonio, the granddad in Eduardo de Filippo's *Saturday Sunday Monday* (played onstage in London by Laurence Olivier); the old git who advertises Werther's Originals on the TV; Lord Marchmain in *Brideshead Revisited* (played on film by Laurence Olivier); Queen Victoria; King Lear. They're clearly of this world, clearly parents at some level, but at the same time, more primed with meaning than the actual parents themselves, who are too locked into the day-to-day battle to be anything other than functional slaves. Grandparents can draw on a cultural well of possibilities, in which they can assume power, wisdom, frailness, assininity, tolerance, calm, irrationality, reflectiveness, or any combination of these things in a way which parents never can.

Roald Dahl (a classic oldster himself) was keenly interested in generational differences, and whereas characters in his books from the parents' generation are often dullards or monsters (Mr and Mrs Wormwood in *Matilda*; Aunts Sponge and Spiker in *James and the Giant Peach*), the grandma in *The Witches*, being *in loco parentis* but old enough to be freed from the constraints of being a parent, can be wise, resourceful and engaging in a way that parents would find impossible. She smokes cigars, carries a gold-topped cane and interprets life with the same fervent enthusiasm as a kid ('Are you or are you not going to allow my grandson to keep his white mice in his room?') while at the same time displaying the wisdom and shrewdness of old age. So once our family members start to go grey, they automatically tap into that reservoir of oldsters we've come across in the past, borrowing bits off them and doing their grandparent thing almost by association. I recognised my parents as grandparents (once they became grandparents) not only because of biological reality, but because they resembled the iconic figures I'd previously encountered.

Of course, once my parents became grandparents, I expected them to behave in some way like an ideal of grandparents, something more narrowly defined than parenthood, but equally emotionally imposing. Looking at it from their point of view, this must have been a burden. Especially as *being a grandparent* is something grandparents can only really do once the grandchildren are old enough to understand that they *are* grandparents and are qualitatively distinct from parents. As it turns out, my mother does this by being the comfortable, provisioning grandma, feeding the kids bushels of stuff that's bad for them (chips and ice cream and sugary biscuits) and not having any fruit in the house (a big plus). She also loads up on *Beanos* and other easy reading, has a TV set twice the size of the one we have at home (and twice as loud), never shouts at them, treats them with absolute indulgence and even lets them clamber up her diseased apple tree and wreck it as part of a warlord death mission. They like all this very much. Away from the rigours of their own home, with all its irksome regulations and evil-tempered parents shouting and cursing, this is like a rest cure. This is grandmothering in the traditional sense: I also recognise it because my grandmother used to do it to me, although her pleasant grandmotherliness was vitiated by the surroundings in which it operated. Her house was, basically, Edwardian in outlook – lots of cold, hard parquet flooring, defective central heating (if any), mountainous brown furniture that it hurt to sit on. The only thing to do there, apart from get her in conversations about gravy, or visit my bedridden and frankly none-too-appealing grandfather, was to attempt to peer up her skirt and catch a glimpse of her bloomers. Modern grandmothers at least offer soft armchairs, tropically furious central heating and fitted carpets as deep and absorbent as a bath sponge.

At the other end of the scale, you have the preternaturally vigorous grandparent, as exemplified by my father-in-law. Displaying the energy of someone half his age, and unquestionably more than

I have ever displayed *in my life*, he romps and chases and wears the boys out without getting short of breath. They think this is pretty good, too, except when he presents them with a long list of necessary and urgent tasks to perform in the back garden (lopping branches, building bonfires, tying up errant bushes: the inheritance of a lifetime spent as a company manager). I find his industry astonishing. Once, he even got my lads to uproot a tree stump from the clay in his back garden. He had them using a ten-pound sledgehammer, an axe and a road-mender's pick. They could barely lift the things, but he hauled them out there anyway. It was like a detail out of a Brueghel, the bare tree stump, the frosty mud, the bowed figures, my father-in-law marching around in a mildewy tweed jacket, staking a claim to the next generation but one. I skulked around indoors, trying not to be spotted. 'That's it!' he kept shouting, 'that was a good one!' each time Alistair or Tim managed to strike a shuddering blow into the wood. 'Come on! Give it another one! It's starting to shift!' The boys strained away, trying to prove their toughness and manliness, while he enjoyed their company and just a hint of that old managerial sting. I'm not even sure that in the back of his mind he wasn't trying to transfer some of his own energies into his grandsons, to make them preserve it and see it through well into the next century, by some symbolic process of transference known only to him and other buzzing oldsters.

In my family, conversely, age inherently meant a voluntary or involuntary decline in powers and vigour. When I was young, the grandparents had either died before I was born (my maternal grandfather), were largely bedridden (paternal grandfather), were shadowy hypochondriacs (my maternal grandmother – who came to stay with us, once, in a cloud of talcum powder and decongestant rubs and proprietary remedies and who kept her false teeth in a glass, like a specimen out of a medical museum), or were just nice but uneventful (paternal grandmother). The concept of a vital, active grandparent in the Jennings family was simply beyond imagining.

Of course, their grandparenthood and your parenthood is a two-way street. It's not as if they merely turn into loveable old folks with cardigans. You start having to look after them in a certain way. I don't mean in the straightforward caring sense – although that may well come later – but in a purely social sense. Before you have children, your relationship with your parents more or less goes on as an ageing version of whatever went before. You are still their offspring, with all the hopes and annoyances that entails – still theirs, in some tiny way, still a kid to them. They are still your parents, exerting all kinds of overt and hidden pressures on you.

Once you have children of your own, however, a distance begins to open up between the generations. You are a parent now, much less a kid. Your relationship with your own parents has to move onto a different footing. The decisions you make are going to be the key ones; the weight of responsibility has now officially landed on your shoulders. So my parents have become more formal in some ways. They can't treat me as quite the child (however old I am) that I was before I started my own family ('Darling, are you sure you *should*?'). Equally, I can't treat them quite the way I used to. If they must keep their distance a little more, then so must I. I can't unthinkingly dump myself on them any more, because – in practical terms – I now have a partner and one or more small children with me; and because fatherhood has made me a grown-up at last, however they may think of me. I can't throw sulks or tantrums or moods or general stupidities, partly because it's a bad example to my children, partly because the grandparents are making an effort to accommodate my new circumstances, and I have to reciprocate. If I want them to do something for me (which usually means looking after the kids while we go away, sometimes for weeks on end) I have to maintain a degree of civility. I cannot, as I used to do, lean heavily on their dining table, forking in facefuls of roast lunch without saying a word, followed by an abrupt and monosyllabic departure from the meal to go off to the pub. Manners suddenly become more prominent than they ever have been in the past. I now, for instance, offer to do the washing-up after a meal – something I could have done years ago, yes, but which I only do now because as a householder and meal-provider I appreciate the drag that washing-up represents. We have conversations in which I say, 'How are you, then?' as I might to an acquaintance whose good opinion I valued. When I get up from my chair I grunt and mutter at the effort of it all and say, 'Wait till you're my age, *ha ha*.' Which is a curious feeling, after all those years of treating your mother and father like a couple of bits of furniture. Having to moderate my responses to them is a real novelty.

But on top of that, something else begins to emerge. The sense of separation that requires me to act somewhat differently from the way I did pre-children encourages me to take a step back and look again at my parents and wonder if what I see in them, my kids see in me. It's a truism that we turn into our parents as we get older, but there's something in the new grandparent/parent axis that sharpens that identification. Deeply worrying, on the one hand, to catch sight of myself in the mirror with the same perplexed frown and round-shouldered stoop as my father; obscurely reassuring to see myself locked into the great cycle of genetic inheritances. Even now, I've started prodding the incipient buttocky cleft in my chin and wondering if it's my father's and will mature with age; while the few streaks of grey around the temples have grown overnight into fields of ash, thanks to my stress-inducing children. It's quite obvious that in comparison with my kids, I'm becoming a physically rather depressing old man: deteriorating muscle tonus, skin getting to look like a well-used wallet, mottled patches, rheumy pink eyes. I always thought of myself as being pale and slim and taut, despite the evidence of hundreds of family photographs. But the unimpeachable youthfulness of my kids confronts me with the truth about my physical appearance. Which leads me to guess that they might tolerate my ageing with the same oxymoronic mixture of affection and faint repulsion that I tolerate my parents' physical old age.

And, just recently, I've started to wonder what I will be like as a grandfather. Grouchy, I reckon.

The good news is, we have got shot of the highchair. The boys get older, they walk, they talk, and gradually start to grow out of the hardware that surrounded their early months. The buggy goes (ours got nicked, actually, like the video camera: a beat-up Mothercare buggy in scarred grey; *why?*), the cot is dismantled and stored in the garage for those notional grandchildren of our own, while the car seat that got vomited over at least three times, the indefensible baby backpack for carrying the child on long walks and the highchair all go to a shop in Chiswick which claims to sell second-hand baby things for you, but which silently and stealthily goes out of business one day, taking our chair, backpack, puked car seat with it. That was the second time I ever cleaned the highchair, before dragging it off to Chiswick. The first time I cleaned it was shortly before Tim was born. God, it was encrusted. It was like the caves at Cheddar Gorge, only with bits of half-year-old Heinz stew and potato mash instead of limestone formations. I went at it with a screwdriver to prise the stuff off and Susie said, 'Couldn't we just burn it?' Not only was it a cesspit, it was a kind of instrument of torture. The children were lashed into it by some filthy restraining straps – ostensibly to prevent the young son climbing out and falling on his head, but subtextually as a way of reinforcing the regime of absolute parental control. The straps were so momentously stained that they wouldn't clean up in the washing machine, so when I went to Chiswick, I tried to bundle them up in an efficient knot and hoped the shop owner wouldn't notice.

Well, that is all over: and when the baby paraphernalia goes, you sigh with exquisite relief, because slowly, slowly, your children are getting to be fully functioning humans, who can walk, talk, sit, eat, sleep, without any special equipment, and without any additional expense to you. They are *boys*, now, not toddlers. They are really growing up, and if I can ever find the time and space to stand back from the endless rackety drama of parenthood, then I am unbelievably, fathomlessly proud of them.

Round about now, we also get into childcare. The next wave of adults to enter the world of my children, after the grandparents: the carers and nannies. We started off with a child minder, the way so many do. She was a terrific, *big* woman with five children of her own, and so agreeably middle-class that she made us feel low-rent. We sent Alistair off to her, three days a week, six months old (six *months*!) with that mixture of the blithe, the desperate and the heedless that you feel in the first year. She didn't last for ever, though. Tim turned up and we knew we had to import help on a one-to-one basis. We had to get a nanny.

I can remember the first one all right. We gave her a car – a beat-up VW, blagged off Susie's former company. A small red one, nice enough car, brakes didn't work but it had a sunshine roof. And the radio was fine. She got the car on day one and started nannying. On the third day, she destroyed the car at a road junction, rang us up to say that she'd destroyed it and then hid in her flat in South Wimbledon for a week, not returning our phone calls. 'I was too scared of what you might say,' she said later. 'I couldn't face trying to explain it to you.' We had hired her because she struck us as a reliable type. We then bought her a poxy blue Fiat which was for sale three doors away. This was virtually brand-new, or so it seemed. It even smelled of new plastic when we tried it for the first time, and the dashboard had that tactile sheen you only see on newish fascia materials. After a couple of months, though, it was grimy, the paintwork was dulled, the exhaust rattled and a few spots of rust were starting to show around the door edges. She complained after a while that it was too horrible and shaming to be seen in at the school gate when she did the pick-up, so we shelled out for a repulsive very old small grey Volvo which, like the VW, had no brakes, but unlike the VW, was impossible to steer. It was also extremely fuel-inefficient and had clearly been used by a previous owner to transport spoil or loose aggregate, or maybe even manure. On the other hand, it did have four headrests and headlamp washers, and the heating and ventilation system was extremely good, especially in cold weather. At seventy on the motorway, it gave the driver the feeling that he or she was about to leap into the nearest crash barrier. But in traffic, stuck at lights, you could really appreciate the knob in the seat back which adjusted the lumbar support. While the nanny went negligently through these three vehicles, we were stuck with our own cars, the cars we started with, one each, ageing without grace. Then she quit. Then she came back again. Then she quit again. On and off, she was with us for, what? Three years? Four? She was our longest-lived nanny by a wide margin.

There are families who have nurtured fantastic relationships with their nannies, keeping them for eight years at an unbroken stretch, watching them get married, start families of their own. They bring their nannies along to family functions. They live with them. We have never managed any of this. Indeed, I can only remember the nannies by summoning to mind the cars they drove. In fact, I can remember the cars much better than the nannies. The nannies themselves are always shadowy creatures with curiously impermanent characteristics – but then this may be a product of the fact that we are too horrible to sustain a relationship over more than a month or so in normal conditions, and so the people we get never become much more than ghosts. What we have always wanted is a tough-minded professional who comes in, does the job and goes off again – someone as ruthlessly competent as you believe yourself to be, but who masks their hardness with amiability and an absolute, unquestioning recognition that they are lower in the hierarchical order than you, and also lower than the children they look after. They are there to be alternately worshipped and despised. Despite this, they must be cheerful, motivated and scrupulous. We've never really wanted anyone to act the part of mature older sibling with our kids, a person for whom we feel any sense of personal responsibility. There is a lot of room for hypocrisy.

That said, it was surprising the number of would-be nannies who turned up at our house, completely willing to feign an interest in our perceived way of doing things. I've lost count of the number of nannies we've failed to employ. I can only remember a sort of seasonal wave of humanity, generated by *The Lady* magazine, with its mendacious small ads section ('Cheerful family seeks bright, enthusiastic nanny for lively five- and two-year-olds. Own car' – in other words, short-tempered misfits with illegal wreck seek scapegoat). We started when Tim was about nought and Alistair three and have been going, relying on increasingly small nanny interventions, since then. One enormous raven-haired candidate came to our house, crossed her legs like a resting navvie and shouted at us for twenty minutes. Another – a bitter fifteen-stoner – carped on and on and on about discipline while terrifying our boys into silence with one brimstone glare. A third simply lay in a chair like a piece of fish on a slab and said, 'I'll do whatever they want to do.' I quite liked the fifteen-stoner, to be honest, but I could see that she offended against the ethical tone. Susie put a stop to her anyway. There were never any pretty ones for me to lech pitifully over, and, with one exception, we never had a nanny living with us, creating embarrassments around the bathroom in the mornings. (Or, for that matter, worse than embarrassments. I know of one couple who kept a virtuous-seeming nanny in the basement where she lived quite happily, until one night the husband and wife were awoken by shrieks from the bottom floor of the house. The husband nerved himself up, went downstairs and found the virtuous nanny having a three-in-a-bed with two guardsmen she'd picked up in a pub. She was fired the next morning. Well, what would *you* have done?)

On the other hand, one male nanny turned up who was so sweatily keen to be liked that we at once assumed he was a pervert and threw him out. His eyes bulged and he wore an off-white jacket with a T-shirt underneath, and seemed curiously interested in our boys' amusements – rather than indifferent or hostile, the reactions we normally hoped to see. Taking him for a deviant was doubtless a vicious misassumption, but we live in a climate of hysteria, so what else was there to do but assume him to be weird?

Weird or dangerous. The Louise Woodward saga has concentrated our attention horribly on the sheer blind faith it takes to put an absolute stranger in charge of the thing more precious to you than anything else in your life. It has also left us with the queasy certainty that nannies are no longer the semi-sanctified kind you get in A.A. Milne ('Nan and Me are friends'), but are capable of being more or less anything, anything the human condition can encompass. The fact that thousands of us just go ahead and pick nannies out of the hat and keep our fingers crossed is only a particularly acute manifestation of the inconsistency and helpless compromise at the centre of modern parenting. 'An employer might think it safe that all the obvious duds and kooks have been eliminated by careful telephone interviewing,' says our copy of *The Good Nanny Guide*, 'and that she is now going to view a parade of suitable candidates. You may be in for a shock.' Well, we shocked ourselves practically every time.

Note that *she*, incidentally. Plainly, *The Good Nanny Guide* is written for the wives of real husbands, locked in with their kids and their tough schedules of ferrying children around in immense cars. The fathers are barely expected to have an opinion when a nanny turns up to pitch for business. And you know, even though I was there on the spot when our regular parades of duffers and no-hopers and social derelicts came round (punctuated by the occasional gilded talent – a giantess with copper-red hair and wrestler's shoulders; a small and powerfully self-motivated blonde, who wrote down a menu of the day's activities in a neat, curving hand) I did my best to fade into the background, to dissolve into the upholstery, to be a distant patch of light playing across a wall. *I frankly didn't care who we got.*

This was me doing my best to revert to the old male archetype. This was me trying to pretend to be the bluff, disengaged dad-who-knows-nothing-of-such-woman's-things. I was desperate to give the impression that even though I was involved in the business of domestic life, I wasn't spiritually a true part of it. So I just loafed around at the interviews. Once we'd got someone, I simply did my best to look friendly but somehow permanently distracted by the cares of my work. Even with our longest-standing nanny, the car-crasher, I made it my job to bustle about the kitchen, fixing myself my umpteenth bladder-wrecking displacement-activity cup of coffee, swapping the lightest banter with the crasher, before lurching out again, back to my room.

I was also perpetually terrified by the thought of being thought to be a leering old twat ('One lurking drawback to the family,' as *The Good Nanny Guide* balefully puts it) and imposing my cheesy sexual presence on any female who wasn't my wife. Not that it was ever really an issue, but intentions can be mistaken, or you can simply go mad and make a pass at the woman nearest to you. One unreconstructed father (City worker, dandruff, weight problem) with an au pair at home actually once said to me, 'You must come round and look at her tits one day. She's *Swedish*. Goes round in a *towel*.' These terrible accidents of personality can happen almost without you noticing.

But neither Susie nor I had much to do with our nannies. We didn't nurture them. We didn't really want to know about their interior lives. We only wanted them to turn up, like helots, or automata even, and take our children away from us. And because that's what we wanted – no involvement with them and, for about six hours a day, no involvement with our kids – we felt guilty. And because we felt guilty, we tried to treat the nannies as if they weren't there, or were somehow not entirely real.

The only time we found ourselves inextricably entangled with our nanny was when we had a very tall lad from Yorkshire to look after our children. He'd been some kind of teaching assistant at one of the local schools and wanted to make some cash in the holidays before going to university. I mean, he was a nice enough guy, but he had to stay with us for five punishing weeks (the only time we ever bent our rule about never having live-in domestics) and demonstrate his arrant cluelessness when it came to looking after two nasty-minded and insubordinate small boys. Moreover, although he claimed to be able to drive, when we gave him the nanny's wreck to churn around

London in, he turned out to be a novice in anything except his mother's automatic Metro. He burst in on me one morning, shouting, 'The car! The car! I can't move it!' He had, in fact, parked the car neatly right up onto the pavement so that he could step out of the driver's door and enter our house in one stride – indeed, the car was virtually inside the house – but he couldn't get it back *off* the pavement. It took me twenty minutes to wrestle the car back onto the road. Then he couldn't understand southern supermarkets and their contents. 'What's *that*?' he would say, pointing at something I'd brought in – an avocado, or a piece of provocatively shaped pasta. He would load up with sliced white, fish fingers and lemon curd, and come to eat his high tea just at the time when I was mincing about the kitchen in the evening, drinking and laughing silently at my own jokes. He would sit extensively at the table and be Yorkshire about my children and London and the traffic. I found myself being bracing and adult and, essentially, *in loco parentis* to this teenager, and while I couldn't exactly begrudge the effort, it was still enough to bring on a kind of mild breakdown. Particularly since he saved every penny he earned (Yorkshire) and only went out on the town once in five weeks. Which meant that most nights, he was down at my table, eating sliced white and jam and tinned peas and drinking tea made in the teapot and yapping on at me. What does it all mean? It means that whatever age they are, all nannies are additional, paid children, a living paradox – an extra emotional drag which is meant to make life simpler, the embodiment of a professional arrangement conducted anti-professionally. And I suppose the thing that the Yorkshire boy did that most pissed me off was the thing that all nannies do: he reminded me, constantly, that I am nowhere near the nice, tolerant, liberal, easy-going person I imagine myself to be. And that when my two children are his age, between us we will make the house unbearable.

*   *   *

It occurs to me that it was a lot easier to write about those events which occurred before we'd had any kids. Things then were done in the adult mode: discrete, planned moments that had beginnings and endings, and lived neatly defined existences in the pattern of our lives. A pregnancy test here, a visit to the fatuous specialist there, a birth there. Adults (or *grown-ups* as I now find myself helplessly referring to them) can do this with their days, but only if they have no children.

It's now been over ten years since that was last a possibility. The moment Alistair arrived, followed by Tim, it's been another full-time job to go with the first, paying one – the difference being that this has no convenient form, or plot, or sense of appropriate climax, and only the most rudimentary sense of structure. A classic parental ambivalence: if anything has given my life purpose, meaning, achievement, it's having children. Now they're here, life without them would be – unimaginable. I don't proselytise at people who haven't got kids; I would never dream of plugging the fatherhood thing, except to someone who was seriously contemplating it. Then I would insist that it is the biggest and best thing you can do, other than sell the film rights for a million bucks. But at the same time, I quite often feel as if I'm the ball in a pinball machine, ricocheting off the bumpers, hurtling across the surface of the table, constantly in frantic motion without ever actually getting anywhere. Sometimes I simply feel that life just goes on, daily (nightly, from time to time) in a massive, formless kind of sprawl of interactions and moods, slowly expanding like cosmic gas. I know, rationally, that I must be making progress, learning, acquiring wisdom. I must be in the process of becoming a more experienced father. In fact, I sometimes suspect that if I ever become a grandfather, I will be dazzlingly good at it, a storehouse of lore, wisdom, sympathetic hints. I may even be a pretty good father by the time my kids leave home. You learn *something* all the time you're with children. But it doesn't feel like that. There's no *sense* of linear progression. And instead of having tidy, well-shaped moments to recall at leisure, I'm left more with long passages of time whose beginnings are now forgotten and whose endings never quite came, but turned into something different but equally pressing. It's like trying to think about the sea, or the human brain, or how much money it would take to live a nice life. It simply will not fit into a handy space or reveal its deeper organisation.

FOUR

A kids' clothing store in a small-time mall: we are in there with Alistair and Tim. There must be at least eight other families or family combinations milling around the same premises, yanking and tugging at the goods, barely keeping their tempers, scrutinising the gear under the shop's spotlights. Tim is plainly too young to have an opinion about what he wears, but Alistair is locked in a battle with his parents.

'Why can't I have *this*?' is what he says, generally. He tugs at something which is okay – how could it not be? It's hanging up in the middle of a middle-market chainstore, it's been programmed to be *okay*. It's a T-shirt with a picture of Taz, the Tasmanian Devil, courtesy of Warner Bros. But Susie shakes her head.

'What about *this*?' she replies, holding a sombre navy blue garment up to his chest. I take my cue from her and nod stupidly.

'Yeah. That looks fine,' I say.

'But what about *this*?' Alistair insists, moving on from Taz to a Donald frigging Duck.

'No, no,' says his mother. 'That won't do *at all*.'

Here, I'm tempted to go either way. On the one hand, Susie

has a point: maybe what she's chosen is more appropriate, more serviceable, versatile. It probably is a better bet than Taz or the Duck. But then, he is only four. What does it matter what a four-year-old wears? He could wear a red Taz top, orange slacks and a yellow sweater, provided they were clean and not full of holes. I'm not sure I didn't wear something similar when I was young. There is, or ought to be, no culture of good taste in children's clothes. I can remember wearing a yellow short-sleeved shirt with domino patterns together with a green knitted tie when I was his age, and I felt like Tony Bennett. Indeed, I'm just cranking myself up to make this point when Tim turns hazardous in his pushchair, so I take Susie's side to speed things along and just say '*No*' to Alistair. Another twenty minutes of this and we will be out of the shop.

Now we are seriously out in the world, we have to make an impression on it. So what do we do? We dress our kids up. Now, we know already what sort of people our children are shaping up to be. We have held parties for them and whiled away years of our lives playing baneful games on drizzly afternoons. We have fed them and talked to them and watched them grow. We are gleaning a sense of what they will be like. This is what everyone does and all parents are to some extent bound together by these commonplaces. But even in the great freemasonry of parenthood, not everything is done according to the same immutable principles. Things are done for effect, for social positioning, for distinguishing and categorising ourselves, declaring our aspirations for our children, and what we think they might well be *if only everything goes according to plan*. And, in fact, clothes and toys, being the only things a small child can really be said to possess, have real hierarchical significance.

When we were in the market for young kids' clothes, there was a clearly understood league table of labels. At the bottom was a company called Adams, whose cheapish and brightly crammed chainstores we used to find ourselves in with startling frequency. And where, I might add, we bought an unsurprisingly large number of clothes. Above them was Mothercare – really the only supplier in the very earliest months, when you needed those baby-grow all-in-one outfits and poxy little bootees. Later on, though, as the kids got bigger, Mothercare's range seemed to get smaller and more arbitrary, although this may have been a function of the Storehouse early Nineties restructuring programme. So far as prestige and status were concerned, I don't know whether their line was deemed especially banal or the quality was considered off, but for whatever reason, Mothercare never had any real impact among those whose approval we grovellingly sought. Perhaps the store's ubiquity counted against it. You wouldn't expect special praise or admiration for buying your food at Sainsbury's, for instance.

At the other end of the scale, you had something called OshKosh B'Gosh. I mean, I never understood at the time what this was all about and I never dared ask. It simply sounded like some kind of baby-talk. I suspect I subconsciously strove to keep it at that level. Only now am I aware that it's the name of an American company which has been making overalls for over a hundred years, and was founded in Oshkosh, Wisconsin. Indeed, it claims to sell more bib overalls, both for large American men as well as small suburban children, than any other company in the world. The fact was, though, that it was only ever the name printed boldly on the back of tiny working men's overalls and boiler suits and miniature farmhand all-in-ones and was only ever seen on the children of quality and status-conscious mothers. The less we could be bothered to find out what it meant, the more fetishistic its importance became. The only time our kids ever wore this stuff was when it was given away to us, third- or fourth-hand, and God did we feel strange with it on their backs. In fact it still gives me a jolt when I see the label now, reminding me of a time when worldly pressures really started to make an impact on childhood.

Our native meanness is such that we almost never buy ourselves designer label clothes, let alone designer clothes for the kids – who, anyway, will have grown out of them or ruined them within six months – and any suggestion of designer priorities at any age makes us feel self-conscious. And yet, according to the yellow press, there are people who will spend £150 on a Moschino plastic jacket for their ten-year-old, or £125 on an Armani top, on the ethical grounds that they'd buy clothes for themselves from such retailers, and that to deny their kids the pleasure of something equally well-made and fashionable is a vicious inequity. This is the reasoning of the mad, of course, since children's clothes are not worn in the same way or with the same intentions as adult clothing. When you dress your tot up in something as ostentatious as an Armani T-shirt, you're explicitly using the kid as an advertising hoarding for your own wealth and self-regard. The kid can't know the full significance of *Armani*. He can't know as an adult would know – with all the vanity and cupidity that it entails – that he wants to wear this in preference to something from Tesco. This is the most extreme imaginable instance of an adult exploiting the child's potential as a walking, and unconsulted, billboard – a tendency which you reveal the moment you put anything more than basic kit on him.

Because this is what they are: human advertisements for your taste and accomplishments, the moment they get beyond about one year of age and are mobile enough to demonstrate your fashion sense to the world. Up to that point, a romper suit is a romper suit, whatever happens. Beyond that, children's clothes look just enough like adults' clothes for the style intentions to show through; and kids are just about human-shaped enough (instead of being lumpy and deformed with fat, as they are at six months) for the smartness of the design not to be wholly compromised by the wearer.

Well, I admit that even we fell under the influence of peer pressure, and were nudged into this territory, but only once, and then only with a very marginal piece of designer labelling, a tangential one, a wild card. This came from a local boutique for kids' clothes, where Susie clapped eyes on a tiny, stylish blue corduroy jacket – a sort of Italian academic's jacket, chunky cut, a little bit *la lotta continua*, a little bit social history lectures, University of Milan. It was approximately three times the cost of anything else we might have used to cover up a three-year-old's torso. It was only wearable (by Alistair) for six months before the season changed and it got hot to wear, but in that time I can remember putting it onto him and standing back in a kind of awe at what I'd created. He pushed his hands into the stylish square-cut pockets and stomped around in a resolute way, as if he knew that this was really an adult garment, miraculously on loan to him, and that he had better wear it with the right kind of self-importance. And at the end of summer, of course, it was too small. So it was pressed into service when Tim came of age, a little more worn by now, the Milanese academic only used it for gardening, maybe, but it still looked good. And it got three months' wear and some buttons came off and that was the end of its usefulness. (This is one of those areas where that bourgeois inverted snobbery you sometimes come across of ostentatiously using something very old and worthless to proclaim your higher, anti-materialist sensibilities – clapped-out Volvo estate, knacker's yard TV set – simply didn't apply. You just do not put your children in worn-out clothes if you can possibly avoid it.) The jacket was so very expensive, though, and so rare and unusual a purchase, that we still have it, folded up in one of the upstairs cupboards, even though it will never fit anyone in this family again, or not until we have grandchildren. By which time it will be about as much use as a collapsible opera hat or pair of Victorian riding boots.

About forty-five years ago (judging by my old copy of *Illustrated* magazine), children wore shorts, little patterned dresses, sweaters and tassled scarves – with school variations (caps and hats, serge and ties) – until some time in their teens, when they abruptly became pocket adults and adopted double-breasted jackets, long trousers with turn-ups, A-line skirts. There were only two states, and there was an acute demarcation between them. And both embodied the values of the older generation, the parents' generation. Why, even when I was a child, in the Sixties, I was not only ponced up in corduroy shorts and short-sleeved shirts with wobbly abstract patterns, but had to wear *sandals* on my feet, Start-Rite items, with inoffensively snubbed noses, air-holes for your socks to breath through, soles made of a wanky rubber compound that frayed at the edges, little chromed buckles which snagged on things. Shoes (with or without laces), proper black leather items with proper soles, were such a token of maturity that I can still remember the first pair I ever claimed as my own; and I only got those because they didn't fit my brother. I realise this must make me sound like Catherine Cookson or Charlie Chaplin, born into grinding poverty, no shoes for my own, ragged britches and so on, but I came from a comfortable, suburban middle-class home, in which these rules applied for me as they did for everyone else I knew at the time. Your clothing, a generation or so back, exemplified your condition as immature person. Real shoes were something you only got after years of apprenticeship with the buckle-up sandals. Freedom from this yoke was one of the things people fought for in the Sixties: the right to dictate your own clothing preferences, once you'd reached an age at which you *had* clothing preferences.

But grown-ups hate to yield what little powers they have, with the result that today, we still use clothing as a way to demonstrate our authority over those in our care. The difference between then and now being that we conspicuously dress our young offspring, not so much as little children (as we would have in the 1950s), but as little adults; or rather, we dress them as we dress ourselves – in other words as slightly younger adults than we really are. The result? My kids have the same mistrustful aspect as the children in Bronzino's paintings of the Medici family. They have that slightly jaded look that you get in *Don Garcia de' Medici* and *Maria de' Medici* – that unspontaneous, organised air about them, that look of resentment at yielding to another's tastes, of being togged up for the benefit of the outside world. That look on the face of young sixteenth-century Maria (the first-born of Cosimo I de' Medici and Eleonora de Toledo) is precisely the look on the boys' faces at that moment when they've been got up in the same chino trousers/blue sweatshirt/chunky boots combination that *I* am wearing and are standing by the front door, ready to go out and perform. She may have been painted in 1551, in her eleventh year; and she may be wearing a double rope of pearls around her neck, a dress of sombre velvet trimmed in brocade, with a cream-coloured silk stuff emerging at the shoulders where they join the sleeve, pearls hanging from her ears and a pearl-studded band on the crown of her head. But I would say she's unashamedly pissed off at having to get all this gear on, just to satisfy the perverse and arbitrary requirements of the grown-ups. It is a look which has persisted for 450 years, more or less unchanged: *I'm only going in the car: why do I have to wear laces?*

This is particularly true where Gap clothes are involved. Gap nowadays is what OshKosh B'Gosh was about six years ago. When you buy Gap, you enter that world, wholesale (at $5 billion per annum and rising, Gap's total sales make it about the same size as the economy of, say, Cyprus) and you live the values, however distorting they might be. I once disregarded house rules and bought a costly Gap sweatshirt for Tim. I was told by Susie never to do such a thing again (particularly since she'd found a miraculous supply of bargain sweatshirts in a branch of Tesco a hundred miles away). Sticking your child in Gap makes him look even more like a smaller, more resentful version of you than any other range of clothing – grown-up somehow, but also perpetually and playfully childish, thanks to the uniformity of the Gap look. It locks him into your compromised, adult world, making him appear hunky but twee, grown-up but cute, a dwarf in a baseball jacket and roustabout jeans. And of course they've now started a BabyGap line in an attempt to plant the seed even earlier.

But then, why should I bother about this so much? As long as my children are reasonably clean and warm, what does it matter what they wear? I suspect that my feelings must have something to do with the fact that clothing is one of those areas where I *simply do not have much to contribute*. That, for some reason, choosing the kids' clothing is a job appropriated by Susie (and, I suspect, by most mothers) and where I am strictly a bystander, carrying the odd armful of clothes around the places where we get our cheap stuff and following instructions as to which items go on the children if I have been left in charge of getting them dressed. It is not what you would call a full participation in the dream of an egalitarian household. And I don't think it's entirely to do with my notoriously poor clothes sense (not as bad as it used to be, though: I like to think, as Martin Amis once put it, that I dress not so much with taste as with insight). It's something to do with the fact that most British men have some sort of ingrained irresponsibility when it comes to clothes – the tendency to splash out on *that* tie, *that* sweater, *that* jacket; the tendency to partner unsuitable shirts with improper ties and socks – and women know that the same irresponsibility will be as bad when it comes to choosing their children's clothing. Makes no difference whether you have boys or girls, either. A friend of mine with two daughters is no more limited than I am, just because he has girls: he is limited to precisely the same degree, i.e. entirely. He once bought the elder daughter a dress, whereupon it immediately disappeared, only to reappear years later, hidden in shame at the bottom of a drawer. Like me, he is not even allowed to select clothes for his kids to put on in the mornings. 'Their carefully matched outfits are painstakingly extracted from the drawer by my wife,' he says.

And then, where does this manly irresponsibility stop? Getting them dressed at all? Feeding them? Making sure they don't die in the traffic outside? This is one of those paradoxical situations, in which I feel that I am being deprived of something I don't particularly want (the right to buy children's clothes, or choose them in the morning), for fear that it means a greater circumscribing of my powers – many of which I don't mind losing, either. Which, in some ways, just about sums my position up.

It sounds inhuman now, but without a doubt, Alistair was two and a half years old when we first started the long and madness-provoking haul towards a better education. I'll level with you, although Susie may disagree with me: we thought, this kid (it goes double, incidentally: Alistair *and* Tim) has got to go to a decent university. Therefore, he must go to a decent secondary school; which in turn means something acceptable at around the age of four. Which means getting him the best start possible the moment he can walk, talk, handle a crayon. Susie, I know, would say that this reductive, mechanistic approach was the last thing in *her* mind at the time, and that what she wanted was somewhere fun and nurturing to bring little Alistair/Tim to an understanding of the possibilities of learning and to get some early work habits installed for later life.

But I maintain that here in the suburbs – in the borough of Richmond-upon-Thames, a real hothouse, a real bourgeois snake-pit – this is the way we're all thinking. And you can tell that this is on everybody's mind by the frightening number of nursery schools all over the place: at least seventy within realistic driving distance of our front door. In fact, there's one just across the road from us, with a persistent knot of tense, laughing mothers outside at midday, whisking their bleary tots off for a snack, followed by violin lessons, or horse-riding, or tennis, or aikido, or swimming, or ballet. They look as brittle and highly-focused as the parents of a bunch of Harvard Grad School applicants. The fact is that we can barely move for pre-school nurseries around here, because this is a breeding-ground of middle-class desires and ambitions, which are then projected onto thousands of young, middle-class children.

I too once went to a nursery school (in laughable Whetstone, actually, North Finchley way) so when the time came to start looking for a place, I thought I knew vaguely what to expect. Actually, what I went to wasn't called a nursery school. It was called a *Kindergarten*, a nice Germanism (that whiff of advanced Continental Froebel practice) which you don't find any more, and it was run by our friend, Mrs Woodyatt. One reason you don't find it any more is that *Kindergarten* is a little unambitious for today's kids. Indeed, you couldn't have called it a *school* at all, certainly not in comparison with today's nursery institutions. It was so benignly untaxing that images of my time at Mrs Woodyatt's still stick in my mind, decades on, with the same carefree persistence as holiday snapshots. The suburban front room she turned over to the ten small children in her charge, its furniture ranged against the walls, a sandpit generously lodged in the centre; my first true love,

Julia Brown, whose glance I would try to attract by singing along with *The Laughing Policeman* on the gramophone and miming to the clarinet solo; the constant need to pee; the possibility of jelly from the kitchen; hand-clapping and swiping paint on bits of paper; the time I turned up one New Year wearing the Christmas-tree lights draped round my neck like a priestly stole, so attached was I to them. Those were blithe times. But we didn't *learn* much, except how to be away from Mum and be in the company of other children without having a breakdown. She was a nice woman, Mrs Woodyatt, and I'm sure I'd have turned out worse if it hadn't been for her. But her *Kindergarten* was principally a socialising experience, not the first step in an academic career.

This is no longer possible. When we were toiling around the local nursery schools, there was a permanent menacing undercurrent of competitive expectation. Indeed, the ones we inspected were all gussied-up like miniature big schools, with academic agendas and programmes of work, no matter how scant. And they all had worldly, appraising headmistresses – however much they tried to sell the line that the object of the game was to be with other kids and have fun.

One place in particular made a deep impression on us. It was the second nursery school we had ever looked at, and it was in the church hall of a vast Victorian redbrick Early Gothic palace of worship, with the woodwork picked out in deep green, just to reinforce the atmosphere of sombre concentration. And it was just like a tiny English public school, with its dim-wattage bulbs and its lancet windows and the leading in the panes and its melancholy institutional colour scheme. What's more, it even had that authentically grim, ripening smell of feet and food and fart which hangs around our ancient seats of learning. There were caches of thumbed reading books and dumps of things like paints and sheets of paper and glue, held in intimidating open-fronted wooden storage units. And – enough to bring a catch into your throat – there was a line of diminutive wellies all along one prison wall, with a row of coats and sweaters hanging above. I checked the labels furtively and bitterly to see how many OshKosh and Gaps there were. I also spotted that the wellies and other footwear looked a lot smarter and better-finished than what was on our kid's feet. Still: the contrast between these little bits of clothing and the Thomas Arnold mood of the building was poignant. After some dithering, we found the – headmistress? principal? praeceptor?, who then looked suitably bored at our account of what it was we thought we wanted for our two-and-a-half-year-old son. She was somewhere in her forties, turned out in a kind of whiskery business suit, and clearly wanted to be doing something other than opening doors for us.

'We believe in giving them a taste of a formal routine and structure, while giving them a chance to *explore* and *have fun*,' she said. We pursed our lips and nodded. I think Susie had made up her mind the moment she let herself into the building that this was too much the Dotheboys Hall for her child. In fact, all the time that we were looking at nurseries, she felt incredibly strongly either for or against places, in a way which I could almost never manage. It wasn't that I was apathetic exactly. It's just that everywhere we saw looked more or less plausible, more or less the kind of place where any child might do well. It was suburban Richmond, after all, a focal point in one of the biggest single swathes of middle-class values in London. What could go wrong here?

Susie tended to take my easygoingness, however, as a dangerous sign of that lifeless indifference that fathers traditionally display towards all important aspects of their children's development – that same indifference that they show to clothes and food (*Ah, let them eat the cream topping*) and the traffic outside. Fathers tend to argue that this is not so much indifference as a better organisation of priorities. They worry less, but they worry the right amount about these things. Mothers historically worry overmuch. Mothers tend to argue that fathers are either in denial or wilfully complacent: a complacency which goes along with all the standard British male wilful blindness to bullying, musical tendencies, aestheticism, academic gifts, loneliness, that you get from the Eighth Marquis of Queensberry down. Susie saw my emotional recumbancy as recidivism and told me by signs and intimations – shouting at me, hitting me – to beam in on the problem. To see it *as* a problem, in fact.

The mistress of this tiny college clearly read Susie's dislike and my inertia. She pushed us into the doorways of one or two classrooms with a shout of warning to the class leader.

'And this is the first-year class. You can see they're doing . . . *modelling*, here.' There was clay and Plasticine all over the floor. We pressed on, even though we knew that there was no point. There were four different rooms, all filled with large-eyed, wild-haired children in smocks, like a bunch of turn-of-the-century Irish tinkers. The tots were staggering around their classrooms in a way that I guess was meant to be brightly industrious but which appeared both regimented and anarchic, as it might be in a Soviet tractor factory just before the collapse of Communism. They kept poking at each other with paintbrushes or the flats of their hands, shouting and crying. In every room, there was about the same division of efforts. Maybe a third of the kids would be industriously engaged in whatever it was they were supposed to be doing; another third would be listlessly tackling the same problem, but with a load of getting up and wandering around, or chatting to their friends; and the last third would be either running mad, screaming and howling and roaring with laughter, or would be catatonic – with fright, alienation, who knew? – hunched in a corner, staring into the chaos. And they made noises and smells which I hadn't heard or smelt for twenty years, the noises and smells of unsocialised, very small children, the raw smell of digestion. How was my beautiful boy supposed to survive this?

'Well, let me know *as soon as you can*,' said the head, closing the door on yet another vision of anarchy. 'As you can imagine, *there's quite a lot of pressure for places*.'

This was the clincher for most of the interviews we had. A bruising statement of the obvious, the salesman's bait. Mrs Woodyatt never had to resort to that kind of thing, I'm certain – that reminder of the outside world with its incessant demands, the dig in the ribs to point up your vulnerability and your kid's defencelessness. But it was always a part of the encounter, no matter what sort of nursery school it was – and we saw a few – veering from the Thomas Arnold place to a completely free-form romporium a mile or so away where it was like the UFO club with the Soft Machine as house band. Here there were wild patterns everywhere and people wandering from room to room looking for the party. Many of the adults wore beards. And yet, there too (after we had flinchingly pushed our noses an inch into each open doorway) the cottage-loaf proprietress narrowed her eyes and got businesslike and explained a great number of complex regulations and requirements concerning the payment of debentures and the rigorous tight-but-loose organisational structure of the institution, and how all this would further the development of the entire child. And how places were strongly in demand, and could we let her know as soon as possible? *Two and a half years old.* What was it going to be like at eight years? Eleven? Fifteen?

Our final choice of school was as predictable a reflection of our values and aspirations as you could possibly have wished. We went Montessori. This is one of those admissions which causes those in the know immediately to glance at each other and wag their heads, because *Montessori* – like *Steiner School* – is a brand name as pointedly incriminating as Gucci or Saab. By a nice irony, given the competitive middle-class aura which currently clings to the process, the whole thing started when the Italian Dr Maria Montessori evolved a system of education for children considered retarded or beyond the requirements of conventional schooling. She got results from kids who'd been written off academically, transferred her techniques (in 1907) to a group of pre-school Roman slum children and got even better results out of them, using her puzzles and perceptual training devices in an ordered framework of endeavour and learning. Having started at the turn of the century, there are now thousands of Montessori schools all over the world, millions of satisfied customers over the years.

But there's something about its philosophy of order and structure which pisses other parents off – that and the Jesuitical presumption which insists that there is a Way of doing things, and which tends to make converts out of those parents who exploit it. Montessori herself said, 'I studied my children, and they taught me how to teach them.' But what one tends to notice about a Montessori nursery is what's known – disapprovingly, or with awed reverence – as *the equipment*: little pieces of standardised kit for measuring things, relating items to one another numerically, *the number rods*, which are all kept in tailor-made holders on the classroom shelves. A lot of parents just look at this complex of tools and read into it a repressive, over-formal insistence on academic skills attainment from a cruelly young age. Worse still, you get the occasional newspaper article claiming that not only are Montessori kids academically hothoused, they're also forced to practise their manual skills with socially divisive tasks like tying shoelaces and polishing silverware. Well, this is nothing new: according to one version of the Montessori legend, the urchins of Rome actually applauded with delight when Montessori taught them the correct use of a handkerchief. For supporters, this is all building brand reinforcement, and no one can ever justify their brand loyalty to a consumer of a different product. It also points up the philosophically unbridgeable distance from the modern Montessori, back to the origins of nursery education. Whereas Johann Oberlin's first semi-*crèches* were for the children of eighteenth-century farm labourers, and Robert Owen's community for the offspring of mill-workers, started in New Lanark in 1816, was as much a safe haven as an educational establishment, the modern Montessori is all about the steady transfer of economic power from hand to head.

Our local Montessori actually looked much like all the other places we'd seen, if not even more unprepossessing. It was a dog-eared single-storey building by a bowling green, a lot of toddlers staggering about in cute gingham smocks, childish daubs pinned up on the walls. I didn't see any silverware; although one or two of the teaching staff were so PLU (in a laidback, suburban manifestation) that I found myself bending slightly at the waist when talking to them, my hand reaching deferentially towards my hairline. As for the rigours of the Montessori system, its bricks and rods and measuring devices and formalised language instruction, there was only the most discreet evidence. Nor was there an entrance test, as is the case in the toughest nurseries in the most pressured London education authorities. Even the headmistress seemed normal, without being worryingly so. And there was this enormous benefit, so far as I was concerned, that when I told other parents that our boy was going there, they immediately parroted their concerns about its academic leanings and its intellectually competitive ethos. I'm ashamed to say this was music to my ears – just as it was music to hear the way they argued that their own kids were much better suited to somewhere more relaxed, informal, undemanding – somewhere where the emphasis was on social skills rather than number-crunching or letter formation. Immediately I felt that all that time visiting other nurseries had not been wasted, that we had taken the first steps towards engineering an academic superman. The more I thought about it, the crazier I got. I saw my boy as bracketed from the word go in the fast stream of schooling, a boy who will go to the top, an intellectual, part of the high-flying Montessori set, like Martini drinkers and friends of Frederick Forsyth.

Was this no more than a by-product of the hysteria and misinformation that envelops all middle-class families when their kids reach school age? Does everyone feel like this in some way? Was it just my need for vicarious aggrandisement? My sons' triumphs compensating for my banality and inadequacy, Russell's 'Hope that one's children may succeed where one had failed'? My sons, like Dustin Hoffman in *The Graduate*, urged into swimming pools in full diving kit to show off the proud genetic inheritance, the genius cultivated by the efforts of the parents ('This remarkable young man is going to perform for you some amazing feats of daring in water that is over six feet deep!' as the dad says – and it is the dad, isn't it, always)? Or was it just our version – my version, not even Susie's – of the OshKosh boiler suit, the Armani top – my way of grabbing a spot in the Big Race, not by using my boys to advertise my material good fortune but to advertise *my* cleverness, *my* driving academic purpose, the one thing that you can't argue with? Who was I doing this *for*?

I asked my parents about this. I asked about the guilt and the anxiety and double-think that wells up in these circumstances – school, the first steps into the greater society, status. They didn't seem to know what I was going on about.

'It was all very straightforward,' they said. 'There wasn't any great pressure.'

But what about the competition for places? The remorseless

jockeying for position with other parents? The clothes? Society has become more intensely competitive in the thirty years it took me to grow up, and the comfortable rigidities of the early Sixties are now just stuff for OU degree courses, but surely it hasn't changed *that* much?

'Oh, no,' they said blankly. 'You just went off like everyone else. It wasn't a problem when you were young.'

So I'm sitting in my car outside the nursery school, debating how long I can stay in there before I have to get out and face the mob. There must be about twenty of them, thronging the patch of grass in front of the main door. Some have got minuscule toddlers with them; one or two are even in headscarves. They all know each other and are locked in complex and limitless debates about nannies and holidays and other schools (especially other schools). They are all mothers. I am the only father.

It turns out that all this time, I've been worrying about Alistair's interests only marginally more than my own. And now that I'm the one on the spot, I'm hardly worrying about his at all. Instead I'm fretting about the collision between ideology and practice which has got me trapped inside my foul car. Indeed, the foulness of my car epitomises the problem. It's not so much his socialising that bothers me now, as mine. As I said before, Susie and I have always been (we like to kid ourselves) at the cutting edge of gender politics, in that we both work from home, split the bills down the middle, share the drudgery of housework more or less evenly and look after the children with hair-splitting equality of labour. And while this does not necessarily make me *happy*, it does make me feel that I am doing the right thing, both philosophically and personally. But not many other couples (see above) do it the same way. In fact, once we'd integrated with the rest of our community to the extent of sharing a nursery school, it seemed that absolutely *none* of the other couples was doing it our way.

Instead, it looked like it used to when my mum collected *me* from school: the all-women cabal, the jolly intimacies, the absence of belching and farting and sneezing that normally accompanies any gathering of men. And there was the car. My car was a horrid old VW (still is, unsurprisingly, just a different model) while the women owned glistening Volvos and Renault Espaces. (There were, in reality, plenty of other crappy cars like mine, but rendered invisible by the overweening presences of the smarter ones.) Although I couldn't detect any major non-material social distinctions between me and them, the fact was that they were women whose husbands had bought them swanky cars to drive around the suburbs in while I was trailing around in an old nail which I had bought myself. I was their geometric opposite, barring the fact that I was still white and not black – which would have made me so exotic as to be more or less incredible. I was a man, apparently unemployed in the middle of the day, driving a tatty old car. No matter that Susie turned up in my stead on other days (driving a car rather less tatty than mine) or that in the course of conversations she'd managed to have with some of these women, she would have explained some of the nature of our domestic circumstances. I felt absolutely unable to account for my presence. I felt that they would just not be able to get the point.

So I would hide in my car, sometimes affecting to do some paperwork in order to convince any roaming mother that I too had business cares, however idle I may have appeared. Then I would check my watch for the fifth or sixth time, conning the scrum at the main entrance to see if it was moving (which meant that the kids had been let out) and then sprint towards the school with what I hoped was an engaging, abstracted smile on my face. Sometimes mothers would throw back a half-smile, as you might to any disabled member of the community you knew by sight (*Yes, he's a human too*). Sometimes the same mothers, depending on caprice, would cut me dead, so I would have to turn my half-smile of acknowledgement into a puzzled frown of thoughtful introversion, a kind of Prince Charles Thinking expression. Once I got to whichever child I was collecting, it was usually okay because I was pleased to see him (the way one always is after a separation) and I could devote my attention to him and blot out the mothers. I also told myself each time that this wouldn't last and that at the next school up, the whole institution would be bigger and there'd be more people at the gate, some of whom would inevitably be fathers, and I wouldn't be so conspicuous any more. I was wrong, as it turned out. I was still burdened by the problem at the next school (where, even though it ended at half past three instead of midday, and I could *just* have been there legitimately, I still felt like a leper), and to some extent am even now, even though my boys have reached the big time and there are lots of people milling around and lots of places for me to hide. Even now, I am still usually the only guy among the cars, save for an occasional beaming workaholic dad, come to pick up his kid *just this once*, patrolling the tarmac like a male lion out on the plains of the Serengeti.

But what exactly was I fretting about? What was so bad about all this? After all, not all these women were harridans or pitying traditionalists. Some, indeed, were friends – one of the spin-offs of having kids is that you do meet people like yourself, bound by the same crushing obligations and soul-plundering emotional ups and downs. Some, inevitably, I was delighted to see. What was the problem?

Well, there do seem to be two distinct camps here. I merely fall into one of them. Other fathers I know who have dragged along to pick up their kids from school (none, I would point out, as often or as diligently as me) divide evenly into those who dutifully loathe every second and run past the mothers as if trying to get out of a sudden downpour; and those who claim to find the whole thing a hoot, a laugh, a moment of relaxation in an over-regimented day. *They* claim that hanging about with strange mothers allows them to play-act and explore a cute, gender-transgressing, playfully domesticated side of themselves. 'Oh yes,' they say, 'I love to hang around and gossip with *the other mums*. We talk about cooking!'

I know of one guy who actually took his modern egalitarian principles to the stage where he gave up his job completely in order to look after the kids (four of them) while his wife became a skull-crushing Stakhanovite City banker. Thus, he took over the cleaning of the house, the cooking of the food, the washing of the laundry and the maintenance of four small children. But while I applaud his conviction, it makes me feel shifty inside. On the one hand, this is progressive and good insofar as it spurns traditional gender roles. On the other, simply switching the tasks round and giving the woman the out-all-hours big-money job and the man all the arduous sub-contracted labour of family-building is not the way forward in an ideal society. What are we striving for? Equality? Or merely the chance to participate in someone else's drudgery?

In fact, the awful dislocating recognition of someone the same age and sex as me doing nothing but traditional housewife stuff was too much. Basically, I just don't believe in it. I don't believe that in an ideal world, in a Utopian society, anyone should do it. I think it's bad for you. Add that to the atavistic shock I felt when I first considered this particular dispensation, of seeing *a man doing a woman's work*, as some neanderthal inner voice cried out, and it brings me face to face with this central problem: I believe in desegregating the family jobs, but I don't feel it. It still sounds phoney to me when a man comes out with distaff stuff – best prices for supermarket sweetcorn, getting the kids' hair cut, clothing details, scandals involving teachers at schools all over Greater London – the kind of self-consciously mumsy schoolgate talk I sometimes overhear. You can't do it (I blurt out, unable to still that inner voice) without either sounding camp or insincere.

Of course, when the other dads did show up in any numbers, the pressure became unbearable. Why? Because they did so specifically for the nursery school sports event at the end of the summer term. Mostly, this involved very small children milling around a patch of greensward, doing egg-and-spoon races and three-legged races. The fact that they were mostly hopelessly ill-coordinated, and on occasion had to be pointed in the right direction as well as physically helped over the finishing line, didn't matter. They were small, they were running about in the open, they were in tears some of the time. It was good to see them being natural and expressing themselves. But as is the way with these things, after the tinies had run their races and fallen over and cried, the adults had to compete.

It really all comes out when the parents take part in the sports-day races, as Amis duly notes in his short story collection *Heavy Water*. The headmistress storms towards the grown-ups, clapping her hands and baring her teeth in an ugly grin and shouting that the time has come for everyone else to take part. *Everyone* else: no room for recusants here. Well, the mums are bad enough. People you knew, if only by sight, to be limp, inoffensive creatures wrestling the wheels of their tank-like cars, suddenly tear off their shoes and crouch by the start line like the original Olympic trackmen. The whistle blows and they all rush off to the far end (the course suddenly quadrupled in length for these leviathans after the tinies have been on it) screaming and whooping. For a fraction of a second, you can glimpse among the khaki shorts and floppy white shirts the teenage girls who must be still inside these frowning suburban mothers, catch a ghostly hint of the sexual charge that must have drawn their husbands to them.

But then you get the husbands themselves. They get their own race and they love it. The first time I found myself at a nursery school sports day, I actually managed to butch it out and refused to have anything to do with the fathers' event. I stood my ground at the edge of the track, smirking uneasily. Fortunately, there were a couple of weaklings there with me (crippled by holiday accidents or squash games) so I got away with it. The second year, though, absolutely *every* father who'd turned up volunteered for the long-distance race, right round the perimeter of the borrowed cricket pitch on which the games were taking place. There was a lot of vicious joshing, a lot of evil-natured *How are you, David? You feeling UP TO IT?*, a certain amount of glancing spitefully in my direction. I had nowhere to hide. All the mums rounded on me (the deviant father, always around to collect his son) and jeered me up to the starting line. The other dads were already pulling off their shiny loafers and loosening their ties and smoothing back their hair and gazing down the grass track with a murderous fixity. Some of them had evidently been waiting for this moment for some time. I could tell that they had been practising. I tried to get into the mood by hitching up my socks and wiping my spectacles, but instead of fearsome competitiveness, nothing much entered my heart except dread. It was one of those calm, slightly sultry English summer days, a good day for lying on your back and staring thoughtfully at the sky. I thought I might be sick. The headmistress of the Montessori nursery said *go* and immediately a pack of grunting men shot past me and ran off into the distance, their ties flying out behind them, their heels flashing in the sunshine.

I found myself right at the back, alongside a very old man – a late father, or possibly even a grandfather. His thinning grey hair flapped around on his crown. He looked into the distance with watery eyes. 'God,' he said, 'I must be mad.' We trudged round for a while, until it dawned on me that even he was moving slightly faster than I was. Another minute went by and the gap between us grew wider, and then he had deserted me and I was alone, stumbling along, the distance between me and the rest of them widening until they were two-thirds of a lap ahead of me, in a three-lap race. I struggled and sweated and groaned for air as I tried to close the margin between me and the old man (that affirming lard I had been carrying since Alistair was born coming back to haunt me), but he got further and further away, closer and closer to the rolling, jostling backs of the fit men, leagues away. Eventually, after they had all crossed the finish line, I was still yards off, lurching along, nearly in tears.

But then a wonderful thing happened. Alistair, who'd been watching with the rest of the children, corralled into a fairy ring next to the teachers, took pity on my state, ran up beside me and jogged along, making encouraging remarks. 'I thought I'd keep you company,' he said. And he did. I don't know whether I was more ashamed for myself for being a fat turd, or for Alistair for having to be seen with a father like me. But at the same time, and more than either, I loved him for being generous and companiable and brave. He saved that day from being one of those memories that cause me to yelp with uncontainable embarrassment in public whenever I suffer a flashback – and turned it instead into something bathed in a glow of fondness and hope. At last I staggered and wheezed over the line, to a smattering of sarcastic applause and ironical *well dones* from the nastier-minded teachers, while Alistair gave my hand a squeeze. I can't tell you how grateful I was to him for being there, and I still feel grateful to him, just thinking about it now. I hope his kids will do the same for him one day. It's typical of everything to do with children, that while some situations can – out of the blue – turn into disasters when emotions get out of control or when expectations get unmanageable, disasters such as this one can just as abruptly be filled with love and gratitude.

(Despite Alistair's greatness of soul, that race prompted a desire in me never to do such a thing again. And I managed it at the next school up, too, until I got bullied into taking part in the dads' three-legged race. I was paired with a short, dark-haired man whose head came up only as far as my armpit. He tucked it firmly in there and we blundered off towards the tape. 'Oh shit,' he kept saying. Really, I should have just picked him up and carried him, but instead we tried to do it by the rules. We crashed to the ground three times, came last by such an astonishingly long margin that most of the spectators assumed we were limbering up for the next race. Then I really gave up.)

So the *Guardian* – natch – recently added to my internal debate by running a piece on fathers who bring up their children – either as single parents, or because they've opted to be househusbands. Turned out that the piece was written from America, the laboratory of social change, and where, supposedly, the number of traditional households – man goes out to work, woman makes home – has fallen to seven per cent of the population. Now, if you have a topic worth consideration (or, more likely, a topic not worth consideration), it'll end up on the Internet. And this was largely the thrust of the piece: the Internet as resource centre for full-time fathers. Spurred on by this article, I spent ten minutes diligently researching the matter. I found a website called *At-Home Dad*, offering articles like *No, No, NO!* ('I looked at him . . . and said, in a low but Fun voice, "Do you know why you cannot go outside, John? Because it's raining out, that's why!"'); also something called *Crib Demolition*; and a selection of heartfelt encomia – 'I surveyed the park with a smile on my face and thought, "I wish every at-home dad could experience what each dad here today felt, SPECIAL for being part of a growing minority, the at-home dad!"'

Getting bored, I looked around for some more Dad material. I found a Net version of *Fathering Magazine*™, in which A.A. Talbert wrote a poem, *Our Baby Is A Boy*: 'The doctor took a picture showed his beating heart/ And showed that little place at which his manhood starts', while Barry Koplen ruminated on the way his kid chucked his food about, concluding that the child should 'Spill and create', since there had only been

> 'before your return,
> a mopless kitchen, empty
> without your colors
> all but lost to memory's fade'.

Then there was *Full-Time Dads* ('Because parenting is not a hobby!') and *Slowlane* ('The online resource for all Stay-At-Home Dads') which puts you in touch with *Dad-to-Dad Southern California, Main Home Dads, Minnesota Dads At Home, Inc.*, and the *At-Home Dad Handbook*. And there were still more, waiting in the ether, only I'd had enough by this time and went back to my computer patience.

Anyway, it is a rich seam to mine, and Americans (currently the most on-line nation on earth, with one person in three wired up to the Net) are busy pushing the boundaries forward. Which is fine, I'm sure, as a way of enabling the greater society. But it also has that tendency to see itself as the voice of a neglected minority whose rights are in danger of being traduced – only valid up to a point, and potentially full of diminishing stridency. More than that, it makes me conscious of my own partial Stay-At-Home-Dad status

(Stay-At-Home-Dad or SAHD: the morose acronym suggested by *Slowlane* – and why *Slowlane*, by the way, with its air of terminal inertia?) and resentful that I should identify, however slightly, with a bunch of sentimental, solipsistic Americans. I don't want to be part of an interesting cutting-edge social subgrouping. I am deeply conventional and I would like to lead a deeply conventional life – not just for the sake of my own sense of belonging, but because I feel – as a product of my own upbringing, I suppose – that fathers should ideally be dull, stolid people who draw little attention to themselves but against whose tolerant drabness the light of the child can shine all the brighter.

Two? How come two? Two is now considered the bare minimum, almost parsimonious, as one was a generation ago. These days, three is your basic package, with four as the luxury version. I have even come across a couple of families of five: the mother of one family (startlingly healthy-looking, not at all the haggard wreck you'd expect) said that they were going to stop at four, but the gap between numbers three and four was so small, she somehow forgot that she'd even *had* a fourth baby, and had to have another one, to get the benefit. For a man, four is pretty status-ridden, demonstrating not only your over-active generative powers, but also your staggering capacity to pay for your children. Once the dust had settled from Tim, though, we stopped. I now dread the thought of another child, because I know that I would still have to do a large part of the looking-after; and I am simply not lively enough any more to cope with the horrible demands of a very young child. Besides, I quite like the rowdy dynamic we have already with two. Maybe this makes me selfish. I like to think it makes me socially responsible.

Nevertheless, I do detect a ghost of *hauteur* in the four- and five-child fathers. We have long gone beyond the stage where it was enough simply to sire a child and push it around in a buggy and declare yourself marvellous. That's no longer adequate. Several years on from our first births, we are all familiar with the idea of generating children. There has to be a new test of manhood, an effluxion of that ritual competitiveness (could be cars, pay packet, golf club membership, foreign holidays, attractiveness to women) which distorts male relationships, turning them into covert wars of status and potency. There are times when you feel that if you're not like, say, the late Joe Kennedy – nine children and the resources to keep them in style – you're not adequately fulfilling your destiny.

The way I see it, this is a competition which you cannot win (unless you really are like the late Joe Kennedy). Stick at two and you can have a nice life and not have to give up too many things, whilst at the same time seeming cheapskate in the eyes of larger families. Have four or more and your tribal authority goes through the roof – you are a *victor ludorum* of those *ludi publici* – but you might die early in the process, trying to earn all the money such a brood requires. At the very least, you might end up like Mr Quiverful in *Barchester Towers*, the divine with fourteen kids and a clergyman's income, gloomily contemplating 'his young flock, whom he could hardly take to church with him on Sundays, for there were not decent shoes and stockings for them all to wear. He thought of the well-worn sleeves of his own black coat, and of the stern face of the draper from whom he would fain ask for cloth to make another, did he not know that the credit would be refused him . . .'

And there's the question of making the love go round. At the risk of sounding like a page off *Dad-to-Dad Southern California*, I wonder at my ability to love both my children equally and still have a bit left over for my wife. Before I had children, I would have questioned my ability to love anyone much more than I loved myself. Now, however, I see that it is feasible – but it's not something I would want to be presumptuous about. I can remember quizzing a father of three as to how he managed to spread himself around among his family, and he put it as a matter of differentiation, rather than quantity: 'I love them all differently,' he kept saying, in a mantra. 'They all know I love them, because I love them differently.'

I didn't buy this. In fact, I think I subscribe, quite deeply, to a nineteenth-century, mechanistic understanding of the psyche, which sees it as something like a steam engine or a plumbing system. You can load it up to full pressure and be surprised at its strength and endurance. But it has a finite capacity, beyond which it may not go; and I have reached the limit of my emotional boiler and have no technology to extend my range. I am, if you like, still at the Richard Trevithick stage, rather than the Arthur Woolf stage, with the principle of the compound steam engine, extracting more energy from the same source.

But here's a weird thing. A couple of years after Tim was born, I thought I might as well have a vasectomy, in the way a number of my male friends have toyed with this solution to family planning once they reached the right-sized family. Susie and I went down to the local clinic, had a consultation with a doctor which consisted of the doctor reading questions off a check list, nodding occasionally and murmuring *uh-huh* into her clipboard. It took about twenty minutes to get through the interview, at the end of which she said that she could squeeze me in next week or would I like to wait a month for the following batch? The encounter had actually been sold to us as a *counselling session*. I had pictured it as a fretful puzzling over the issues raised, lasting hours and with a deal of soulful introspection. Twenty minutes of call-and-response struck me as perfunctory, but then, as a pair of middle-aged middle-class degree-holders, I suppose we must have looked like exactly the kind of thoughtful, responsible citizens who would have done all their cerebration beforehand and require no further prompting to see the consequences of their actions. I let the doctor put my name down for the next month's batch and we went away.

But in the car on the way home, we both burst into tears. It was inexplicable. I wasn't unduly worried about the possible physical complications (some kind of nodules are apparently known to form in your testicles, sometimes, as a consequence of a vasectomy) although had I interviewed the East End comic Jimmy *'Kin 'Ell* Jones (*The Guv'nor*) at the time, I might well have thought harder about this. When I *did* interview Jimmy Jones, a few years later, he explained that he'd had a vasectomy which had ruptured while he was onstage, perched on a Val Doonican stool and reaching for a high note in *Danny Boy*. 'A warm feeling down me leg' was how it announced itself. Blood everywhere. No, the feeling that overwhelmed us was one of superstitious dread, that by (literally) cutting off the chance of any more children, we would challenge fate, jeopardising the two we had. One of our boys would be run over by a bus and the other would die of some illness. It was an overwhelming sensation, and as we blubbed in the car, we both mentally cancelled the appointment I had made half an hour earlier to have my *vas deferens* severed. In other words, it was suddenly brought home to us how impulsively we made our decisions about our fertility and how we approached these decisions far more irrationally than we liked to kid ourselves. Two has symmetry but that's about all. There is no such thing as a rational number for a family. Four or one is no less sensible or stupid than two. All families are both ridiculous and a brilliant idea.

FIVE

Drinking, smoking, arguing, taking liberties with the truth, evasion, bad temper, sloth, greed: all things I've been guilty of in the past, am guilty of now. I switch on the TV after a stupid, awkward day and watch it uncritically for an hour and a half. When my children do the same, I nag them and complain that they're wasting their lives. I pig out on dairy products at the dinner table and reproach them when they beg for treble ice cream. What kind of example does this set my children?

Things have moved on from the nursery phase. Now they're at the age of four, going on six, they can spot these discrepancies, inconsistencies, thoughtlessnesses for themselves perfectly well. Before then, kids are just young and innocent/stupid enough not to conclude that you're a bum. Management from nought to three is less about leadership by example, more about basic training – food, walking, bowels, object manipulation, sleep. Once these are out the way, though, your kid begins to explore the potential of consciousness and reasoning. You get into the more refined area of not *what* to do but *how* and *why* to do it. A.A. Milne's *Now We Are Six* seems not just from another age, but from another planet ('I think I am a Muffin Man. I haven't got a bell, I haven't got the muffin things that muffin people sell'). Instead, now we are six we are into good practice/bad practice, justice/unfairness, selfishness/social consideration. The Larkinesque horror of *They fill you with the faults they had/ And add some extra, just for you.*

In fact we are well into the long haul, and are getting to know one another pretty intimately. I am irretrievably lost in middle-age, writing a book about the north of England, which takes me away to Wigan, Cleethorpes, Blackpool, South Shields. Had I been a little faster on my feet, it could have been Trebizond or Santa Barbara. But I accept my fate with good grace and spend some months sitting on murky trains and waiting on railway platforms. The disruption this causes to the domestic routine is very exciting for everyone ('Did you stay in a hotel? Did you have a kettle in your room? Is Wigan full of rich people?'), not least Susie, who complains vigorously. She gets her revenge vicariously though, when Alistair catches chickenpox and gives it to me. The first I notice of it is on the train back from Blackpool, where the air-conditioning seems unusually powerful and I have difficulty swallowing. I get home and my skin comes up like the surface of the moon. The nanny we have at the time (long hair and a bust like a roll-top desk) goes around saying *Here comes Spotty, Spotty Muldoon, he has spots where others have none.* Both boys contract the illness but recover quickly, leaving themselves unblemished. I am so poxy, though, that when I take myself to the doctor, he hunts around for a camera to take a few dermatological snaps. 'I've never seen so many spots in one place,' he says, admiringly. 'The backs of your knees are incredible.' I don't care much either way, as long as they vanish somehow, and as long as my boys' good looks remain. They're now at an age when they are almost astonishingly handsome, with clear eyes, glossy hair, faultless lightly browned skin, an aura of well-being and vitality radiating from them like some kind of peculiar cosmic light. In many ways, they are at their most loveable and cherishable: entering that golden age of childhood which all older parents look back on with such fondness. I have to admit that I get homesick for them when I'm dragging around Northern England.

But at the same time, they are also morally ugly enough and shrewd enough to start picking holes in my campaign of internal domestic discipline. The result is that if I rebuke Alistair for, let's say, allowing a Duplo tower to fall on his younger brother's head, then the conversation will go:

'You just let that fall on Tim's head.'

'I didn't know he was there.'

'You saw he was there.'

'He shouldn't have been there. He was in the way.'

So I think *Ah Jesus, it's going to be one of those insanity-provoking ritual confrontations.* I must be strong, stronger than I've ever been before, and keep my calm and imitate the kind of reasonable, firm, rational, humane father I know must exist somewhere beyond mere imagining.

'Yes, but you must look before you tip a load of Duplo over. You see? You've hit Tim on the head and made him cry.'

Sententious crap, of course, but I must try and make him understand something about cause and effect, reasonable and unreasonable behaviour.

'But you do things without looking.'

'What do you mean? What do I do without looking?'

'You drove the car in front of another man's car.'

'*When?*'

'When you brought me back from school.'

I'm torn. On the one hand, I get a *frisson* of pleasure at the clever little swine's quickness in pointing this out to me. On the other, he's answering me back. This is uncivilised. At his age, he should understand that I have good grounds for whatever I come out with, whereas he is still a social primitive. I press on with my impersonation of a reasonable man.

'That was a mistake.'

'So was this.'

'I think you did it deliberately.'

'I didn't.'

'I think you wanted to make Tim cry.'

'That's not true.'

'I—'

'That's not *true*—'

'I—'

'And anyway, Duplo doesn't hurt. If I'd wanted to hurt him, I'd have done something else. I'd have thrown it at him.'

This is where the discussion starts to unravel. This is the sort of *non sequitur* which kids come out with at precisely the moment when you're trying to garner some sort of sense, build some sort of meaning out of the exchange. I must, I think to myself, turn this sorry encounter into a lesson for us both. I don't *want* to get into a discussion about ways to hurt your brother. That's not the *point*.

'That's not the *point*—'

'He was annoying me anyway—'

'So you did it deliberately?'

'He was *annoying me*—'

'And that's no reason—'

'How d'you like it when he annoys *you*—?'

Now we are starting to shout at each other. So I say, 'Oh for God's sake—'

'It's *true*—'

'*Look* – that is not the *point*—'

'That *is* the point—'

'The point *is*, you have to *understand*—'

'Why *should* I—?'

Various things can happen. We can calm down and we can have a discussion about the moral questions raised by one child knocking down a load of plastic bricks on the other. We are now, all of us, just old enough for this to be a realistic possibility. We are grown-up enough to resolve our disputes through dialogue. Or, and more likely, we can take the brakes off and just yell. This, in turn, will lead to a seismic tantrum (from both children). Which then sees me picking up the screaming child, tucking him under my oxter, stomping upstairs like some monster out of Goya's *Proverbios* and throwing him onto his bed to consider the wrongness of his ways, while I stomp downstairs again, shouting at the walls. It's like the battle with Tim's watch, but with violence against the person. In the past, Alistair and I have come close to injuring one another in these encounters (that awful recklessness of child-driven rage), and I am glad to say that he is now so large that picking him up and throwing him around is no longer possible. Tim likewise. I am grateful for this, as I am grateful for all the deliverances that Fate has obliged me with. But even if I don't pick Alistair up, even if I just yell, then I have lost whatever it was I had hoped to gain. I am a savage, he is a savage. What's more, I am a clichéd savage. I find myself saying *Well just do it!* and *Because I say so!* and *Don't ask questions!* – formulations which I would have sworn not to use five years earlier, formulations which just spring out of some well of unconsciousness and jump from my open mouth.

(Is there any fundamental difference in this process between one child and another, between Tim and Alistair? Do I need to bear two distinct strategies in mind? Does one child run off the rails in a way markedly unlike the other? Tim is more mercurial – either much more conciliatory or instantaneously hysterical, depending on his mood. Alistair is generally a little more restrained, more quietly bitter than his brother, but when violent, much more so. It's hard, normally, to anticipate which way either will turn in an argument. The only certainty is that if one is vile with temper, the other will be implacably sweet. A process of yin/yang, automatic counteraction, which occurs spontaneously and has been doing so ever since Tim was old enough to read a situation.)

Maybe my stressedness, my inability to contain myself, is a generational thing (as I said before), a product of the more labile, random, disorganised society I live in. I know for sure that my parents never lapsed into such ravings with me as I do with my kids. Their technique was just to sigh (with disgust or bitterness, depending), roll their eyes to the ceiling and say nothing. In fact, doubtless as a result of this – the *status quo* inevitably being found in one's childhood world – I've always found the selfish frigidity of Charles Ryder's father in *Brideshead Revisited* defiantly appealing ('I am giving a little dinner party to diversify the rather monotonous series of your evenings at home') and sometimes try it with the boys. Usually without success. They just point at me and stare and say, 'Why are you looking like that?' The alternative seems to be a rant, breaking down sometimes into wanton use of force. There is no middle ground. It's like a switch being thrown, an instant inversion from one state to another. What I can't do, to impose my view of how society should be organised, is be sweetly tolerantly generous.

Not in a million years could I be like George Crabbe, the eighteenth-century poet, as memorialised by his son: 'His fatherly countenance, unmixed with any of the less lovable expressions that, in too many faces, obscure that character – but pre-eminently *fatherly*; conveying the ideas of kindness, intellect and purity; his manner grave, manly and cheerful, in unison with his high and open forehead . . .' There then follows some business about insects and shells, culminating in this: 'Coming lightly towards us with some unexpected present, his smile of indescribable benevolence spoke exultation in the foretaste of our raptures.'

Note the way the older Crabbe comes *lightly* towards his son. He doesn't stamp on the ground with his sweaty feet, or stumble uncertainly through drink, or smack his forehead with the heel of his hand going *God! God! God!* See how he is both grave *and* cheerful, pure *and* fatherly, expectant at the prospect of taking pleasure in someone else's pleasures. Everything about him (and this was the man who wrote, 'I've served the vilest slaves in jail/ And picked the dunghill's spoil for bread') confirms a type beyond human capacity, a figure on the cusp of angeldom, a blithe human reproach to the rest of us. I, conversely, live in a seamy hinterland bounded by the philosophical extremes of, say, Kenneth Tynan (booze, fags, sex), William Dorrit (pomposity, imprudence, financial uselessness) and Uranus. Did George Crabbe ever betray weakness? Did he have any trouble getting his way? Did he have difficulty prevailing?

The problem is multiplied by the fact that once our boys got to the stage where force and blind command were not options, I had to do two mutually contradictory things. I had to menace my way around the house, policing aberrant or anti-social behaviour – be a negative, restrictive force – and I had to offer some kind of pattern to follow, some kind of design for living for my inquisitive four/five/six-year-olds.

But all I have to turn to is *bien-pensant* bourgeois liberalism for my design for living. This currently seeks to underpin itself ethically through the argument that morality is a function of the genes, and that societies which do best are those whose members are genetically inclined to observe the rules of *quid pro quo*, foresight, tolerance, accommodation, non-violence and the repression of those who don't obey these rules. *This, boys, constitutes right behaviour.*

Or we might talk about Piaget, the pioneering child psychologist, who argued that younger children (say, from four to eight) have a morality which he termed *heteronomous*: subject to another's law. The younger child takes its lead from adults, and regards the adult law as more or less sacred. After about eight years, an *autonomous* morality takes over: the morality which is subject to one's own law. In other words, group agreement, mutual respect for one's peers, a growing intellectual awareness of the world combine to enable the child to work out a moral code. The progression from heteronomous to autonomous is independent of direct adult tuition. There again, even allowing for the fact that Piaget was Swiss and working sixty years ago, eight sounds old to be in the heteronomous phase. Our boys started to get autonomous from four onwards, and nothing we can do (Piaget was right) seems to alter things.

But this is not the kind of material I can immediately lay my hands on. In a crisis, or at a turning point in what I think of as my child's development, I do not want to discuss Piaget or morality in a post-theistic liberal society. What I want to say is something like, you may not think much of *me*, but there is a big, implacable, supernatural version of me somewhere in space, a *God*, and (like Jules says in *Pulp Fiction*) he will strike down upon thee with great vengeance and furious anger if you hit your brother/foul your room/steal food from the kitchen. This is the middle-class parent's (at least, *this* middle-class parent's) persistent conflict: the certainty that *rules must be obeyed*, but no certainty of what the rules should be, or how severely they should be imposed, or why they should be obeyed, or how they can be made to be obeyed.

Can I fall back on my parents' moral schemata? Yes, except my parents were themselves falling back on a world of pre-War and wartime moralities, which even by the Sixties seemed a little retro. Why, when I pinned up a picture of The Beatles (the groomed, mid-Sixties Beatles at that, not even the halitotic, whiskery Beatles of *The White Album* and *Abbey Road*) it sent my generally placid mother into spasms of anger at John Lennon, a man whose sarcastic rowdyism had clearly got through to her. 'That dreadful John Lenin,' she said and still says, thus killing two monsters of the twentieth century with one blow. Given that my father was a solicitor, there was never much discussion of the wrongs and arguable rights of theft, violence against the person, any of the things that might happen in an average schoolday. The climate was just wrong for daring to think the unthinkable thought and turn it into radical action. In fact (and this now seems somehow terrible, a lack of something in my own childhood) I can't even remember a time when they chided me or berated me for any misdemeanour or gross provocation. They *must* have, but the chiding was either so mild as to be dismissable, or so awful as to be consigned to somewhere in the pit of memory. Which means that either I was perfectly well-behaved (completely timid, for sure: that may count for a lot) or they never punished me when I was badly behaved, relying entirely on example to direct me in the world.

So how about friends and acquaintances? How do they manage? Well, I have seen it done by an expert, as it were: a primary school teacher who very earnestly took her five-year-old daughter (who had just beaten up her younger sister and then stormed out of the room) to a quiet spot, knelt down so that she was at the same level, rather than towering intimidatingly over her, and said, 'Now, do you want to tell me *why* you did that? Don't you think Lucy is upset by what you did? Would you like it if someone did that to *you*?' And so on. The child whined for a bit, like a mosquito in a bedroom, but, to my surprise, came round and had a dialogue with her mother about her feelings and insecurities. Little Lucy was corralled into the discourse and they resolved the problem. I went away from this feeling very bitter and envious until eighteen months later, by which time the same child had had a personality transplant and would now no longer listen to any kind of instruction. Instead, she preferred to scream and pout and quit the room in mid-sentence so jarringly that even her teacher mother started shouting back at her (*Come back here! I'm still TALKING to you!*).

Okay. Any other examples for me to imitate? Well, I can think of one acquaintance (father of two sons, like me) who strikes me into awed silence whenever I see him – which isn't, it has to be said, that often. This is because he is an off-puttingly complete traditional father, updated for the end of the century, but, at source, built along the lines of the 1950s model. Thus he holds down a serious professional job, brings home a load of money, drinks like a fish and puts on about a stone in weight every year. But once at home he does all that *Parents' Magazine* stuff. He *reigns*, by building tree houses, constructing rope swings, getting his boys to do sordid tasks in the garden involving wood and mud. He lets them play their awful TV pop music at full volume about the house. He shows them how to perform manly chores with fishing lines and raw bait, practises rugby with them, helps with their singing, gleefully buys them treats from the corner shop. He is an all-round guy and they adore him for it, quoting him *ad nauseam* as the only valid authority in disputed matters. Of course, bad behaviour happens, of course he shouts at them. But the relationship is predicated on this positive, inspirational approach, rather than on the aggressive narkiness which usually characterises my technique. Which makes him as much use as George Crabbe.

Nor can I picture to myself (for any decent length of time) a perfect domestic arrangement, in which everyone is in harmony with the rules and everyone understands everyone else's point of view and accommodates them accordingly. This is less to do with the nature of discipline and more to do with the fact that it's almost impossible to imagine *any* ideal state which involves one's children. I can just summon into being an ideal world in which Alistair comes up and says, *How are you today, Father?* And I reply, *Just fine and dandy, thank you, my boy.* And he wanders off to eat a punctual breakfast before Tim appears, kisses me on the cheek, says, *I hope you slept well. Can I help you to your coffee?* And I say, *Thank you, my son.* And then he joins his brother for a quietly involving conversation about the previous night's football across the breakfast table. But I can imagine this for only a second or two, before reality returns like a bounced cheque and I find myself uncontrollably conjuring up the usual scene of fighting and badmouthing. I can, on the other hand, easily lose myself in a long-term daydream of a perfect adult and childless existence because adults are to some extent predictable and malleable, both in one's dreams and in life. And if they're not, I can always move on in my dream to some who are and so extend the dreaming process and project a perfect state of being for myself in quite extensive detail. But I can't conjure up a perfect, imagined world involving my children because I cannot change them. I am stuck with my real boys and the threat to public order that they represent. I love them because they are so utterly and absolutely themselves; they drive me barking mad for the same reason. As a result no wish-fulfilment dream involving them lasts longer than a sneeze.

Yet another go. How do I set a positive example to my children at this crucial age? After long and empty meditation, something springs to mind from nowhere, quite unbidden and completely horrible because completely negative and counterproductive. The opposite, in fact, of a good example. It's the way I *hide* – something I did when the boys were fiveish and which I still do now. I hide when one of my children wants me for something urgent but inessential – admiring a new bit of Lego, maybe, or some daub on a piece of paper. I hide when there is homework that needs hearing. I hide when it is time to go to the corner shop for a sugar treat. I hide when I'm feeling mentally confused, ungiving, preoccupied, slack. Which is an unduly large part of the day. I can see myself doing it. I give them the *Just one second* routine, in as loving a voice as I can manage and busy myself ostentatiously with whatever it is I want to do. Then the child comes and hunts me down, plucks at my sleeve, quizzes me. I nod and grin and hurry to get away from them, perhaps carrying something upstairs, a cheerful cry of dismissal drifting over my shoulder. The child comes and tracks me down again. I have nowhere to turn. I say, *I'll be there in just one minute* – and go and hide in the lavatory. And there I sit, the door locked, a timeless peace hovering in the air. I am safe. I hear my son pad up and down, calling out, *Haven't you finished?* To which I reply, *Not yet.* I look out the crossword puzzle book. And the child pads away, giving up, and goes and switches on the TV, the nanny in every house. And I look up and see my murky reflection in the mirror over the washbasin.

Surely I can think of something better? Still racking my brains for positive examples, I have a last try and come up with a string of differently nuanced negatives. I don't drink to excess (not often, anyway). I don't chase after other women. I don't gamble. I don't beat up my wife. I pay my way. Maybe in this day and age, this small litany of restraint constitutes a precedent. Maybe that's all you can do for a five-year-old child: show him or her what a reasonably socialised adult looks like – unexceptional, just-about-coping, not-entirely-dehumanised-by-life. Heaven forbid that I should be so remarkable or outstanding in some way that I set my children an impossibly high standard to rise to in later life and consequently ruin their sense of self-worth before it's even properly matured.

It was during these complexities that I began to appreciate the symbolism of Dettox. *Wipes Away Doubt*, it says maternally on the label, and ever since Reckitt & Colman brought it out in the 1980s (a mixture of antibacterial cleanser, cationic surfactant and nonionic surfactant) it has been lurking in corners of our house (bogs, bathrooms, the kitchen) for the last decade. Does it work? Well, yes. It's fine in its way. It's a kind of junior, sweeter-smelling Dettol, that hideous matter my mother used to tip into the bath to cleanse cut knees, and which clouded the water like absinthe. Dettox is to Dettol as path weeder is to Agent Orange. But it has a handy pistol-grip dispenser to give you the sensation that you're actively murdering germs with a kind of anti-bacterial gun. It visibly cleans things up and it cleverly masks the odour of the crap in question with a smell both disinfected and curiously neutral.

We got through gallons of it in those early years. But it's that *early years* association which is so special about Dettox. It's in there with a whole sub-order of products which haunted the first years of life: baby shampoo, talcum powder, wet wipes, formula milk (that sterilisation business with the creaking plastic bucket, the punishment for relying on formula milk at all), baby food (made to resemble *exactly* the shit that came out as a by-product, uncannily so, a philosophical truth about the nature of matter and the dross from which we came and to which we will return), Calpol – a kind of paracetamol for kids, kept in a palatable liquid suspension: banana flavour, at times. Of course, there were loads of other bits of crap and garbage, mountains of the stuff – pushchairs and carrycots and baby clothes and little bowls and mugs with pictures of cavorting rabbits on them and all that clanking hardware. But whereas the clothes got too small and the buggies unnecessary, these smaller items never changed. They persisted in the backwaters of our home, gathered dust, hid in medicine cabinets, came out to surprise us now and then by reminding us of their existence.

Of course, by the time Alistair was six and Tim was three, the baby food and formula milk had long gone, as had the wet wipes with their spectral clag still hanging over them. Likewise the baby shampoo and talcum powder. Now, only the Dettox and the Calpol remained. The Calpol by virtue, mainly, of cunning marketing by the manufacturers, Warner-Lambert. When I was five or six, I got Disprin – proper, adult Disprin, the rank-tasting stuff in a small powdery white lid-shaped pill. This was given to me in fractions of a tablet, whenever I had a fever that needed fixing or a headache that made it impossible to play with my *Man From U.N.C.L.E.* shoulder holster and U.N.C.L.E. areas of specialisation and identity cards. I didn't get anything sweet-tasting (bananas!) in a teaspoon. But Warner-Lambert have not only devised a new way of delivering pain relief, they have cunningly extended the life of what was originally a baby/toddler product by bringing out a version for older kids (a picture of a child looking like a worked-over Alistair on the label, so there's no confusion). And so *that* product was still with us, and indeed, still is, as they find more and more ways to extend its active life.

But even the Calpol is marked for obsolescence as our boys grow up. Eventually it will go the way of the baby-bouncer and the very small Wellington boot, and leave us only with Dettox. Which is ageing now, getting out and about less than it used to, yellowing with the passing of time (was that the Dettox itself, or the plastic bottle?), gathering dust, beginning to look a little furtive. It reminds us of when we were younger, when our children were harder work but also simpler; when dramas were mainly physical things that could be resolved with a damp cloth, a certain amount of fuss (yes, you *do* have the power to affect my life) and a bottle of disinfectant. Six years on, and already we are in the grip of a nostalgia triggered, in the Proustian manner, by the contemplation of objects.

Sooner or later, we won't have carol concerts either. I don't mean just us as school-going parents. I mean that another few decades and two thousand years of Christian trappings will finally be out of the window and we'll revert to a simple semi-pagan celebration of the midwinter solstice, a Saturnalia in the suburbs. As for now, though, we have to go through the business of the Nativity (and the philosophical problem of Father Christmas, who does not exist), mainly at the prompting of the kids' schools. Which may or may not take a strict line on the need for Christian faith. And this really bursts into your life, and that of your kid, with the school carol concert. Alistair has by now made the move into the primary school stage, with Tim dogging his heels. No longer tinies, they will soon both be wearing little uniforms (encrusted with food and dirt) and doing bits of arduous homework in which they, mainly, have to make things out of cardboard and poster paints, with the galled assistance of their parents. And they will no longer be babies doing a shambolic re-telling of the Nativity story in a borrowed sports club members' bar ('And the shepherds saw the star, and they were sitting down, and, and . . .'). They will both be in a church, belting out songs and reading homilies from the Good Book.

The Christmas carol concert is massively better in comparison with the school sports day, because you don't have to do anything. At our boys' school, the headmistress used to cut a deal with the local vicar and ponce his church off him for an evening. All we had to do was turn up and look pleased and appreciative and not faint or be sick or start a fight. Where it wasn't okay was because the parents came impiously sweaty after a bitch of a day at work, or flagrantly dolled-up and glaring around with hostile, dark-rimmed eyes – either way, radiating secularity and material obsessiveness.

I can see our last ever primary school concert now, in my mind's eye. All the parents are astonishingly together in one place. The atmosphere is solid with competition, neurotic self-critique, worry over which new parent friendships are going to turn out to be phoney in the full glare of mutual competition, anxiety over which parents greet whom first and how, whether or not you look on a par with your contemporaries or whether you've stupidly over-dressed and look like someone at a Royal garden party/stupidly under-dressed and look like someone come to inspect the wiring. There are handfuls of fiercely proud grandparents prowling around, finding fault. There are other handfuls of apologetic grandparents, forever getting out of people's way. There are not enough seats. We only ever managed once to turn up early enough to get a good place. You stumble around looking for a chair and end up miles away, behind a pillar, and sit and worry and try not to stare. And you feel that you are all part of a community of souls who should have everything in common, but, paradoxically, only share a desire to see your child do down the other children.

But then the kids themselves troop in, clutching their song sheets, and all these appalling thoughts vanish. What a crucible of emotions! So small, so vulnerable, yet so independent, so clearly themselves! They're herded in by their teachers (suddenly drenched in sanctity, radiant with the cares of their work) and their headmistress picks her way among the mob. She has a scowl on her face and a smear of green eyeliner which we never see her wear at any other time of the year. The church seems overbearingly large, Gothic, marmoreal, in comparison with the children. We hold our breath while they all sit down on a big patch of carpeting in front of the altar, like a couple of hundred pixies in a fairy glen. Then, one after another, the different classes get up and are egged into performing their party pieces. Alistair uncomprehendingly reads about the Annunciation. A child farts.

Here, two contradictory sensations take over. You see your child separated from you, physically distinct on the dais, affirming his or her independence as a human being. But as you watch him or her from the shadows of the pews, with the perspective of unaccustomed distance, you see at the same time how much your wonderful offspring owes to you and your genes. Or rather, you tend to sit there and scornfully remark how much other children owe to their parents' genes. When I look at my own boys I see only them, someone unique; just occasionally a glimpse of something they might have inherited – or, more likely, a habit that they've copied off one of their parents. Ever since they were born, they've only ever been themselves, rather than a loose aggregate of several generations of middle-class families. It's only when one of them makes a joke or employs an ironical look that I ever see something of myself.

But when I look at other people's offspring I see the faces of the older generations gazing out in miniature from their kids, like reflections in a trick mirror. I note how some brick-chinned five-year-old is the exact image of a greying, brick-chinned thirty-eight-year-old tucked halfway back in the sea of faces. Works in a bank? Lawyer? If wearing a pullover and no suit, then what? Media type? Creative artisan? Shiftless hack? Daughters are smaller, pinker equivalents of their mothers, but with the same pinched noses or fretful eyes, the same hair. And I say to myself, *Well that one's going the same way*. *That* one's off to be a lawyer/get married and get pissed off/run a shop/get into the acting business *just like his parents*. It is a strange conviction I have at this carol service, this certainty that I can see their futures written on their faces this way, that they are locked into the future in a way that I could never predict for my own kids.

And then they get up and battle their way through one of the evening's featured items. The headmistress's big thing is to get the children to sing awesomely complicated Yuletide rounds (in sixteenth-century French, sometimes), accompanying themselves on recorders, cowbells, tambourines. These are generally terrible and frightening experiences, in which the audience sits, as jumpy as cats, while the music threatens to implode on the platform in front of us. The kids stare wildly into the crowd, anywhere but at their music, looking for support. The idea is to stretch their capabilities. When it works, which it sometimes does, either through luck or conscientiousness on the part of the teacher involved, it is a triumph of intent over chaos. The kids writhe around and tug at their fingers, looking pleased. The headmistress breaks her scowl. The parents let out a low moan of relief and pleasure, a mass exhalation of tension. And in that moment, everyone can see that, so far as their own little mite is concerned, anything is possible, from now on.

They are starting to be different, become unalterably themselves. At the same time, though, they reflect you back to yourself. A résumé: by now, Alistair is giving my own lip back to me. He says, *You're just being totally unreasonable*, and, *That's not MY problem*, and, *You should show some consideration*, and, *I've had enough*. Tim, at the same age, has a penchant for his mother's special brand of hysteria: *I can't stand it*, and, *You're killing me!*, and, *You're a complete waste of space*.

The good thing is that this makes them more fun to be with, nicer company: because they can talk more like adults. The bad thing about this invective is not just that it's yourself you hear being replayed to you, but that it seems to come out in moments of crises, of extreme rage or frustration. It comes out at moments when your child is at his most unreflective and therefore candid. And if what enters his head at this moment is something that *you've* come out with, months earlier, what does this mean for the rest of your kid's personal development? There you are, bottling up your furious sarcasm in order to try and resolve your difficulties in a sensible way, and abruptly the implications of everything you've been doing for the last five years is shoved in your face: *You should show some consideration.* Jesus! What kind of sanctimonious buffoon would come out with *that*? It's what you'd expect David Tomlinson's Mr Banks (quite a hero of mine, actually) hoping to say to his dismal-looking kids in the film version of *Mary Poppins*. It's completely in accord with his *It's high time they learned the seriousness of life* and *Outings ought to be fraught with purpose and practicality.* This, like the helpless *You'll do it because I say so* is the sort of discredited trash that I wordlessly vowed, in pregnancy and in the first few months of life, that I would never utter. And yet, here it is, not only coming back at me as proof of what a fraud I am, but out of the mouth of my own son, who should be above these things.

But it doesn't stop there. As part of their growing into separateness, my boys start to adopt attitudes that I find weirdly familiar. Absorbing my tendency to make a joke rather than deal with an issue head-on, they tend to become joke-minded. If I say that football is garbage and there's no point in supporting a football team, they will let it be known that football isn't really their thing, either. Whenever I lapse and giggle and point frantically at a passing car (because it is rare, or interesting, or simply flash), they start to quiz me lazily on aspects of that same car, dipping their toes in the soiled waters of car-fancying which I have long given up hoping to share with anyone else. They express political sympathies that I would not disavow. They get to be deeply fascinated by the various drinks Susie and I consume at the end of the day: gin, whisky, beer, wine – sniffing them, admiring them against the light.

'What exactly does gin and tonic taste like?' a son will ask.

'Go ahead,' I say, in my Liberal Parent voice, 'have a go.'

I proffer the sparkling beaker. Always that second of doubt, as the child leans forward to inhale the scent of juniper and the sharp pinch of quinine on the top. What if he gets the taste for it? What if he starts to sneak the stuff into his apple juice? This is what happens in teenage, not now. Why do I have to be so candid about this?

He takes an insect-sized sip and sneezes with disgust.

'This stinks,' he observes.

'Well give it back,' I say.

They even start to take a superficial interest in books, or the process of reading, without actually doing an awful lot of reading themselves. It's flattering.

Naturally, I try to encourage them to become even more like me in certain ways. Being a father means that I have a duty to bore them with my music collection under the pretext of readying them for the world. In practice, this means that I tie myself up in Hornbyesque knots trying to decide whether it's better to start at the beginning with Chuck Berry and Little Richard, go in with the greats (Beatles, Beach Boys) or start at the present day and work back (formerly Blur, Nirvana; at the time of writing, The Chemical Brothers, Propellerheads). But then this leaves no room for any of the jazzers, who present their own chronological difficulties. Start off with Louis Armstrong and Jelly Roll Morton and move through seven decades up to free form? Just plunge in with something accessible (Fats Waller, Benny Goodman) and work out, sideways? And then what about the whole world of serious or classical music? I made a conscious decision not to turn my boys off the world of the highbrow by forcing them to listen to *A German Requiem* in its entirety. But am I being over-optimistic to assume that they might get into it by degrees like I did, starting with The Beatles' mixolydian cadences and gradually moving backwards? I wasted quite a lot of spiritual energy over this, and still do, playing what I hope is an eclectic rag-bag of sounds to tempt them into the righteous path. I bung on a record and caper around to it (or look solemn, pained, if it's Bach or Debussy) and invite their responses.

Me (capering embarrassingly): *What do you reckon? Jumping, isn't it?*

Boy: *Is he playing the bagpipes?*

Or—

Ideal Boy: *That's terrific. What is it?*

Ideal Me: *One of Beethoven's late quartets. Recognise that instrument? I'll give you a clue—*

Ideal Boy: *—It's a viola.*

Ideal Me: *Well done!*

Some they like, others – more often – leave them cold. But for some reason I see it as necessary to go through this even though (a) they can make their own choices perfectly well and (b) it's a kind of half-arsed programme of intellectual refinement, something I vowed (along with all the other things I vowed) not to inflict on my own children.

Worst Case Me: *What do you reckon? Good, eh?*

Rebarbative Boy: *No offence, Dad, but it stinks.*

Worst Case Me: *You cultureless little yob—*

The reason I go on with it, though, is because I see it as more than just learning, more than just an education in culture. I see it as essential to their development as people. It is so important in my life that I can't believe that anyone can be a complete person without this stuff. I want them to be like me, in other words, at the same time as I want them to be completely different from me. This is nothing to do with the accidental frisson I get when I spot some inherited or adopted equivalence between me and them. This is a compulsion to replicate part of my experience through the next generation. It even has a moral force. I believe that these things are positively good, however senselessly prescriptive it may be to force them on others, and that maybe this is one of the few truly affirming examples I can set.

For other fathers, it's other things. Could be football, could be scouting, could be ballet. It all comes into the broad conspectus of culture. One guy I know takes his daughters regularly to art galleries, and has done this so often now that they regard such an activity as a completely normal, even satisfying way of spending the time. Another guy I know is assiduously bringing up his boy to be a Chelsea supporter, because that's what fathers do and it obviously never occurs to him to question the rightness of this activity. For him it's – again – almost a moral good to have the sense of belonging, shared partisanship, devotion in your life that comes from following a team. It's not worth wondering whether the kid might want to support Arsenal or Liverpool, because – on top of the general rightness of football fandom – the dad *knows* that it's right and proper to support Chelsea, just as I know it's right and proper to have a working knowledge of The Kinks and The Smiths. In fact one of his proudest moments was when he took his little boy off to a Chelsea–Wimbledon derby. They walked through some grimy tunnel to get to the ground along with hundreds of other Chelsea fans, chanting abuse about the Wimbledon team. The son slipped his hand into his father's hand and together they marched down the tunnel carolling about what a bunch of fuckers Wimbledon were, enjoying the interesting acoustic effects of hundreds of boozed-up Chelsea supporters echoing off thousands of encaustic tiles. One of those moments.

Part of this is just the closeness, the companionship of being with someone you love. But part of it is undoubtedly the feeling that you're with a younger version of yourself, a younger, much improved version of yourself, to whom you want to extend all of life's advantages and enriching possibilities without the need to go through any long, tiresome process of selection or solitary, arbitrary discovery. An earlier generation of fathers wouldn't have felt any ambivalence about it. Now, conscious of every individual's right to determine his or her own life preferences, we feel more uneasy. But we still do it, because we're fathers and it's what fathers can't stop themselves doing, and it sometimes feels like the best thing in the world you can do.

Improvement, improvement . . . by now, the toys we choose for them (Xmas and birthday) are starting to look like this:

—**Lego**: all forms, little spacemen who laugh and grin in their air-tight helmets, bucolic tableaux with dappled semi-articulated horses and haywagons, garbage collectors, motor-racing scenes, helicopters with winches whose cords get tangled up and then lost.

—**Scalextric**: in fact something not called Scalextric as such, but a latter-day miniaturised version, not like the elephantine outfit I wrestled with when I was young. The new stuff is less than half the size and twice as fast. It clips together better (the old track was made of some cloddish rubbery plastic which always bent into a series of gentle undulations instead of lying flat on the floor) and the cars don't fly off at corners. On the other hand, it doesn't work, in the sense that you can't have a race, as such, on it: true to the personality of the original. No matter how nicely patterned and delicately moulded the cars, one will always be pointedly quicker than the other; which sometimes won't go at all. My old set was the same in this respect, but made up for it by offering optional extras like plastic marker cones you could fit into the hillocky track, and moulded spectators, including a man with a box camera. It was essentially a solitary toy, even though the boxes always showed two cars pitted against each other at awful speed, a millimetre separating them, the contestants in the background having seizures, their eyeballs popping out etc. It was only really useful for setting lap times against yourself and arranging epic crashes. At the time of writing, Scalextric were re-launching the game specifically at dads, so that they could reconstitute a part of their youth, and then pass the inheritance on. But I remember it as being a lonely, thwarted pastime. (Plastic model kits fit in thematically, here, by the way. Like the Scalextric, I've tried those on the boys, to try and get them to share my brilliant past – latter-day jet fighter, field cannon, WW1 biplane, WW2 Hurricane – but no go. They just don't see it: a rejection which hurts even now. As Geoff Dyer puts it in *Anglo-English Attitudes*, 'The Airfix era . . . retains its power because it was something we went through *together*: a unifying experience that has become part of our collective consciousness.' How can the boys be complete without having savoured the pong of plastic cement? Without having blown a Lancaster bomber apart on the lawn with a carefully-preserved Guy Fawkes banger? Without having daubed themselves in Humbrol? We came close to the classic toy experience with the latter-day Scalextric, but, like the old Scalextric, it was basically frustrating. But Airfix – and indeed, the big, hyper-complicated Tamiya car kits I moved onto in later years – this was wholly satisfying, a wholly realised world. Perhaps they'll get onto it later.)

—**Jigsaw puzzles:** only because Alistair went through a craze for them.

—**Wooden dinosaurs:** like the jigsaw puzzles, a blatant and so foredoomed effort to capitalise on a passing fad and give it a puritanical impetus towards self-improvement.

—**Books:** goes without saying. The only snag with books is that they can irritate you till you choke and still be good books, books worth having in the house, books you must read aloud to encourage verbal skills acquisition. This is true especially of those early things you read to your kids – the Spot books, or the Mister Men books, or indeed anything with the pages made out of laminated cardboard and a wipe-clean surface. Like early toys, they were a shortcut to dementia, because so empty of content or meaning (and a bit like Sesame Street: admirable, really admirable, but I know that Bread begins with B). Richard Scarry's little square books were okay, though, because we liked the scrawny graphic style and the character called Lowly Worm, who wore a *Federhut* and was often seen hanging upside-down from moving biplanes, embodying the human condition. It was elements like Lowly that stopped us going over the edge. After that, though, we had to suffer the pain of rejection when our boys got old enough to express preferences and scorned something we'd loved in our own childhoods. Beatrix Potter got canned right from the start, even though someone gave us a handsome christening present of the complete Potter in a boxed set. And I'm still hurt that no one loved Winnie the Pooh as I had, except in the Alan Bennett taped version. Why didn't they relish the twisted humanity of my man Eeyore? Why didn't they spot the political relevance of Tigger? How could they even contemplate watching the bastardised Disney version? And why, conversely, could I never find it in my heart to love Roald Dahl, while they did? Evidently a genius of some sort for generating such intense loyalty among his young readers, he never genuinely turned me on – never as much, at least, as the Quentin Blake illustrations that came with his books. A generational thing, maybe: post-Just William, post the Buckeridge Jennings books, I was always put off by Dahl's intentional coarseness and fondness for anarchical cruelty, and missed the comforting verities of the earlier stories. On the other hand, Dahl and I (or at least, Dahl's estate and I) used to share literary agents, and I was always grateful for the fact that Dahl's millions saw to it that I got to sit in a nice office with a decent mug of coffee.

—Complex build-it-yourself electromechanical kits and chemistry sets/discover-the-world-of-science outfits: these are still coming in. In the last few years, we have had an electric doorbell kit, a crystal radio and a bendy wire game. In this last, you have to pass a metal contact along an awkwardly twisted wire without touching that same wire. Make contact, and a tone generator (the real point of the kit, containing two transistors, some capacitors and a packet of resistors, each no bigger than a grain of rice) goes off like an air-raid siren. Pure chemistry sets are almost unobtainable these days, but there are general science kits around with weather vanes, shreds of litmus paper, elementary gear for pulleys and leverage experiments, that kind of thing. (I, of course, had a large and elaborate proper chemistry set, with which I used to make a tough brownish residue in the bottoms of test tubes, until all the test tubes were clogged with this residue and couldn't be used for anything sensible or realistic.) Well, we had one of the modern equivalents and the weather vane went out in the garden for a few years until a gale sheared it off its post. The accompanying rain gauge cracked in the first frost. The doorbell kit was never made and I think got binned a while ago. The litmus paper was lost or eaten, while the bendy wire game was made entirely by me, on account of its insane complexity, far beyond the capacity even of an unusually bright six-year-old child. The crystal radio set is still in the box, about three years on, waiting for me to move upon it like the great Creator. Someone – not me – did manage to build a simple car with a battery-powered motor out of an engineering kit. This was a hit, but was very rapid and had no steering. So it shot under furniture and down stairs and mainly destroyed itself, which made everyone quite tearful.

And what did *they* want? What did they get as palliatives from their parents, clearly troubled by what tedious presents they'd chosen to give off their own bat?

—**Gunge:** ever-popular, plastic pots with fluorescent elastic muck in. A friend of Tim's once shoved a handful into Alistair's tape recorder and permanently fucked the mechanism. It also turned out that if a child got it stuck to any piece of clothing or bedding, it never came off, but metamorphosed under the influence of heat in the washing machine into a tough, brightly coloured, cement-like matter. This denatured gunge was a trial to whoever wanted to clean it off. It was also, I guess, a betrayal to the child who owned it. If you want to play with a sanitised version of your own excrement, then the last thing you want is for that generous material to turn stiff and unyielding on you.

—**Guns:** Susie and I patrolled this one fairly rigorously, and since most of the people we know are wet liberal types like us – taking a nicely sanctimonious stand against the coarsening effects of violence in our culture – guns were not always freely available. We didn't get them, most other people didn't get them, but one or two mischievous adults (Uncle Stephen, for one) did like to pander to boys' instincts. And when the guns appeared, they brought violence with them, just as if it had been Compton or Medellin. Not through fake shootings, but because there is always a hierarchy in weapons and the hierarchical disputes which result from this are always nastier than the guns themselves. Some guns, either because they are bigger, or have more features or more realistic detailing, are high status. Others, because they demonstrate the opposite characteristics, are low status. If you have a low-status gun, you have to beat the other guy up – either to get his weapon off him, or just to reassert your authority. Since Alistair is, at the time of writing, larger than Tim, and will be for the next few years, he usually managed to beat up more than he got beaten up. And so got the high-status gun. This meant that we had to get involved, as parents, which meant that all the guns got taken away or redistributed, according to us, more fairly. Sometimes Tim would end up with a huge yellow and blue crossbow which used air pressure to fire half-metre-long sausages of foam plastic. Alistair got a small black plastic handgun which did nothing but rattle. Tim could fire foam plastic sausages at Alistair, sometimes hitting him in the eye. Alistair would then strike Tim a blow with the butt of his handgun. Tim would kick him. Alistair would push him down the stairs, and so on. It's not so much that guns encourage children to be violent: they are, anyway. It's that they channel the violence, like a torrent of water, into a confined space, at which point it gets dangerous. The guns become irrelevant in themselves, the violence becomes everything. Conversely, kids will also use things that aren't guns to stand in the place of guns, if they absolutely need to enact some kind of shooting drama. Fingers, sticks, Biros, will do. I have even heard of one child using a sausage as a shooter, when all else failed. The positive side to all this gun warfare is that it provides a medium through which boys can express aggression without *necessarily* physically harming one another. It is, they say, a transition in the process of becoming a fully socialised person. Impossible, though, to overcome that feeling of unease whenever the rods came out – an unease, I imagine, equivalent to the unease felt by fathers with daughters, whenever they encounter the full horror of the Sindy/Barbie doll collection. Guns and dolls: both painfully expressive of those early gender obsessions. But at least I could understand guns. I was never in the position of one father I know who came upon his daughter's entire collection of Barbies, 'All spread out against a wall, all in different clothes, or sometimes nude, *twenty-five* of them. I didn't know she had *twenty-five*. They looked like that necropolis in Sicily with all those mummified aristos.'

—**Stupid costumes:** Batman, a cowboy, a policeman, Captain Scarlet, Troy Tempest, a Crusader with a plastic shield and a hollow plastic broadsword, a medical doctor. Almost never worn complete, but dismantled into their components and then reassembled in mutant, *Mad Max* forms: Captain Crusader; Batboy; Dr Scarlet; a cod-mediaeval *Stingray* commander; a policeman wearing a cape, a six-gun, a broadsword and a stethoscope; a space bat with an heraldic shield.

—**Power Rangers:** a craze, some years ago. You had to get the plastic action figures for your children to leave lying around on the floor, twisted and broken; or jammed down the back of the sofa. These were unplayable-with toys, toys that you simply had to have, whose possession you could prove. Like Spice Girls memorabilia later on, or Pog collections, you didn't even have to like them. You just had to have them in your house. This is peer-group ownership, and it is so powerful a force that it has even, in the past, got us into the worst shop in the world – Toys 'R' Us – hunting for Power Rangers tat. Is there an adult equivalent? Something like an acclaimed book that you're never going to read (*A Suitable Boy, A Brief History Of*

Time, Vanity Fair) or a gadget that you never use (video camera, rowing machine) or item of clothing (linen suit)? *Something you have to have an acquaintance with*. And if that necessitates ownership, then you do that, too.

—Computer and computer-related games: I don't think the jury is out on this. I am certain that computer games and their relatives (Nintendo, Sony Playstation, GameBoy, even the primitive Tetris games that are lumped in free with tape players and wristwatches) are positively bad. Nothing, of course, more clearly indicates the generational gap between me and my children (or the fact that they are boys) than that they think that computer/video games are smart, while I think they're cretinising. Much of this is to do with the fact that I have no purchase on these games from my own past – I was, of course, footling about with Scalextric, Airfix and clagged test tubes at this age – and that however much my kids try and explain their attractions to me, they're exclusive, dividing me from my own offspring. Which is part of the appeal for them. But they also fry your brain and make you into an unsocialised wreck. I know this, because I have played them from time to time (Mario, the Tetris game, a motor-racing video thing, a shoot-'em-up on the computer and a compulsive old Space Invaders thing called Crystal Quest, which had terrific gastric sound effects) and I have felt my senses winding up tighter and tighter as the game progresses, my vision locked onto the screen. The world around me shrinks and shrinks, until the only things left are the screen and the figures flashing across it. I can tell, viscerally, that I am going *tonto*. Now, I know that something like this happens to my kids, only more so, judging by the symptoms they display after some time has elapsed. In one instance, I come across Alistair and a pal solemnly and silently sitting side-by-side, staring into the screen, only their fingers moving over the control buttons, like a couple of run-down animatronics. In another, mesmerised by a particularly stupid beat-'em-up video game, Tim (especially prone) *will not* relinquish the controls. He stares at the screen for as long as there is electricity coming out of the wall, fighting a vicious inner battle as he punches and kicks the oriental robot who *will not lie down and die*. So I ban this game, physically chuck it away. But then he descends on a basketball game – ostensibly fun, harmless, instructive even – and again wires himself up so badly that he ends up bouncing up and down vertically as if on a pogo stick. He is galvanised. This is nothing to do with hand–eye coordination or rapid tactical thinking or anything else that apologists for these games might advance. This is mania, and it does not occur in the context of any other pastime.

So there's a tension between what I want for them and what they want for themselves. How could there not be? It's part of that process in which I want them to grow into themselves at the same time as I want them to be the same as me, be my mates even. But with the exception of the Lego, they want their toys to demonstrate their otherness. What else could I expect?

I suppose what I expected was that I could profit from this interlude between the incredibly dim and thwarting toys of the earliest days and whatever they'll have instead of toys in a couple of years' time (drugs, cigs). I could become that smiling father from the old Scalextric ads, or the Hornby Double-O promotions, or the Mammod miniature steam engine catalogue of thirty years ago. Ageing now, and unable to do much, if anything, with the highly physical baby toys of a few years back (too fat and stiff to get down and crawl around the playhouse; too fearful of checking out with a heart attack from pushing the stupid handcart around; that *oof!* I now make whenever I bend down), I did promise myself the compensation of becoming a smiling greasy Fifties Dad. I saw myself in tie and cardigan (I would have taken up a pipe if I had to), delighting in the delight of my sons, and in the toys themselves, once those toys had become more a matter of thoughtful dexterity than physical ebullition. I looked forward to what I imagined were those traditional father/son pastimes. No matter that in the real world at the end of the century, there's no time for pastimes in the traditional sense. It is, nevertheless, the idea, unformed and unarticulated, which was somewhere in the back of my mind, and which Power Rangers and Gunge and weapons have cheated me of. As I suppose Scalextric and *The Man From U.N.C.L.E.* may have cheated my father.

Time is accelerating – and there is nothing like the aggregate of several years' toys to make it plain that the thing you thought brand-new, that you can remember your son yanking out of the box, is three years old, and only kept for nostalgia or museum reference. The boys themselves know this, and will fall upon some piece of defaced, frayed plastic with cries of grateful recognition. They are conscious that time is passing for them too, and that they are now old enough to have a history. So the toys are freighted with meaning for all of us, and all the wealth and power and material influence of Toys 'R' Us, with over 1,400 stores worldwide and sales around $10 billion per annum, and with its awful, sub-human chaos and madness each Christmas – even Toys 'R' Us can somehow be compressed along with the rest of human experience into a very slightly shitty plastic helicopter which no one much played with when new, but which now sits in the obsolete toy drawer, painfully necessary, but like a *memento mori*.

Where I come into my own, though, is answering the hard questions. The exchange goes like this. Alistair says, 'Where's Patagonia?'

And I answer, 'South America.' But this is my chance to shine. I cannot let the question rest there. I must tell Alistair as much as I know about Patagonia – which is, frankly, almost nothing. But I know that he will already be losing interest in the subject from the moment I tell him it's in South America, and so my super-detailed reply will sound imposingly long-winded.

'A lot of Welshmen there. Because of the resemblance to Wales – Atlantic coastline, hills, sheep. Royal Academician Kyffin Williams – a Welshman, you will note – has painted it many times. His flinty, sombre colours and his boldly masculine use of the palette knife . . .'

Not all of this may be accurate. Some of it may be completely wrong. Why doesn't it bother me? Why do I enjoy sounding off about this? Or about something even more traditionally manly, fatherly, like the internal combustion engine, or Jimmy White's brilliant but erratic form as a snooker player? Just thinking about it, I can feel myself getting an anticipatory thrill, the thrill of being an expert. That fact that I am nothing of the sort is not an issue to my six-year-old son. To him I must appear to possess an incredible amount of random knowledge, as well as the ability to understand French, drive a car and cook a chicken. It is one of the few unadulterated privileges of being an adult, and it really only comes into its own in this time when the kids are old enough to have a need to know, but young enough not to be entirely cynical about the person informing them. In fact, it's something I've unconsciously been looking forward to since the time when *I* used to quiz *my* father, believing him to be an absolute repository of all knowledge, even when – most of the time – he hadn't a clue. For some reason, I can still remember asking him what football teams were (I must have been pretty young at the time, or startlingly naive, even by my standards). He said, confidently, 'There are two teams: Spurs and Arsenal.' That was it for footie. Two teams. And for years, I believed him.

But it goes beyond simple improvisation. Even when I have no idea what the answer to the question is – or such a shaky grasp of the subject that I am not prepared to try and butch it out – there's an intense pleasure to be had in *looking the thing up*.

'The Encyclopedia!' I shout, a cross between Joyce Grenfell and Heinz Wolff. 'Let's see what it says!'

There was once a chance that I might have become a school-teacher. It was a chance I revoked in one of those Existential moments in life, one of those moments when you make the *acte gratuit*. The interviewer for the teacher-training course asked me how I would feel, facing a class of fourth-form boys. I said the thought filled me with *nausea*, and they didn't offer me a place. But I wonder sometimes if I couldn't have got something out of being a pedagogue. Is this why I love to flick importantly through the pages of one of those Dorling Kindersleys, shouting out items of interest on the way? Partly that; partly because it's one of the few times when I really feel in control, benignly in control, of my own children – for the time that I have their attention. And partly it's because I have a chance to reduce my own almost limitless ignorance by a fraction.

'The Black Death,' I say. 'Did *you* know that a third of the popu-lation of Europe died from it. *I* didn't know that.' Or, 'Canada is the second largest country in the world.' Or, 'Anole lizards inflate their red-coloured throat sacs.' Sometimes, emboldened by this sudden rush of information, I get carried away and start to extemporise, dangerously drawing parallels between, say, the Anole lizard and the bagpipes; or between Canada and Mandelbrot's fractals. I want to enthrall my boys with the scope of my learning and at the same time instill in them a hunger for knowledge. I want them to see me attempt the high-wire act of intellectualising. I want to impress them, in short: I want their admiration, and this is one of the few ways I have of doing it. And if this leads me to over-reach and claim acquaintance of something I actually know nothing about (a high probability of this), then I can give them a useful lesson in humility (it's *okay* to admit to being wrong). I can purge my soul and hope that they won't think I'm a fraud.

But it's a book thing. The arrival of a computer and the *Encarta* CD-sized encyclopedia – made so that kids can roam around on the end of a mouse and find things out for themselves – has dealt this a blow. There's nothing companionable about a computer screen. You can't wave the thing around histrionically, brandishing pages and flipping with fierce keenness through the index. And the process of investigation is necessarily less encumbered with serendipities and fruitful chance encounters. You can't turn to the wrong page by mistake on a computer disk and find yourself looking at the Hapsburgs instead of Hibernation. And what's the point of pursuing knowledge if you can't do that?

It must be costing me at least £400 a month, per child, to bring my boys up: although I suspect it's much more, depending on what I include. Do I add in the initial cost of the house, which has to have two kids' bedrooms, both of which need furnishing and decorating (as little as possible, admittedly: pigsties most of the time)? Plus, say, the cost of owning a four-seater car instead of the leery two-seater runabout I could have if I didn't have children? Although the two-seater would probably cost more than my austere Volkswagen, so forget that. Figures of £50,000, £60,000, £80,000 have been quoted at me in the past, as the total cost of raising a child, extended over a period of, say, eighteen years. The last sounds plausible, but even then, there's no allowance for inflation, or for the fact that unless I shoehorn my children straight into a post-school training scheme, I've got at least another three years of colossally expensive university education and board & lodging. And even after *that*, there might be some costly professional qualification to pitch for. Or they might want to go round the world. Or at the very least, may well just ponce unrepayable loans off me.

Sometimes I look guiltily at couples who haven't got children – contentedly gay men in nice Central London apartments; blithe old hippies in big houses filled with nice things – and I dream of what it would be like if I'd kept all the money I'd ever made, for myself. Tens of thousands of pounds I wouldn't have spent on baby-walkers, football boots, computer games, ice lollies, videos of *Space Jam* and *The Jungle Book*, school trips to Sutton Hoo, sweatshirts, Big Macs. I could be sitting, here, now, surrounded by entirely adult paraphernalia and order, ranks of gleaming CDs (say) beside an audiophile's music player, all the knobs and switches open to the air, unafraid of being bumped into, pulled off, fucked with chocolate. I could have a BMW lounging outside. I could take regular holidays abroad, none of which was in any way compromised by the school calendar. I could live in a room of monastic austerity on 500 a month with white, unfingered walls. Or I could splash out on some Versace cushions and pretend to be Donald Trump. And if I had never had children, had never had my boys and known how beautiful they were and how exactly they seemed to fit into the space in the universe allotted to them – if this had never happened, how could I miss them? What if that concatenation of circumstances at the very beginning had never been? Would I be any less fulfilled? I wouldn't be writing this book, for sure. But then I wouldn't need to work nearly as much, anyway. Or I could do something on food or travel instead . . . In fact, it struck me that having two children is something I would have thought of as simply *impossible* when

I was eighteen or twenty years old. Something that others were able to do, evidently; but not me. Way beyond my capacities. Earning a bare living was the summit of my ambitions. I would have considered my life a triumph if I managed to keep things just ticking over. Being financially and emotionally responsible for two children is *so* awesome a notion – so breathtaking, so remarkable, such a wonderful *achievement* – that I must stop thinking about it before I panic.

We're standing in the yellowing transit lounge of the airport in Antigua, having just stepped off a huge British Airways jet. Our hair and clothes are wrecked, full of sweat and farts and the sort of drifting, grimy polymers that airplanes fill up with. We have been travelling for a day. We are dehydrated, we have no idea what time it is. We still have several hours of travelling to get on with, in a smaller, dirtier plane which will take us to Barbados. This is one of those once-in-a-lifetime, let's-go-crazy family holidays: unrepeatable, complex, above all expensive. Two weeks in which to have a good time, absolutely without compromise or the possibility of failure. Which is why I find myself grabbing poor Tim's hand and smacking it *really* hard, raising a jet-engine scream from Tim and a rumble of disapproval from some ladies standing a few feet away. When I see other parents smack their children in this way – unthinkingly, purely as a reflex of anger and frustration, wholly without justification – I usually feel awful. I feel all the injustice that the smacked child must feel and I feel ashamed for the parent. In fact, it's worse when I see someone I know personally, losing control and shaking their child, or making it cry, or smacking it. It feels worse because the nakedness of their rage and loss of self-control is as bad as if I caught them dead drunk or in the middle of some shameful wrongdoing; their humiliation diminishes our acquaintance. At once, I step outside myself, see what I have done, and like the ladies standing next to Tim, understand my smacking as a straightforward barbarism of which I am at once ashamed and for which I would like to apologise both to some higher authority, and to Tim himself.

So why do I hit him? Because he *will* not stop running round and round an island of pouffes and potted plants in the middle of the airport lounge. But we are on holiday, our time is our own, why shouldn't he fool around? He's been stuck on a plane like the rest of us. He too feels tired and sweaty and tainted with bad air. What have I just done to him? I have just let him know that *I* am on holiday, and that means that I am a ragbag of nervous anticipations and money worries: heightened by the fact that this is altogether more of an investment of time and money than, say, a rented cottage in Devon, and that, as the stakes go up, so does my terror of failure. Which is why I strike him, shamingly, in a small, sweaty airport, in front of about thirty people.

But even in the rented cottage in Devon, the tension is unsuppressable. Not only do we have this one brief moment in which to shake off all the cares of the world, we have to drain it of experience, savour every instant of it at the same time as we are stuck together in each other's company for the whole day. No school, no work to lighten the social burden. *I am paying good money to be with my kids all the time*. Of course, my peculiar circumstances – working at home, collecting from school, being on hand – are going to exaggerate this effect. I guess that traditional working fathers are going to see it differently, maybe relishing the chance to get to know their kids after weeks of separation, bond with them, rediscover them as human beings.

But then, does anyone really want to go to sleep in a huge dormitory of a communal farmhouse bedroom, with the kids snoring away in one corner, the parents in another? Before waking up at dawn with the July rain glistening on the windows and the smell of the countryside drifting down the chimney and your eyes gummed together with damp and your ears full of the chattering of the rooks? Your children are still snoring away, the bedclothes by now looking as if a rhino has trampled them.

And they're so ungrateful. In Barbados, they complain about the food (okra, flying fish, mango, deliciously and painstakingly prepared by a maid whose sorrowful dignity nearly drove me crazy) and the absence of funfair rides. In Devon, they complain about the cold and wet and the absence of funfair rides (but not the food, which is carelessly and disgustingly prepared by me, much of the time, but which has the unbeatable virtue of being totally familiar). What's more, at the time of Devon, Tim is still very small and I have to carry him around in a backpack for children – the kind like a rucksack, but with a space for the child to go in instead of your sweaters and kagools, the one I ultimately tried to flog in Chiswick. It is a very bad product: grey, slack, shaped for something like an economy packet of cornflakes, rectilinear, boxy, not at all for a large baby. Indeed, we have to cram bits of soft packing down around the sides so that Tim doesn't get knocked around against the metal frame every time I take a step. And it hangs low on the shoulders, so low that all the weight seems to gather in the small of my back and makes me want to fall over backwards. With this burden, with the damp in my clothes and the smell of my awful cooking hanging round me like a familiar, I lurch around some (literally) shitty Devon fields, thinking about money, having my spine twisted by my younger son.

I can't decide whether enough is made of family holidays in films and books, or whether it's surprising how much actually is. For an audience without children, tales of family life (Dickens excepted) are pretty irksome. For an audience with children, they're wholly gripping, but too parochial, too coy to have a much wider constituency. What springs to mind? *National Lampoon's Vacation*, preceeded by *Holiday Camp* (1947, the film which gave the Huggetts to a waiting world). *Death In Venice*? 'Leave here at once, without delay,' as Aschenbach nerves himself up to say to Tadzio's mother in the Mann novella, 'with Tadzio and your daughters. Venice is in the grip of pestilence.' Kate Atkinson's *Behind the Scenes at the Museum* ('We are still going to Whitby, to spend the half-term holiday in a self-catering flat, as previously arranged')? Bill Bryson's *The Lost Continent* – one of the best, with the crushed figure of Bryson's father at the wheel of the family car: 'He never arrived at an amusement park or tourist attraction without first approaching it from several directions, like a pilot making passes over an unfamiliar airport . . .'

It may be that family holidays are self-limiting as subjects for art. In fact, it's hard to see how they could be otherwise. When they're interesting, it's because they're seen from the child's point of view, affording new emotional challenges, unpleasant changes of scene, unexpected glimpses of the adult psyche. For the adults, holidays are really non-events, anti-events, in which, insofar as anything happens, it should happen so as to make everything peaceful and anodyne so that you know you've had a break. Fine, when you're still pre-children, to go mad and have *experiences* in Vietnam and New York. After that, though, after kids, you want to be liberated from adult consciousness. You want to be slightly bored. I want my children to be there but not there. I want them to become an adjunct to the holiday, rather than be themselves: to come only when called, to be entertaining, to divert me – after which I can go back to lying down somewhere, drinking furtively in the warm shade. The fact that they do not do this – rather, that they create undue extra work (slackening off now, but once a Victorian expedition of folding cots, pushchairs – bundled up to withstand the labours of the baggage-handlers at British airports – sackloads of spare clothes, child remedies unobtainable in Greece or Turkey, playthings to amuse them for the first day and a half) is only fair, even if it seems an undue imposition to me.

In the end, I find myself lounging on a sunbed (this once happened, I finally made it to a sunbed in Portugal) on a terrace with a pool behind me and a fridge full of beer a few feet away, and what fills my thoughts? Number one son coming up every ninety seconds to tell me about some huge sub-tropical ants he's discovered and which are clearly about to pick me up and pitch me into the pool; Number two son throwing himself off the terrace and into ten feet of ratty bougainvillaea and screaming and screaming and screaming. And that is pretty well what holidays have become.

Someone I know (two kids) was complaining to me the other day that a friend (childless) of his had been loudly amazed when he (the father) had gone upstairs to look at his children, asleep in bed.

'Why do you just *stand* there,' the friend of the friend had said, 'and *look* at them? They're *asleep*.'

So my pal said, 'I look at them *because* they're asleep.'

Any father will understand what he means. The reason we nip upstairs to check on their sleeping – once they're past the baby phase and into proper childhood – is not, normally, because we're worried they might be uncomfortable, or hot, or restless, or ill. Quite the reverse. We go upstairs trusting that they will be absolutely unconscious, allowing us endless time to look at them and enjoy their beauty – always especially touching in repose – and gaze on them as human works of art, vulnerable, expressive, still. We look at them because this is the only time we ever can look at them, without interruption, without their rushing off, a small word of abuse drifting over their shoulders, without their squirming and looking uncomfortable, without their asking tricky questions. It's analogous to the way we feel fondest talking about our kids when they're not there. The way we reminisce about their triumphs and their adorability without their being present to interrupt and remind us that reality is more complex than that. It's even a part of the same mechanism which makes me feel emotional and homesick at the sight of other children about my boys' ages when I'm away from home – the stabbing sensation which perversely reminds me that I need to have my kids around me, the moment I'm deprived of them.

Sleep is like this, a time of unblemished contemplation, a time when we can uninterruptedly worship the creatures we've made. Sleep and love are, in short, more or less synonymous by now.

SIX

So it's Susie's birthday. She decides that she wants to go down to the sea (with which she has a mystical affinity). The place she wants to go to is Portsmouth because it's got sea, it's easy to get to and because there is the Naval Heritage of Portsmouth for the kids to visit. And this will keep the whole family happily occupied for a day. It's November, cold for southern England, might have been nicer to stay indoors and work up an odorous fug, but the sea is by definition out of doors, and we go. Everyone gets warm coats and gloves, and a huge fight breaks out between Alistair and Tim in the hallway. We have not even got to the car, and already Alistair has called Tim a *stupid bloody prat* and Tim has called Alistair an *idiotic git*. Nine-thirty in the morning (*We'll never get there*) and already the air is turning sulphurous. I suspect I can hear the f-word somewhere, muttered by a boy. Abusive language is enough of a commonplace for us to recognise the sinking feeling it generates in us, but still enough of a novelty for us to experience a shock when we hear it. We force ourselves into the car, the words distantly ringing in our middle-class ears.

★　　★　　★

Arseholes, bastards, fucking cunts and pricks, the way Ian Dury put it in *Plaistow Patricia*, and we loved him for it. We all know – Ian certainly did – that language has the power to convulse us, even though it's nothing, mere sounds in the air, ink on a page. That's one reason why it's so powerful. The source of its influence is invisible and mysterious – we can't understand it, and we can't decide how best to deal with it, or even tolerate it. But when it turns out that our kids – no more than eight years old, even now – know these words too, it feels like a special assault on us and our values and the whole world that we're trying to fabricate around our children. But then, I swear, Susie swears, it's quite plain that everyone at school swears their fucking heads off. Is it hypocrisy to be affronted by my son coming out with *bloody* or *piss* or *fuck*? Why do I go through the pious lunacy of saying, *Well you can do it at school if you must, but not in front of us and CERTAINLY not in front of the bloody grandparents. Excuse my language.* Whose sensibilities (other than those of the grandparents) am I trying to protect?

Well, it's precisely their sensibilities and the sensibilities of every-one like them – oldsters generally, revered family members, well-brought-up people whose good opinion we wretchedly crave. And by extension, my own sensibilities and sense of self-worth. Swearing is one of those shaming random dangers, like explosive crapping used to be with six-month-old babies. It's something that can be hedged against up to a point; but with a one-in-six chance of bursting out nonetheless. In fact the abstract fear of uncontrolled childish swearing is so strong in my mind that it now haunts me in the form of a scene which roams around my semi-consciousness. In this scene I involuntarily limn a rigidly formal imaginary encounter involving me and my family (round a dining table, maybe, strenuously polished and larded with quality crockery and cutlery) and some other austere, venerated personages at either end. In my imaginings, these revered ones aren't quite my parents, but not quite the Queen and Prince Philip. The Duke and Duchess of Devonshire, maybe. It starts off tense but bearable. We sit there in taut near-silence, crushing our cheeks together so as not to fart, picking at our food and exchanging only cautious pleasantries. Everything is going more or less as well as it can, when Alistair – sitting opposite me, so I can't hit him under the table – loses his temper with Tim after a wordless exchange of gurnings and hand gestures. He blurts out, *Piss off, Tim. You're so full of shit*. And the Duke and Duchess of Devonshire jolt in their seats as if they've had a hundred volts up their arses, and I deliquesce into a smear of grease. The nobility get up, leave the table; and I (hating them as much as I hate myself) mouth apologies at their retreating backs at the same time as I wave my fist, Basil Fawlty-style, at my children. *Wait till I get you in the bloody car*. In other words, I am less concerned about the actual fact of my children cussing than I am about the loss of face it would involve me in. It's not the words, it's the atomically minute chance of the words happening in front of the Duke and Duchess of Devonshire. So whenever my boys remind me that they know those words I suffer a small death at the thought of what they could do to me at some point in the future, at the same time as I genuinely fear for the well-being of my parents and in-laws, who will not be so relaxed as I believe myself to be (in normal circumstances) about such language.

Plainly, all this free-wheeling anxiety is as much about my loss of control as about attitudes to emphatic idiomatic speech forms. Bad language points up the fact that now my kids are not only of an age where they can dip into what was once an exclusively adult world of effing and blinding, they are of an age where they will go ahead and assert themselves in a pre-teenage manner any old how. And of course, pre-teenage implies teenage, which in turn implies a complete breakdown of parental authority/decency/the rule of law, the full ordeal of later parenthood. Each swearword contains the seeds of something much bigger and much worse. Every *shit* holds the prospect of future anarchy, condensed and focused into one illegitimate rebellious act. For God's sake, it's already happening. One of my sons (I shan't shame him by naming him specifically; just say that he was six at the time) left us a note on the stairs once, indicating his displeasure at his parents. *I hate you*, he wrote, *you are worse than fucking stonefish*. Actually, he wrote *fuking stonefish* and I did haver around for five or ten minutes, wondering whether or not to correct his spelling. The other son (seven going on eight this time) scrawled a streak of graffiti on his bedroom wall one afternoon, while under the baneful influence of a particularly dirty-minded friend. What was worse in this latter case? The vandalism? Or the appearance of the words *tits*, *shag* and *fart* in a room which not that long ago was decorated with a plastic mobile of some sheep dancing around the moon to Brahms' *Lullaby* and an amusing pink pig with a clock in it? I was so incensed by this that I ordered the offender to paint the words out – just like some petty provincial bigot faced with a desecration of the town bus stop. I produced a tin of paint and a brush before realising that giving my son these tools was like giving a can of petrol to a pyromaniac. So then the very tall Yorkshire nanny boy came in and offered to do it and that made a worse mess than my son would have made. But I couldn't shout at him afterwards.

Where do you start to draw a line? Clearly, *piss* and *shag* are too old and coarse for a seven-year-old – in my presence, at least; not at school, though. *God* itself has long ceased to be a real verbal shocker, just as *damn* did years ago. I have a feeling *Jesus Christ* (which I still try and expel as *Jeepers Creepers*, or *Gee Whillikers* or *Jiminy Criminy* or some such inoffensive downhomey expletive when it threatens) and *bugger* will go the same way. And then, what about *bloody*? If I let that through (and if I do, Susie may not, having a much lower tolerance to foul talking, from anyone) what next? If *Jesus* and *bloody* and *God* are sanctioned, then will the whole lot, the whole bestiary of abuse follow? And will that betoken the beginning of the end of whatever authority I thought I possessed? Yes, I know, all these words are daily made more and more anodyne through greater social use, yes, we swear like pressed sailors around the breakfast table in comparison with the way we spoke around my parents' breakfast table – and in comparison with the way we spoke when our children were tiny and we were still-new parents: when we were piously eager for everything around our kids to be nice and pleasant and not sordid, and didn't blaspheme at all. Social conventions change. But it symbolises something too big to be ignored when your eight-year-old stubs his toe on the step and a scarcely repressed *fuck* comes hissing out.

Not than they learn it from us. They learn it at school. When the boys were around four, they knew *damn* and *bloody*, courtesy of the playground *souk* of swearwords. By six, they were well up to date with *shit* and the other bodily functions. By eight, they are not only in the big league (bigger classes, bigger work, bigger friends, bigger problems), they have a full grasp of the lexicon of swearing and only natural good taste prevents them from using it. And so it's not only the threat to my authority that upsets me. It's the loss of their prelapsarian, pre-abuse childhood. Not long ago they were learning how to ride a bike. Now they sound like off-duty policemen. How did we get here so quickly?

The row grizzles on all the way down the A3. Tim has a way of yelping Alistair's name, when he's annoyed, in such a way that your ears sting. Alistair has a way of tormenting Tim in a suppressed monotone that brings on an adult headache of impotence, as well as making Tim scream back. If I were able to look at our car as it churns down the road, I would see that we have become one of *those* families: portly, middle-aged dad, flecks of grey in the hair, dewlap under the chin, scowl of nameless displeasure on the face, shouting over his shoulder at the back seat; mum staring out of her side window, lips pursed, nerving herself up to make another UN-style appeal for peace; kids in the back, squabbling. The full *Simpsons* accreditation. If I could go convincingly bald, and thus add to my air of harassment, I would. We are also going to be late for lunch when we get to Portsmouth. A problem compounded by the fact that we have no idea if you can even *get* lunch in Portsmouth.

So the rate at which childhood passes has accelerated massively in the last twenty years or so. As Steven Spielberg once put it, 'The years of childhood have been subject to a kind of inflation. At sixteen, I was the equivalent of a ten-year-old today.' When I look back at myself aged eight, the worst words I ever employed were probably *willy* and *bum*. I was well into teenage before *fuck* ever got a look-in, to say nothing of *shit* and *piss* and all the rest. And now I wonder at myself for being such a retard. What was I doing all those years? Wandering around in short trousers at the age of eight, playing with toy cars and not even knowing the word *fuck*, let alone using it? No wonder I always felt out of the swim of things! How *parochial*.

When I reflect on my past like this I do of course worry that I'm incorporating into it elements that really had nothing to do with me, but which I've retrieved from advertisements of the time, or from films or books. Hence I nostalgically recall a composite, innocent, semi-fictional me, my shorts held up by one of those elasticated belts with a snake clasp, fishing for newts (which I actually used to do), making Airfix kits of Dornier bombers (as we know), going camping (which I didn't), and scrumping apples (never). I compare this *Eagle Annual* version with what I suspect my real life to have been like, beneath the glaze of selective memory, and I wonder who I'm trying to kid.

So I worry about my kids losing their childhood (being sensible about it, this *is* their childhood, no matter what I think; that they will, in all probability, look back on it as a period of innocence, a period when they were protected from the real world in a very slightly boring cocoon of family life). And I worry about having retrospectively lost my childhood when I compare it with theirs and find it somehow lacking, somehow diminished. But most of all I worry about the way time itself, not just childhood, is speeding up. It's not just that six months ago my baby boys were struggling across the carpet in nappies and now they're mouthing the kind of dreary insults you get in pubs. It's that six months ago I was starting to do a book about the North of England and now that book has come and gone, and I am struggling to write a book about posh people and I know that in reality two years of chronological time have elapsed between these books but it's six months of perceived time and before I know it I'm writing *this* book and whole years have come and gone in the time it takes to get my hair cut. *My children are eating time up.*

Maybe we are in the wrong bit of Portsmouth for lunch. Maybe it's the wrong day. Maybe we're blind to the possibilities in front of us. There are three places on offer: a scuzzy-looking boozer; a restaurant with a full menu outside; a murky kiosk flogging chips and hot dogs. No one can agree on what to do. Our boys are not only old enough to hold opinions about what they do and don't want to eat; they are just old enough to make it necessary to listen to their preferences rather than shove them through the door of the first place the grown-ups can agree on. Alistair, incredibly, is developing an aversion to chips. This is astonishing, not only because he is an English boy and all English boys gorge themselves on chips, almost as much as American boys; but because at other times he will eat (and this is no less amazing) just about any other kind of food, including the sort of green vegetables that even adults are afraid of. No one except me wants to go into the scuzzy pub. You can see why. It looks like the sort of place returning seamen would have reduced to matchwood regularly in the early years of the century and still has a reek of barbarity about it: brown, gluey carpets, slaughtered furniture, ex-professional wrestler behind the counter. No one except Susie wants to go and sit down in a restaurant with tablecloths and napkins and purse-lipped waitresses. Fifteen minutes go by while we argue about whether to go further into town to see what else is available, but the daylight is precious at this time of year and if we are to see anything of *HMS Warrior* we need to see it while the sun is still out. So we rule out a time-consuming walk into the city centre. Which leaves, by default, the kiosk of fat at our elbow.

'Great,' says Tim, conning the selections (eggs, burgers, chips, dogs, jumbo sausages, tea) with an expert eye.

'Tim, you're a stupid idiot,' says Alistair.

We get dogs and chips and Styrofoam cups of tea (made, from the taste of it, with the frankly available sea water) and sit in a bus shelter to eat them. Tim is old enough to command our compliance with regard to what he eats, but he is still young enough to make a bollocks of eating it. Pretty soon there is ketchup everywhere and bits of soft roll blowing down the tarmac. We beg the wrecky kiosk for more paper napkins, which get scrunched up against Tim's face and then, like the soft roll, escape from us in the frozen breeze. Alistair sulks in the next section of the bus shelter, emerging from time to time to call Tim names. I march around with my own collapsing dog, making gestures at Tim and refusing to let him use my freshly laundered handkerchief to clean his face. Susie, aware that this is her birthday treat, urges us to be more pleasant.

'Just let him use your handkerchief.'

'*I* might want to use it. I can't use it if it's got food on it.'

'Can I borrow your handkerchief?' says Alistair, ever the older-brother opportunist. I swear under my breath. Food is flying along the front and towards the barren concrete of Portsmouth's Naval Heritage, Tim is starting to cry with rage and frustration as his chips blow away, Alistair is shouting at him and me, my hotdog mustard is going over my feet as I gesticulate crazily at both of them, Susie is shouting at all of us. A group of unhappy-looking Americans pauses for a moment to look at us in our filth and disorder, before moving on quickly.

According to my copy of *The Young Man's Companion* – a reprint of the writings of Edward Turner, from 1866 – 'When you are helped to anything at a dinner table, do not wait, with your plate untouched, until others have begun to eat. This stiff piece of mannerism is of frequent recurrence in the country, and indeed among all persons who are not thoroughly bred. As soon as your plate is placed before you, you should take up your knife and arrange the table furniture around you, if you do not actually eat.' Good news to my boys, of course, who not only don't wait for everyone else before starting, but also have been known to eat by shoving their faces flat onto the plate and sucking the food up. On the other hand, 'Avoid taking upon your plate too many things at once. One variety of meat and one kind of vegetable is the *maximum*.' Boys learn at school to heap cones of food onto their plates, doesn't matter what sort it is: fish, gravy, spaghetti, cabbage, an egg, all together. The main thing with school food is to get a load and then sift through it to see what you want to eat, keeping the rejects for trade. And then the same thing, with variations, happens at home. Pile it high, go for scale.

Like the bad language, too late to do anything now. Penelope Leach doesn't offer any advice. The first entry under M in our *Baby & Child* is not Manners but Masturbation. My own upbringing? I'm sure my folks nagged me about elbows on the table (*All joints on this table will be carved, ha, ha*) and saying *please* and *thank you*. But the only time I can recall them getting worked up about manners, genuinely aggrieved, was when I said *Pleased to meet you* to someone I was being introduced to. My father became intolerably irritated in the car on the way home. 'You don't say, *Pleased to meet you*,' he said, to my amazement – since I'd gone to all the trouble of opening my mouth and being polite in the first place – 'you say, *How do you do?*' My father hardly ever gave advice of any sort, but when he did in this instance, it was a piece of advice I found entirely useless. In the real world, you – I – say neither *Pleased to meet you*, nor *How do you do?* but opt generally instead for a neutral *Hello* or a *Hi there*, if the mood justifies it. Either way, never anything more formal than that unless for some reason you're being introduced to a duke or ambassador (Your Excellency!). You'd sound ridiculous.

But that was my father's piece of advice. And I think this little moment was actually responsible for my having a down on manners of any sort for quite a long time afterwards. Having been corrected for a misdemeanour I hadn't committed, I worked up some sort of insane theoretical justification for not being mannerly on the grounds that it was condescending to others at the same time as it made a falsehood of interpersonal relationships by creating an artificial distance. This ratiocination has now come back to haunt me, in that (a) I have no manners at all, even though I enviously respect them in others and (b) I am unable to set an example of mannerliness to my kids, or even train them in the rudiments of formal behaviour.

Does it matter? Do their friends have better manners? Are my children being sneered at because when they eat, it's like Jan Steen's *Twelfth Night* or *The Egg Dance* – arms and faces and bits of food and stained clothing in one energetic mass? I doubt it. The shit flies around whoever's children are eating, however smart their parents are. Kids shout, argue, run around waving mashed potato, pillory their siblings, charge up and down stairs, break things, fail to say *Goodbye and thank you* when they finally go home. They behave, normally, like animals, which a part of me applauds as a sign of their carefree youthfulness. The people who will sneer at my boys, though, are the parents of the friends, no matter how aware they are of the realities of bringing up modern children. *They* will see my splendid boys as animals, primitives, and complain about them when they've gone home, and will draw all sorts of inferences about us. Yes, of course, it's them that I have in mind when the notion of good manners enters my head. It's the car-borne mothers at the school gate, fierce, judgmental, hunting for advantage, who fill me with a need to civilise my children. It's like the swearing, all over again. It's the Duke and Duchess of Devonshire. *I* don't mind; it's *other people* who are the problem.

But when the other nasty judgmental people aren't there, when we're grappling with two vicious-tempered children on a November day in Portsmouth, somehow the need for politeness never seems so materially significant. All I think about then is getting the food, swallowing it, getting them to swallow it, pressing on. And sometimes I think of myself, transported miles away from all this to another country altogether, and sending a postcard home. But the mood quickly passes.

HMS Warrior was built in 1860, and was Britain's first iron-hulled armoured battleship, powered both by steam and sail, and designed with a fortified citadel to contain its main guns. It got up to seventeen and a half knots in sea trials and cost a staggering £400,000 to construct. What a vessel! As it happened, *Warrior* never fired a shot in anger, and was quickly superseded by other, newer battleships at home and abroad. Soon it was taken out of active service, had its funnels removed and finally became a floating oil fuel hulk at Pembroke Dock, in Wales. Where it slowly, but with dignity, spent fifty years turning into a rusting heap. But that was not the end of the story. A trust was formed to put this historically charged old tub back together; restoration work started at the beginning of the Eighties, and now it is magnificently back in Portsmouth, in one huge piece, black, sinister, its timbers and ironwork echoing to the sounds of visitors. The fact that most of the gear inside and on deck is no more than twenty years old, and that it is almost on a par with the Globe Theatre in Southwark as a piece of imaginative rebuilding, is neither here nor there. It is a fantastic object, and just original enough to make that hour and a half down the A3 worthwhile.

So we wipe ourselves down, buy our tickets at the visitors' centre and go aboard. And then one of those totally unforeseeable emotional inversions occurs at the point when the boys actually get on this boat. It's as if they've abruptly thrown their tantrums and animosities into the rubbish bin, like the residue of their appalling lunch (which took some doing, I might add: the litter-bins were pretty full to start with and by the time we'd finished looked as if they'd been packed with the debris from a house renovation), and have started with a completely clean slate. Suddenly they're cheerful again. The pictures we took on the day show them climbing over cannons, manhandling the wheel and fiddling with the rigging, all with absorbed concentration or grins of childish pleasure. It doesn't matter to them that some of the stuff is modern, some of the stuff heavily reconditioned original. Authenticity is only something old people worry about. A couple of years later, we went to the Universal Studios experience in California, where even the candidly inauthentic originals (films and film memorabilia) have the weight of history on them in comparison with their plasterboard-nylon-and-animatronic recreations. Did the kids care? Did it lessen the quality of their experience that they were riding around on things that were rough, incredibly recent approximations of things that weren't that old in the first place? Not a jot. The moment is everything. Thus they sit on a *Warrior* cannon and it could have been made in 1860 or 1985. It doesn't matter.

So we find ourselves back on the old roller-coaster of despair and elation, loving our boys the more because they are so awful up to the point at which they become completely loveable. Even better, they have thrown themselves into the semi-educational experience of visiting an old, reconstructed boat with enthusiasm. They may even be gleaning insights into nineteenth-century naval life at the same time as they play among the planking and ironmongery. It is a union of edification and fun, and we slump on a bench, recovering from the strain, and admire them sentimentally. Can it get any better?

So this guy (father of two) said to me, 'You think that if you force your son to learn the piano, he'll be there, ten years' time, at parties with these incredible girls leaning over him and saying *That was really beautiful* as he sits at the keyboard? You're *mad*.' He had a point. Indeed, he had more than a point. He was absolutely, exactly right. That's precisely what I had in mind, because *I can remember seeing it happen*. This is not one of those pitiful wish-fulfilments that middle-aged men succumb to as they get more and more out of touch – I have seen it happen, and more than once. Admittedly, it was a while ago, when I was still in my teens, but I cannot believe that things have changed that much.

How did it come about? It came about through my friend Phil. My friend Phil was the only truly musical person I knew. Despite enduring the handicap of intensely frizzy hair – the sort that grows in a halo of fuzz, outwards at an angle of ninety degrees from the surface of the head and which turns itself into little twists and corkscrews at the end, picking up fag butts, crisp leavings, pizza cheese etc – despite this, Phil could sit and strum at the most dismally tuned family upright, provided it was away from the rumble and thud of whatever was playing on the party turntable in the front room, and draw girls to him like cats to a dish of warm fish. And the girls, having selected themselves, rather than been muscled into the encounter by some greasy chat-up line, were always captivated by the music, and somehow lighter-hearted, more relaxed and natural than they ever were in the main leering, striving throng of the party. They had chosen him, rather than suffer his urgings to make them choose him. *Oh, that was great*, they'd say, a look of dreamy gratitude on their faces. *What else can you play?*

I, too, was massively impressed by Phil and his keyboards. I could see exactly what it was that the girls found so appealing. And yes, I know that guys at parties playing musical instruments (in particular, the acoustic or folk guitar) run the risk of ending up like Stephen Bishop in *Animal House* and having John Belushi come and smash the thing to matchwood against the staircase wall. There's a preciousness that surrounds self-made music – even if it's well-played – and which is frequently hard to justify to others. But I have always been terribly in awe of pianos and anyone who can get a recognisable tune out of them – quite apart from dreaming of myself reconstituted as a master of the keyboard and driving women mad with the sensuality of my playing – and I have seen the effects of piano music on other people. So when I force my boys to learn the instrument (which I do) I am at the centre of a crossroads of ambitions. Some of these involve simple vicarious wish-fulfilment, in which I compel my children to be the cultured, talented person I could never quite be arsed to make myself. Some of these involve a low plot to get them ready for the teenage years when they will need to have something to do in front of girls (or anyone else they want to impress), other than get embarrassed and blurt out random observations about their sexual obsessions. Some of these aims are inspired entirely by veneration of the piano. And some are prompted by stray reports I come across in the papers which claim that research exists to suggest that learning music at an early age can improve aspects of your overall mental performance (e.g. Rauscher, Shaw, Levine, Wright, Dennis and Newcombe, *Neurological Research*, 1996). The piano has, in other words, become central to my plans.

So we splash out a criminal fortune on a Victorian upright which is hauled into our house by three men on the brink of rupture and is left in the hall. I am certain that it will break through the joists and fall into the basement below. On comes the piano teacher, who is not an evil grey-haired dragon who snaps a steel ruler over your knuckles when you make a mistake, but a cuddly blonde. She is so nice and warm and laughing that she could impersonate Bundlejoy Cosysweet in Russell Hoban's *How Tom Beat Captain Najork And His Hired Sportsmen*. But the boys take against her laughing and her cuddliness. Betrayed by their own ambivalence towards the piano, they cannot bring themselves to like her. They don't seem to hate the piano as such – they even get a kick out of getting a melody out of it. But they don't like it, either. Given the choice of learning how to play it and watching the TV, there is no contest – although they will admit that there are times when, despite themselves, they derive a certain refreshment from making music. So they take these hard-to-handle equivocal responses out on her and on us when she's not around. They chuck music about; they shout; they stamp their feet. They cannot look ahead to a time when playing the piano might get them girls.

Nor can they know that I am astonishingly proud and grateful whenever one of them starts hammering out a tune on the piano. I can't really believe that it's possible to play the piano at all. And to see and hear my own flesh and blood extracting music from it is affirming, mysterious, moving. Put that together with my long-term strategy for social acceptance and it *just about* repays all the time, effort, pain and money that goes into it. Just as the sight of our boys leaping across the foredeck of the *Warrior* just about repays the schlep down to Portsmouth and the disgusting anti-lunch and the ill-temper. There is still, sometimes, a correlation between the virtuous improvements we try and foist on our children and the feeling of achievement that comes as a result.

Could be tennis, of course. Or horse-riding. Or the clarinet. The piano, I suppose, is a little obvious, a little clichéd, as a device for self-improvement. The odd thing is, when I was around this age, eightish, neither I nor any of my friends had any extra-curricular lessons at all, apart from Phil and his hair and his piano practice. I don't know why this should have been, but in comparison with my kids' generation, we were a nation of unambitious slugs with supremely indifferent parents. Nowadays the streets of London are choked with cars filled with white-faced kids hauling off to their various gigs. But our broader accomplishments added up to a big round O. What has happened in a generation to encourage this?

I suppose it was to compensate for this clear absence in my life that I encouraged my children in their brief flirtations with horse-riding (in some disgusting bog-filled stables near where my parents had gone to retire) and tennis. We inevitably did the swimming thing for years, dragging our boys down to the local baths, where an instructor would force his voice above the echoing resonance of the building and drive them up and down the teaching pool. In this respect, nothing much has changed since the time when I was forced to learn how to swim by my parents (swimming, riding a bike, tying your own shoelaces: the statutory minimum in order to be able to survive; driving lessons the same, in a few years). *My* swimming instructor was a callous sadist (to the parents, as I now know, no more than a briskly authoritative motivator of others). Every lesson had at least one child looking at a nervous collapse, rivers of tears and snot running down his or her face. I was always too frozen with terror to express any emotions, and just struggled through in a sort of silent, choking blank. On one occasion the instructor told us to line up at the deep end (twelve feet and gloomy too, like the Aleutian Trench) and jump in. We all did, one after the other: I went in feet first, sank straight to the bottom, walked across the floor of the pool to the steps and stoically climbed back out. I didn't say a word, but I felt the wings of death beating above my head. My friend James MacLeish went in and duly had hysterics under water, at which point he had to be pulled out and reflated by the poolside. Both these events made an enduring impression on me, and I was interested to see how teaching methods would have adapted to the modern world and liberal parenting.

The main difference was that a modern training pool turns out to be all shallow end. So the feet-first plunge was ruled out. Secondly, the instructor had been trained to smile a lot and crack gags, in order to lessen the tension. What did come as an interesting surprise, though, was the fierce nervousness generated by the parents yearning for their kids to improve. This made very reassuring viewing as I sat at the side of the pool (the old story – me and maybe one other father, surrounded by mothers; me looking at the other guy, invariably dressed in a rainbow sweater and thrift-shop cords, feet in sandals or splayed trainers, and wondering whether I looked to the rest of the world as he did to me). It allowed me to realise – in a protracted revelation, over a period of several months – that other people's children were in the eyes of their parents as badly behaved, over-excitable, recalcitrant, as my own. In the shrill acoustics of the teaching hall, every raised voice, every vicious little scolding cut through the background roar of the main pool like a firecracker going off: *Debbie! Come back here! Right NOW!* Kids were being hissed at for running along the sides, not getting dressed, flicking water at their friends, dropping their clothes in puddles, having blue-faced tantrums. I realised that I was not alone, that my boys were not the uniquely intractible beasts I'd had them down for. They were, in fact, about normal in their lawlessness and lack of respect.

Better still, it put all these institutionalised improvements in a new light. I stopped seeing all the tennis-playing, clarinet-practising, five-a-side footballing as indices of any given family's superiority – demonstrating the restless talents of the kids, always searching for new challenges, fresh outlets for their physical and intellectual genius. Instead I began to see them as signs of how imperfect the other parents considered their offspring (and, by extension, themselves) to be. They weren't doing this because they knew their kids were going to be showjumping champions and tennis aces, like tennis-player Mary Pierce and her appalling father. They were doing it to stop their kids getting any worse than they already were. These performances were more like aspects of the Finishing School life, necessary to tame and civilise unsuitable youth before they were ready to go out into the world.

The more I saw of it the more consoling it became. You don't see your children actually functioning in the company of other children that often (except at parties, which are semi-sanctioned anarchy anyway). So when you do, it's one of those encounters with other parents in which you recognise – with an illicit sensation of relief and gratitude – that you share similar problems and experience similar rage and despair. Seeing other people's children debasing themselves is one of the great pleasures of having your own.

Is it the case that everything we do as men is, essentially and in the final analysis, meant to impress women, to gain their attention and probably their company? If this is true, how much of what I consider to be my effort in bringing up my kids is directed towards this end? The whole piano question is symptomatic of various related ambitions. It's part of a broader social striving, to keep up with my peers and the peers of my kids. It's part of an attempt to make good my own deficiencies through the next generation. And, yes, it's an effort to get my boys in the position where they're most likely to make it with girls (and so, ultimately, to perpetuate their genetic inheritance; there's a utilitarian side). In which case, how far does this covert motivation spread? When I tell the boys to do certain things, or not to do them, is the long-term objective (if I'm being honest) to make them, as far as I can tell, reasonably appealing to the opposite sex? I don't have a concept of *manhood* that I particularly want to instil in them – in the sense that I don't want them to exemplify manly traits like being a hearty fellow, or being good at fighting, or being thuggishly self-determined, or very muscular, or cruelly ambitious, or handy with jokes, or notoriously sexually promiscuous, or brilliant with mechanical objects, or obsessed with any one particular football team. All I want them to do is somehow embody that sense of manliness which makes itself most obvious by being broadly attractive to a range of women. Plainly, I've never managed it myself, and may or may not recognise it when it appears. It's just something I've had in the back of my mind. Jarvis Cocker discovered that he had it when Pulp suddenly took off with *Different Class*. Humphrey Bogart had a pugnacious version of it. Shelley clearly had it. John F. Kennedy had it, but used it unreflectingly and indiscriminately, like a cheap car, just to get to point B. Ditto Jimi Hendrix. Dudley Moore went through a phase of certainly appearing to have it, in the early Eighties. Come to think of it, Peter Cook *must* have had it. And so on. Hence playing the piano, which I *know*, in my heart of hearts, women find attractive, provided it's done fairly well, at appropriate moments, and on an instrument that's in tune.

If I had daughters instead of sons? I know a couple of dads with all-daughter or heavily-daughter families, and they seem baffled by their own children. Because they're like that anyway? Or because they're men and they can't understand girls? The dynamics of father-hood change radically when you have daughters. Instead of being the one who leads them on (football matches, cussing, mucking around), while Mum acts like something out of a washing-powder ad (her frowning disapproval – boys! look at all that mud! – turning to forgiving amusement at the japes of her loveable male brood), the set-up is inverted. Dad's job, once his daughters start to reveal their true precocity at the age of eight (nail varnish, earrings, tights, posters of – at the time of writing – Leonardo DiCaprio on the walls, loose talk about parties and boys), is to sit around looking worried and perplexed and irritable. His wife and daughter(s) meanwhile have understanding conversations somewhere else. Susie, I know, feels sometimes trapped by the wealth of smelly maleness which permeates our house; rather as I suspect that the fathers of girls wonder what to do with themselves over a long weekend in a house full of female intentions and understandings. Unless, of course, they end up like Tom Brangwen and his daughter Ursula: 'Everything her father did was magic . . . he was always a centre of magic and fascination to her, his voice, sounding out in command, cheerful, laconic, had always a twang in it that sent a thrill over her blood, and hypnotised her . . .' Later on, Dad will come down and sit heavily on the sofa and scowl furiously at any young men his daughter(s) will bring home. I know it's a little early to bring up this subject – what to do about boyfriends – with fathers of daughters still barely ten, but whenever I have, it's always produced the same reaction: first of all, *I simply haven't given it any thought, I think I've got my head in the sand about it*, followed by, *Any boys come home, with my daughter, I'm going to kill them*. Clearly they can't be thinking, like me, *Must make them reasonably desirable*. Words like *chastity, older men, unsuitable* must drift through their heads instead, like radio interference.

The light fades, the sky starts to turn inky-blue in the east. The *Warrior*'s rigging is etched against the dying sunset, the air begins to bite, my kids want an *ice cream*. In *November*. Almost as suddenly as the mood of robust enquiry overtook them on board the boat, so they revert to type and start pestering me for fats and boredom-repressing sugars. So I tell them to use their pocket money. They point out that I haven't given them any pocket money. I stand on the gently freezing quay, deliberating whether or not to hand the cash over, knowing that when I do so, I lose a little more of what small control I have over them.

That's basically why I give them pocket money in the first place. As an instrument of control and punishment. I've known all along that this sordid rationale is at the back of most of my acts of measured, unspontaneous generosity, but it once came out into the open when we were with another couple and the subject of pocket money came up.

'Why do you give it?' asked the wife of the other couple. I was busy framing a nicely liberal response, along the lines of, to generate a sense of the value of money, to provide the rewards that come through saving for a desired object, to enable my sons to be at ease with their peers (who also get pocket money). Even to show signs of generosity to those peers.

Then the husband of the other couple opened his mouth wide and blurted out, 'Well, you do it so that you can take it away from them.' He paused, looking around him like a businessman caught in a bra. 'Don't you?'

There was a lot of clamour from the mothers, but all I could do was nod as this simple vertiginous truth came bursting out. This is nothing to do with the old Repressive Tolerance rap. This is simple, thick-minded behaviour modification, but with the twist that the more they're used as a way of coercing right behaviour out of your kid, the more your rewards end up burdened with an atmosphere of punishment. In other words, I go about the place shouting, *All right! That's it! Pocket money gone!* (pocket money, or trip to the video games shop/footballing accessories store/cinema to watch one of those cretinising films – *Hercules*, *101 Dalmations*, *Flubber*, *Fly Away Home* – what is it with Jeff Daniels?) so regularly, so mulishly, that any kind of treat or offering comes tainted with the prospect of refusal and denial.

Of course, I only threaten them with the loss of things that I don't much want them to have in the first place. I wouldn't threaten them with no trip to the theatre (e.g. The National to see *Guys and Dolls*; a middle-class treat so middle-class it borders on self-parody) or to Hampton Court Palace (likewise). They don't much want to go anyway, and would rather be at home playing a video game. I can only threaten the loss of something that I don't want them to have. Or with the loss of something they can transform into something I don't want them to have. Which is pocket money.

For some reason, I've never been able to make pocket money contingent on being good. If I've stated that pocket money will only be handed out if Alistair/Tim keeps his room tidy, or doesn't attack his brother, or does all his homework – or is, at the end of it all, simply a nice person to be around – then Alistair/Tim will forget about this conditionality, and be as awful and obnoxious as he pleases. He will then work up a righteous amazement at the end of the week when I deny him the money. It only works if used on the spot as a threat against anti-social action; rather than in advance as a payment for socially acceptable behaviour.

For a long time, Susie railed against this approach. She saw the offer of pocket money as having a binding effect on the parent who offered it. If we committed to pay out, then this was a commitment as unalterable as keeping the water running and buying food. It was not negotiable. She and the other mother at the heart of my enlightening pocket-money discussion thought it was, basically, bent, to try and do it otherwise. But as our boys get older, what do you know but she finds herself going back on this principled position? She loses her temper and finds herself hurling out these threats just like I do. For her, this is a betrayal, lapsing into a discredited masculine routine of threats and arbitrary punishments. This is the kind of oppositional, confrontational nonsense that men perpetrate and which leads to wars, Nazism, football riots. It's the kind of thing that William Brown's father is always doing in the *Just William* books (Mr Brown drawn by T.H. Fisher with a Hitler moustache and coming out with: 'I don't know how he got here or what he's going to do, and I don't care. He's nothing to do with me. I've disowned him. I tell you – I've disowned him'). She sees it as a function of an age so far left behind us that it might as well not have existed. But I see it as the most natural thing in the world. I see it as an inevitable function of having children who grow older and more cunning as you grow older and slower and more vulnerable. So I cling to my pocket-money powers more passionately with every year that passes.

And on the quay? When, really, we want to get home and warm up? Do I struggle around to dig out some loose change and feed them ice creams? It seems so senseless.

'You must be *mad*,' I say. 'Stark mad.'

'We want ice creams,' they answer. I don't want them to have ice creams. I don't want them to make themselves any colder. I don't want them to corrupt their teeth. I don't want to *give* them their pocket money, because it means I won't be able to *withhold* it.

'It's my birthday,' says Susie briskly from behind. 'They don't have to buy ice creams out of their own pocket money. Just buy them some ice creams.'

So I do that, and they are happy. And because they are happy, Susie and I can afford to be happy. In the car on the way back home, if you can believe this, we sing a medley of tasteless old pop hits, including *Hit The Road Jack*, *Wake Up Little Susie* and *She Loves You*. The car lights on the A3 burn in the chilly darkness, but we are safe and warm in the car. The boys are full of fats and sugars, and, after a while, fall asleep so that we can admire them, tumbled on the back seat, sleeping with a careless intensity that we can no longer manage. We gaze on their handsome faces. If you're being a father, what else are you being a father for, if not for something like this? Somehow, you seem to have engendered a family. All in all, this will have been another Happy Day.

A month later and it is Christmas. And the nightmares return. The trip to *HMS Warrior* is over, and we have the pictures back from the chemist to prove how long ago it was. Now it is Christmas, and Christmas means the grandparents and the family as a whole. All the problems of good behaviour, manners, being with people outside our intimate circle of four – they all come back and dog my waking hours. Tripping to Portsmouth, no matter how awful our behaviour, is nonetheless containable: if only because we are relatively isolated as a unit, and used to each other's company. But at Christmas we must show ourselves to an audience. And where are we going to be tested? At the dinner table, eating our Xmas lunch, a house of horrors for a young palate.

Why? After all, the senses of taste and smell don't occupy us full-time, in the way that sight, hearing and balance tend to. Compare the encyclopedia entries for taste and smell with those of sight and hearing and the discrepancy is overwhelming. Taste and smell basically come down to the gustatory receptors – specialised cells with neurons branching among them – and smell detectors, nerve cells with fibres leading to the brain. The gustatory receptors on the soft palate and back roof of the mouth tend to pick up sour and bitter, whereas the receptors on the tongue are more sensitive to sweet and salt. As for the smell detectors, humans have about 40,000 sensory cells per square millimetre of olfactory epithelium, which makes us relatively inefficient smellers in comparison with many other members of the animal kingdom. Nevertheless, this is what we have to work with, and with it we can experience some of the most vivid and satisfying moments of our lives (fresh raspberries, perfume, a really large curry, champagne, the comforting odour of the domestic bed, the distinctive scent of your partner, mayonnaise and chips). Indeed, for something which is really only meant to play second fiddle to sight and hearing, taste can create some of the most memorably intense experiences of our lives. Certainly, many of my happiest hours – possibly all of them – have involved food and drink in some combination.

So it seems reasonable that kids should also have powerful feelings about what they smell and taste. Tim certainly does. How can you tell? Well, it's Christmas, and in a re-run of the first glorious encounter, we have all four grandparents grouped round the table, only now with two grandchildren and Uncle Eddie. The boys ought to be old enough, at six and nine, to have a grip on their emotions. They should see it as their duty to play along with Christmas and make sure that everything goes cheerfully. But Christmas lunch is already in the ragged hinterland of madness before it starts (shagged parents after a four-hour wrapping marathon the night before; grandparents shining with ill-suppressed excitement at watching their grandchildren unwrap their Xmas gifts, followed by heroic wartime punctilio as the grandkids inspect those presents perfunctorily before lobbing them into a mountain of unloved goodies; parents destroyed still more by the toil of cooking). So by the time everyone sits down and stuffs the party hats on their heads, it's like Altman's *A Wedding*. Everyone talks at once, everyone's about to go nuts, everyone's urgently keen not to be seen to do so. The grandparents are steadily filling up with drink until they make distant swishing noises as they walk. They have started to be glowingly affectionate towards the boys. The boys are just moody.

'Why don't you sit here?' says a grandparent, kindly patting the seat next to him or her. One of their grandsons sits down with a grunt. 'Not too much for me!' they all cry as I drunkenly stab at the turkey. Tim bitches at Alistair, or vice versa, about the presents he's got, or hasn't: *You'll never get it to work/ You need to have three people/ I've seen one of those before and they're useless/ Give it to me, I'll get it working* . . . We keep going and everyone gets the food and I slump into my seat and grip my glass tightly—

—And Tim discovers that he has a sprout on his plate. Well, this is the worst possible news you could want on Christmas Day. This is as bad as getting no presents, as bad as getting a Batman outfit when you wanted a computer game. He raises his voice and *demands* that the sprout be taken off his plate. All the grandparents sit up and offer conflicting advice. Some tell him that it's good for him and that one sprout is all he needs to eat to become a superman. Others say that he should do it as a nice Christmassy gesture to the person who cooked the sprout (frequently me, so that won't work in any circumstances, because I am not normally a person worth appeasing). Others turn on me and Susie and say it *is* Christmas and perhaps he could skip the sprout. Tim cries out that we're trying to poison him and that sprouts make him vomit. Indeed, there are substances in sprouts and broccoli which some people, like former US President George Bush, do find unpalatable. I get hardline and abusive and start swearing under my breath and muttering that if Tim doesn't eat it I'm stopping his pocket money for the next decade. The next *century*. Susie starts to seethe and tells me I'm being not just a bully but unrealistic (*Don't make threats you can't deliver*) and that is Christmas lunch off to the worst start imaginable, because of *one fucking Brussels sprout*.

You might argue that is just a by-product of a typically overheated festive season. Emotions are already strained to breaking, and the wrong vegetable merely sets in train something which was waiting to happen anyway. But the thing about food – unlike just about everything else – is that it has this effect all the time, on the most humdrum days and in the most quotidian circumstances. I can't think of anything else that is so antagonising. Not even homework, or music practice, or visiting people you don't want to visit, or trailing down to the shops to buy clothes. Food is an essential, an absolute fundamental of life. But children are happy to see it – literally – go down the drain if it displeases them.

Conversely, they will fight and cajole and plead tirelessly for some piece of junk garbage that barely qualifies as food in the adult worldview. Adults like to make self-mocking jokes about their addictions to Twirly-Wirlies or Rolos, but my kids really are addicted to some of these products. I can at least understand, as a man, the incredibly powerful hold food can have over your imagination. Whereas Susie – as a woman – may have a number of preferred dishes, but nothing that will make her drool and wipe the palms of her hands together, as I do when – for the sake of argument – curry is mentioned, or barbecued fish, or trifle. So I can see why the boys – or why Tim, especially – might go mad for specific foods. What I can't see is why they should go mad for the foods they go mad for and why they should hate the foods they hate, so intensely. *A Brussels sprout.*

Tim's attachment to junk burgers astonishes me, even now. When we were in the States, Tim kept up a litany about going to eat a proper McDonald's – a real, American McDonald's – that persisted for two and a half weeks. Finally I caved in and bought him one. Until then I had managed to keep up a stream of reasonable objections, in which I said, over and over again: 'Tim, you must understand that McDonald's is a global giant, with over 23,500 restaurants in 109 countries. They serve around 38 million customers *every day*, nearly the equivalent of the population of Spain. And McDonald's has based its success very largely on the fact that it offers an entirely consistent, universally standardised product. The whole premise on which McDonald's is built is the highly American one of providing absolute sameness, total predictability. The Big Mac you get in Wolverhampton is exactly the same as the Big Mac you get in Washington. Eating one *here* (in South Carolina, of all places) will not make a scintilla of difference. *It will taste exactly the same.*' As indeed it did, although the ketchup was dispensed from a metal plunger at a condiments bar into a little cardboard cup, instead of being pre-wrapped, as in the UK. Even Tim admitted that his US McDonald's tasted the same as a UK McDonald's. But it didn't make the need any less. He was so intensely fixated that the evidence before him made no difference.

So the Christmas lunch turns into a marathon bargaining session. My dilemma is multiple. On the one hand, as a man, with a man's inevitably gross and uncultured appetites, I can see the extreme appeal of some foods and the contrasting repulsiveness of others. I can see that food is not something you can just take or leave. I sympathise that much with Tim's sprout problem. On the other hand, I feel the need, as father, to impose my authority and force my kid to eat something good for him. At the same time, I feel the old itch to impose some kind of mean arbitrary penalty if he doesn't (withhold the ice cream, no cake). And on top of that, as father, as the master of ceremonies, the person to whom everyone is looking for a lead, I must quell my anger at Tim's bleating and keep the event cheerful. I can, of course, hold out indefinitely, waiting for Tim to crack, because I know that a normal child in normal circumstances will not starve itself to death. It will eat an apple or orange or whatever other pious material you're trying to force down it, even a Brussels sprout, given enough time and resolution. Although, having said that, Alistair has a mate who will *only* eat salami, bread and ketchup and will quite placidly starve rather than try anything different. The crucial thing is, though, that this Christmas meal is in danger of becoming the opposite of what food ought to be. What it ought to be is either a touchstone of familial love and caring – the traditional centrepiece of the emotionally engaged Jewish household, like something out of *Radio Days*. Or it should be a medium of social inclusiveness and integration, as in the endless eating sequence in the first half of Thomas Love Peacock's *Crotchet Castle* ('Here is a very fine salmon before me: and May is the very *point nommé* to have salmon in perfection. There is a fine turbot close by, and there is much to be said in his behalf, but salmon in May is the king of fish . . .'). Instead, however, it's become a token of parental guile and childish perversity, at the same time adding to this by constantly reminding us that our kids' present and future health depends on what they eat now. Broccoli! It stops you getting cancer! Milk! You need it for your teeth and bones! Vitamin A! Carrots! Liver! Sprouts! Roughage! Inedible things! And on top of this, it's an index of the increasing age of our boys as well as being an index of our values. When the boys were small, they had to eat at the table because there was no other way they could get food. For a long time, they had to sit in the highchair and eat (or not) whatever we put in front of them. But now, the boys are starting to get big and mobile and a bit rangy. They don't hang about to sit down. They don't feel the need to behave at a table. They don't care if they eat this or that, or don't eat it. They can get up, wander around, help themselves to something else.

So what do I do with this Brussels sprout? I don't really *do* anything. I just sit and fume, while Susie and the doting grandparents fuss over Tim, removing the sprout and the taint it leaves on the plate and reassuring him that no, he won't have to eat the thing. *Don't worry, dear. You won't have to have it if you don't want it. It's Christmas, after all.* And I have failed to impose my authority, and my children have failed to behave themselves with decorum in mixed company, and worse still, nobody seems to *care* that Tim has shamed me. They just want Christmas to get to the end without imploding messily. And then I catch my father's eye, fleetingly, as he sits at the other end of the table. And I have the strongest impression that he

is conveying the idea, *You were just as bad at his age. Ghastly, isn't it?*
He is reproaching me, Tim and himself all at once. Fair enough, I
think to myself. But then how often did *you* have us all singing in
the back of the car on the way home from Portsmouth?

SEVEN

Now there is only the future, and all I do is worry about it. Alistair has reached that watershed of double figures, no longer a real child, but loitering sulkily on the margin of adolescence. Another year or so and Tim (in a nervous, unintended anxiety pun, I just wrote *Time*) will be there with him. What do I do? I have panics about things that may happen and things that are relatively unlikely to happen. I panic about them more or less equally.

I panic about cigarettes. It's only a matter of time before someone produces that packet of Marlboro's blagged off a father or older sibling and jerks it in my sons' direction. I worry about drugs that I don't know anything about. I don't worry unduly about dope (as we used to call it) because it is a harmless middle-class recreational relaxant. In fact a small part of me looks forward to the day when we can compare old weed lore and I can possibly ponce a fraction off my boys. No, I fret – predictably – about the pharmacopoeia of artificially engineered products, Ecstasy, heroin, crack cocaine – all of which are as unknown to me as deep space.

I fret, too, about their first encounters with drink and the awful messy consequences. This is largely due to the fact that when I look back on my own history of teen alcohol abuse, it is so degraded and depressing (but not as degraded as it could have been, I acknowledge) I wonder how I avoided death or imprisonment. There's a madness about your first few years of heavy drinking which acts as a reproach to you all the rest of your life. But I can't see any way round it. It's just something that happens: the vomiting, the shaming behaviour, the chance to damage yourself physically. And, of course, to get into senseless fights; or just get beaten up in the street. All of which happened to me, all of which I see as an inevitable function of young manhood, all of it awful.

I worry about exams, now, in a way I would never have done five years ago. Exams are no longer something that other people did. They are something that we do, or are cranking ourselves up to do. The consequence of this is that Susie and I now engage in that fretful parent thing and revise in a stricken fashion with our elder son and wonder how, when the younger son is older, we'll find the time to revise with two. Are we doing enough to punish ourselves with vocabulary lists and multiplication tables while darkness falls? Should we be forcing our kids to memorise swathes of the *Upanishads* or *Piers Plowman* on the off-chance it might pep up their GCSEs? I fret about their physical well-being, too. When they were really small, all they had to do was grow. It was a process more or less without adult mediation. We bought the food and pushed it at them and sometimes *into* them. DNA did the rest. But now they are big and they exercise dietary preferences and give way to food impulses, with the result that they are actively harming their bodies. They have fillings. They look pasty-faced after a winter month indoors, bingeing on fruit colas. They plug their arteries with chips and crisps. They listen to my dinner-table counsels with legitimate scepticism, as I angrily ban all choc ices while compressing pecan pie slices and ice cream into my face.

I worry that they may not be making enough friends, or the right friends, or too many undifferentiated friends. I worry that they might be suffering toxic poisoning from the London atmosphere. I worry that they don't use public transport enough, or that when they do, they'll be mugged or kidnapped. I worry that the amount of time I have left to be their father is shrinking: already we have hit the ten-year mark, and by eighteen they will be going away to study (to become plastic surgeons, lawyers specialising in commercial litigation, investment bankers – anything which will make them rich enough to keep us in luxury when we retire), which means that I have had more than half of my time as full-time father. Soon, incredibly soon, they will be gone. And so I worry about what life will be like when we don't have to care for them any more.

I worry about girls, too. Not so much a worry as to whether or not they will be able to *get* girls – or whether they will even *want* to (this latter is something very faintly in the distance: the gay thing, how would I feel *if* it happens, how to relate to something I don't really *know* about, what do you tell the uptight *grandparents*, who cares *anyway*?). Instead, a punishingly stupid and self-indulgent worry as to what will happen to me as and when and if they do get them. I worry that I will start to behave very oddly in the presence of sixteen-year-old females. This is the most absurd fear of all, but it haunts me on a regular basis. What happens if, in a putative existence, a son brings home a girlfriend (assuming that's where his preferences lie; I don't want to be prescriptive about this) and I find myself metamorphosing into a TV dad, this horrible creature with flushed red jowls and a twill shirt and a paisley cravat? I can see it with depressing clarity. I prowl around, inflicting my sweaty aura on the girl by leaning over and saying, *How are you, my dear?* and sitting heavily on the sofa, patting the space next to me, breathing the words, *Don't be a stranger! There's plenty of room!* And I force a gin and tonic on her, mixed insanely strong and hang around, leering, waiting for the consequences. Why am I in the grip of this fantasy? My father never did it to me. He was, indeed, a model of tact and restraint whenever he found me in the compromising presence of women (all right, not something that happened monotonously often). He never lurked around, trying to impose some kind of cheesy sexual presence on them. Why is it such a nightmare? Partly, I suppose, because I mistrust my motives and my capacity for proper behaviour in any circumstances. Partly because what I'm really worrying about – and why I'm projecting this worry into an anxiety scenario – is what sort of person I will appear to be when my sons are old enough to make mature judgments about the adults around them. Up to now, I've just about got away with it because they're too young to know better. But as time goes by and they learn a little more about the world, they'll be in a position to appraise me. Another few years and my cover will be blown.

Piaget again. According to the Swiss savant, we are well into what he calls the *concrete-operational* phase, the stage in which logic and the classification of ideas become apparent in children. Not only that, but we are on the foothills of the next and final stage of development, the stage of *formal operations* – the state which characterises the logical processes of adolescents and adults. In other words, my boys are beginning to be highly advanced in their powers of reasoning, deduction and hypothesising. What they lack is knowledge on which to base their calculations, and maturity. Which they may or may not possess at any time in their lives.

It makes for some spooky encounters. Now we can talk almost as adult-to-adult. There are no big conceptual problems, no difficulty in exchanging ideas. The trick is to remember that my sons are still much younger than me, and will not want to know all about my VAT returns, or why other grown-ups are so irritating, or that experienced airline travellers avoid drinking alcohol on the plane and make sure to stretch their legs at frequent intervals. I find myself drifting off along vague, open-ended trains of thought while I'm driving along and one of my sons is sitting in the passenger seat next to me. I fret over the issues cluttering my mind, as if I were talking to an unusually tolerant, receptive, grown-up friend. It's very nice and relaxing and it's only when a son turns to me and says, with respect to nothing at all, 'What's the biggest piece of food you've ever eaten?' that I realise I have not been having an adult conversation. Conversely, we chew over all the adult topics – drink, women, drugs, sex, money, work – but with the inevitable slant of a ten-year-old. *Did you have any girlfriends before you met Mum? Why haven't you got any money?*

Will it always be like this? I look forward more than ever to the quiet father/son drink in the boozer on a Sunday lunchtime. But I suspect that I will never quite be able to get over the fact that I am the father and they are the sons. And my responses to them will always be modified and restricted by this knowledge. There is no real reason why we shouldn't talk about anything – I don't *think* I've got anything to hide – but, as with my parents and the way they talk to me, I fear that the generation between us will always put some things in the Out tray.

And besides, they may be getting good at reasoning, logical trains of thought, speculative processes; but they still have irrational longings and hatreds, the sort of insane fixations that you can only have when you're really young. Trainers, cricket bats, kagools, Irn Bru chewers, people you know at school, pens with lots of different colours built into them, chunky wristwatches: these can all be things you desire to the point at which you are prepared to pull off your own leg to get them; or with which you will have nothing to do, not even if you are begged, not even if you are paid real money. Parents cannot guess what's in and what isn't. There's no consistency or hidden pattern. There is no hierarchy of wants, in the way that most adults would put a holiday in Mustique above a pair of running shoes. These are just things you love and things you hate, depending on caprice.

Not only that, you can juggle mutually exclusive preferences in your head and make it look commonplace. If you can start to take an interest in girls (and you can at ten these days) how can you simultaneously take an interest in dungeons and dragons type war games? There is no logical consistency here. I point out that girls don't really go for this stuff. Music, I point out (like a broken record) is a much better place to start; although you don't want to get hung up on that, either. Girls want the total personality approach. Girls don't want someone fixated on plague demons and death warriors.

Doesn't make any difference. On the very lip of adolescence, they can keep the Warhammer collection (paintable metal miniatures of spurious monsters with a Terry Pratchett flavour) in their minds at the same time as they memorise aspects of their encounters with girls on holiday. In fact, they can put photographs of the girls in question up on the wall next to renderings of a beast with three tails and a broadsword. I guess for girls of the same age (or younger), it's like putting that Leonardo DiCaprio poster up next to a photograph of a pony. Or wearing nail varnish while you play around on a climbing rope.

Somewhere around here, the world of pure childhood is beginning to turn into something else, a kind of pre-adolescence, an anticipation of an anticipation of adulthood. Which means that while Tim can only look forward to the next big thing, Alistair can look back as well. He can think about the early teenage life that's just about to happen, and even experiment with some of its malpractices. But he can also slip back, out of boredom, or the need for companionship, or even out of goodwill, and do the dumb things his younger brother likes to do, if he decides to. He and Tim will mess around together quite heart-warmingly sometimes, giving me that illusory and short-lived glow of successful parenthood. Then Alistair will decide that he needs to assert his age and status and punch Tim in the leg, quite hard, even though Tim – who fundamentally *likes* Alistair – wants to carry on bonding. I can see why he does it. I just wish he'd make up his mind to be one way or the other: stroppy, angsty pre-teenager, or tousled, messing-around kid. I think Tim feels the same.

They have a way of showing affection which I suppose is tough love. Tim likes to wait until I'm seated, then throws his arms around my neck and tries to snap it. He has come fairly close to strangling me. Sometimes he also plants a vicious kiss on my cheek as a way of levering my head around in the neck lock. At other times, he waits until I'm standing before rushing up, throwing his arms around my waist and digging his sharp chin into my gut. This is exquisitely painful. I cry out and swear at him and tell him never to do it again. But he always does it again. Perhaps he means it as a reproach to my lardiness, which has been coming and going ever since Alistair was born, but is now a pretty permanent silting-up of my body. Alistair is violent, too. He grabs me round the kidneys and crushes me. I have kidney stones, I *know*, because of this. He also likes to jump on top of me when I'm sprawled on the sofa, the way large affectionate dogs sometimes do. He weighs a huge amount, now, because he is a fine, strapping boy, and his weight crushes my inner organs.

So what can I do? I can't tell them to stop, because I love it when they show their fondness, however rough they are. Is this weird? Jacob Bronowski said that 'The wish to hurt, the momentary intoxication with pain, is the loophole through which the pervert climbs into the minds of ordinary men.' Well, I don't *think* it's that, or anything else Krafft-Ebing, *Psychopathia Sexualis*. It's something, I think, to do with the fact that physical expressions of emotion are as strong, literally, as the emotions themselves. You have to crush your old man because that's the only way you'll get his attention and make the point. Hand-holding and cuddling have become jejeune, inadequate; as have hanging round the neck and clinging to the leg. This saddens me, but then cuddling and neck-hanging are things kids can only do when they're really small. Now they have to accommodate not only their maturing feelings, but their maturing proportions as well. Strong affections beget strong actions. So what are they going to do when they're even older? I was once very impressed by an encounter between a dad and his teenage son, at a booze-up I once went to. Son was conventionally surly, indifferent, mussed-up, fifteen or sixteen, par for the course; dad was tall and envy-makingly *décontracté*. I thought that they'd spend the whole event (drinking and shouting: that kind) not talking to each other. At the end, the son would go home sulkily and dad would grin helpless apologies to the other oldsters as they left. But no. The son had his own friends to talk to, as did the father: but now and again they'd pass and smile at each other, and swap a fleeting joke. And on one occasion, the son gave his dad a laid-back kiss on the cheek and dad smiled back. So cool, so undemonstrative, but so affectionate. That must be what I'm hoping for, not least because it fits in with my whole view of the world and human relations: warmth with a cold front, a kind of occluded love, is probably what I'm after. This is why I always feel an almost unbearable tenderness for my boys when they're not there, or when they're asleep. This is why I can miss them but can't always translate my affection into something demonstrative when we're actually together.

   This reached some kind of weird apotheosis when I walked around Finchley on my birthday. It was something I did principally to try and get rid of the mildly recurrent dreams I kept having about my childhood. I thought that by going back to those mundane streets I could remind myself of what it was I was trying to stop thinking about. So I trudged along the enormously long road where we had our first house. I could remember the parade of shops at the roundabout and the layout of the strips of common land where once in a blue moon I used to be taken as a toddler to stumble around and fall over. I couldn't tell which house *exactly* was ours, though. Too samey, too copybook, too Wates the Builders. Still, I had some surges of lost memory washing over me. I got the vibe of being myself and not myself, of accompanying my younger self on the long walk down our road (now some kind of suburban freeway, not the road where I once escaped when very young and where I was recaptured, walking down the central white line). It was all going according to plan. I started to feel sorry for the younger me, seeing a small, solemn, somewhat lonely version of myself walking alongside. I got fairly maudlin and sentimental. It started to rain. I didn't have a raincoat. So I felt even sorrier for myself, for the past me and for the present me. But then the small version of me started to transfigure himself into my sons, a kind of composite of myself and my own children, and I started to feel sorry and tender and protective for *him*, for this compound son. And I wished I could have put out my hand for him to hold, so that he wouldn't feel so lonely and morose, at which point I realised that that would be unfair on whichever son was left without a hand to hold. So I wished that I had both my boys with me, each holding a hand, so that by our collective presences we could comfort each other and remind ourselves that we weren't alone. I was awash with sentiment and rain by this stage. What I wanted above all was that wonderful democratic symmetry of a child's hand to hold on either side, just that wordless affirmation of one another's company, reassuring ourselves that although we were young and insecure, we weren't unloved.

So I trudged on, surrounded by ghosts of myself and my children, wondering where one ended and the next started, feeling comforted and lost at the same time, missing them very much indeed. Then I had enough and caught a bus.

Of course, they know what I do for a living by now. But that's not enough: they want to learn more about the paraphernalia of adult life, the little peripheral *arcana* that adults (no longer *grown-ups*) surround themselves with. They want to know about healthcare provisions (none, in my case) and cholesterol tests. They want to understand something about income tax and tax returns. They love the notion of credit cards. They think electricity bills are smart. Whenever I get a bank statement, I have to wrest it from them if they grab hold of it before I do. In the past, they'd look at the pitiable sum on the bottom line and be awed by it: 'A hundred and forty-eight pounds! That's *a lot*! You could buy four computer games with that!' Older, now, they appreciate that £148 is barely a night out, let alone a working balance, so they wrinkle their noses and ask if I've got any more stashed away (I haven't). *How much do you earn? Are you successful? What do you DO?* It's the school car park nightmare brought into my own home. I have to justify my material worth to my disingenuous children these days, as well as to other parents. Not having a separate office to go to, or a suit to put on in the mornings, or an official job title within the hierarchy, I suppose that what I do must look pretty hand-to-mouth in comparison with the other fathers they meet at their friends' houses. What can I do? How do I raise my status in the eyes of my kids? Do the opposite of Willy Loman (that most tragic of dads) in *Death of a Salesman* –

'Someday I'll have my own business and I'll never have to leave home any more' – and rent a corner in Canary Wharf and carry a briefcase around?

So then they start to speculate about what they might do to earn the money you need to live an even marginally nice life. They evolve strategies in which they divide up their time partly by being sporting heroes; partly by being top-flight barristers; partly by being world-selling children's novelists. I'm deeply worried by the fact that Tim says he wants to write poems and books. I tell him there's no money in it – indeed, I quote to him from the recent *The Cost Of Letters: How Much Do You Think A Writer Needs To Live On?* as a way of putting him off, but it hasn't sunk in yet. Part of me is flattered that they should look to me as a career role model. But I also know that kids automatically first assume that what their parents do is what they will do, before they broaden their horizons and imagine a life wholly other. Unless, of course, they find themselves in one of those medical/legal/academic dynasties which lets no one escape, generation after generation of doctors and doctors. Why, I nearly went for that myself. For years, I assumed that I was going to be a lawyer like my father and his father before him and, yes, his father before him. My parents spent a decade selling me the mendacity that you could be a successful lawyer and writer in the same lifetime. A year at law college taught me that even if I was going to be a terrible writer, I would have made an even worse lawyer: the merciful release of having your options cut down to one. I like to think that I don't have any major plans for my boys' careers: I kid myself that I would be happy if *they* were happy. But I also know that I have, in reality, ruled out careers such as writing, acting, art, singing, playing a musical instrument and juggling – any of the creative/performing careers, in other words. My dread is that one of them will want to fritter away his mental powers chasing the chimera of fame and personal fulfilment. A friend of ours said the other day, wouldn't it be terrible if they ended up doing something boring, like accountancy, or banking, or the law? She must have been mad. I have no problem with any of these fine professions. I will not try and tell my kids that they can be an equally happy investment banker *and* professional sculptor. But I will promote, at the drop of a hat, the incalculable satisfaction that comes from being paid well and having a new car every couple of years.

The corollary of all this interest in my adult business life is an interest in my seedy, personal side. When my kids were half the ages they are now, I could get drunk, or irascible, or dyspeptically over-full of food, or depressed, or hysterical, or just odd, and the chances were that they either wouldn't notice, or I could somehow keep it more or less hidden from them. They were naive enough not to be sure when I was being aberrant, or what was aberrant anyway. But I can't do that now. I have to try to be a respectable human being. This isn't the same as setting an example – doing a George Crabbe and providing a divine template for living. It means that as they have a firmer and firmer grip on the realities of adult life, so I must conform more closely to what an average adult has to do. So I can get slightly drunk, sometimes, because this is an amusing thing to see, and gives the boys some pointers about boozing. I can get fairly irascible, provided I calm down and don't stay that way indefinitely, because that, too, is something that you do in life. I can have rows with other people; and I can find things funny which the boys find pointless and obscure but which they know they will have to find funny at some time in the next five years. It is a gradual unravelling of the mystery of adulthood. Which reminds me that I must make sure that my drawers and shelves are free of contraband/hard drugs/pornography/liquor/secret love-letters, because they will start to go through those next, searching for clues.

And then they will turn their backs on me in disgust and go fully teenage – teetotal, vegetarian, Buddhist. I know *I* did.

Obviously, there was a time when they didn't go for girls. There was a time when you only had to say the word and they made a noise like a clogged wastepipe and held their stomachs. Now, on the other hand, everything is possible. They watch the girls on *Top of the Pops* with their eyes swivelling greasily around almost as much as mine. Tim comes away from his half-hour in front of the TV singing *sexy* and *horny* and gyrating his hips. He is eight. Alistair takes it a bit more seriously, asking which girl singers I find more attractive and why. As an officially de-sexed middle-aged parent, I can't afford to express my feelings too eagerly. So I make some kind of non-committal gesture towards one of the less provocative acts. Alistair chews it over, before going for someone blonde. *It's in the air.*

It's been in the air for a while, actually: the gradual shedding of childish things, the assumption of teenagerhood. Not long ago, we gave their rooms a radical work-over. For a decade, they'd been childish slums. Alistair went through a phase of collecting really big cardboard boxes, huge things, all stuffed one into another to make a beetling kind of tower like Tatlin's *Monument to the Third International*, but without the conference halls inside. Instead, he used all the nooks and crevices to secrete dead toys, drawings, Aeros, vital lost pieces of Lego, orange peel, tapes, socks, comics, glue, severed limbs from action figures, money. Tim had the same feverish mix in his room, but he liked to keep it free-form, at floor level. His room was like one of those terrible apartments you read about in which very old eccentric men discard their consumed matter onto growing garbage heaps, never throwing anything away but allowing it to pile up in mounds, separated only by critical forest tracks to the bed, the door, the table. We'd try now and then to shove the mess into drawers and onto shelves, but after about a week Tim would assert his will and it would all be back around our feet. I suppose if Alistair was Vladimir Tatlin, Tim was more Frank Auerbach, the swirling layers of accretion, the tormented impasto. So we got mad at this one day and repainted the walls, bought some wardrobes, threw out the boxes and the apple cores and debris. Suddenly, their rooms stopped looking like riot aftermaths. They were transformed into young students' dens. We got them desk lamps and noticeboards. We savaged the toy stock and shoved what was left into drawers the size of skips. We stood back and realised that we'd tidied away their childhood and replaced it with the next thing along. These were now young persons' rooms, rooms in which they could spend long hours smoking covertly and listening to – what? The Jesus And Mary Chain? The Pixies? Whatever has taken over from them: depressive new music with which to contextualise your adolescence. They were all at once the kind of rooms that I remembered only just quitting. The rooms in which I'd experienced at least half of my formative moments: now my boys were in them.

And the pattern of play has changed – either because the environment's changed, or because they've changed. Now they spend time skulking in the teenage fashion with and without their mates. They go and make smells and strange noises, privately, for hours. I welcome this. This is exactly what they should be doing. I was never happier than when slouching alone on the floor, watching the afternoon shadows lengthen to the point at which I realised I was actually sitting in the dark. Unless, of course, I was not just slouched on the floor, but slouched on the floor with a girl who didn't find me physically repellent. That was *real* bliss. Indeed, number one son has made tentative moves towards this. Not as far as getting them to come up to his room – but there was a startling afternoon we spent with some friends who had a daughter the same age. We were doing the paired families thing in a pizza restaurant. Tim was somewhere else at the time, which gave Alistair more room to explore his capabilities; otherwise, he would have spent the meal cussing at his brother and sulking. But there was nothing between him and the opposing daughter that afternoon. And there was my boy, fresh out of shorts, sitting at a table talking and smiling and laughing and talking to a *girl*. And she was sitting there, talking and laughing – girlishly – to my boy who was now starting to look – irritatingly – like a very young estate agent. I couldn't believe it. I had to wait *years* to get into that kind of situation. *Years*. So I was deeply proud and envious of his good fortune: but if anything signals the end of childhood, this must have been it.

What's more, I have even had frank sex and drugs conversations with my boys. God, it felt peculiar. I am not in the least a frank person, although I like to think that I have a tolerant outlook on matters of personal taste. It's not so much that I feel we should take a lot of Class A drugs, or necessarily shag one another in odd ways or couplings. But I do think that our hypocrisy about these things is both stupid and unhelpful. This doesn't mean, on the other hand, that we should stray into libertarianism and all the mad right-wing economic and social concepts that some libertarians are apt to be fond of. Ideally I'd see myself just a micron off Holland or Denmark in social and ethical terms, but without the mix of wackiness/po-facedness that can be a feature of their societies. Where was I? Well, I was saying that even though I subscribe to a broadly northern European, semi-Scandinavian tolerance of sex and drugs, I do get sweaty when I have to discuss these things with others. Even sweatier when I have to *explain* them to my children.

I mean, Susie and I have done that free and frank walking-around-the-house-naked stunt before now, and this has prompted the usual enquiries about body hair and the generative organs. So I suppose that's fulfilled its purpose. But it's not something I enjoy doing; and when I try to answer those questions about body hair and the generative organs, I can get awkward about the details. In fact, if I'm caught at the wrong moment, in the wrong frame of mind, I don't answer at all, but do my hiding act (see Chapter Five) and hope that Susie will answer for me. Worse, when something comes on the TV – breasts, TV sex, adult language, mature topics – then of course the guys pick it up with bat-like precision and play it back to me. And half the time I do the pitiable grown-up's dodge of starting to answer and then breaking off to point out (with mad and totally unfamiliar enthusiasm) some item of interest which has taken its place on the screen (*What an interesting tree!*). They know that's what I'm doing, as well. But they can still be distracted by TV at this age; and will always give it the benefit of the doubt over straight human discourse.

So that's how I deal with it normally. But I have, once or twice, managed to have one of those pant-wettingly upfront conversations about relationships, feelings for others, sexual intercourse, conception and contraception. The last time it happened, I was driving the car. This was a breakthrough, because it meant that I could avoid catching anyone's eye in the middle of my speech and embarrassing myself. Being at the wheel also meant that I could use driving as a way of moderating the exchange, introducing delays in which I could check a given train of thought for booby-traps. *Hold on! Let me just deal with this road junction!* Or, *Will you look at that! He pulled right out in front of that van! Moron! Now, what was I saying?* We covered a lot of useful ground that way.

So the sex talk is pretty straightforward. Broadly, we are all in favour of it, but there are certain provisos and protocols that have to be dealt with. Still. This is something that I can speak on more or less authoritatively. Also we have the broad moral catch-all that just about all consensual sex is okay provided it is consensual. Thus I have done my *Forty Years On* talk ('When you get down here, things aren't straightforward at all . . . It's not pretty, but it was put there for a purpose . . . If anyone touches you there, that person is wicked . . .') more or less without tensing myself to death. And I have done my pious *It's the feelings as much as the act itself* rap: about as meaningful as advanced number theory to a pre-adolescent boy. And I'm aware that there are areas of sexual experience that I know nothing about in a practical sense and so can't advance much advice about. But, illness, illegality and injury aside, I have tried to sound fairly up and optimistic at the same time as I have laboured away at my points. And I am going to be an outstanding source of wisdom on the subject of what happens when girls dump you and why they do and why this is not necessarily the end of the world. The wreckage of teen and early twenties love affairs/one-night stands/disastrous encounters is going to be a topic on which I can dilate more or less endlessly.

But I am going to be screwed on the drugs talk. Drugs are tricky. They are tricky partly because I cheerfully tolerate soft drugs and freak at the hard. But what about grey-area drugs – Ecstasy, acid, speed? I've only ever tried the last one, and it was in such confused circumstances that I can't accurately remember what my reactions were. As for the other two, friends have taken acid and had the standard mixture of good and bad trips (the same trip, quite often). I was once stuck in a car going from London to York with a photographer who solemnly and at length told me that he didn't smoke, drink or take caffeine, but downed about a tab of acid per day. This aided his creativity and gave him new insights into the visible world. Then he started staring at the windscreen (I was driving, fortunately) and going on about how amazing the other car lights were in the rain. Then he started photographing them through the windscreen. *Amazing* . . . he kept saying. *Too much* . . . Then he turned the radio on. *Oh wow! Jimi Hendrix! Yes!*

What kind of judgment can I extrapolate from an encounter like this? How can I base my fear and horror of heroin (to say nothing of cocaine, far too expensive, apart from anything) on chance meetings with acidheads and recreational dope fans? How can I hold a categorical opinion about something I don't *know*? Where does my authority come from? And if I express an opinion, how do I know that it won't be axiomatically discounted because it's coming from my mouth, from one of the grey generation? Why don't I know any practising junkies (I only ever seem to meet reformed ones) to whom I can point and say, *Don't end up like him?*

These are all frailties, panics, emotional crises, addictions that might or might not happen in the next decade or so. But what about the crack-ups that have already happened? What do you say about the fact that increasingly large numbers of the boys' friends' parents are divorced or getting divorced? Frankly, it's such a commonplace now that I wonder if they do notice it. Or at least, if they notice it once it's a *fait accompli*. When it's still in the air, or in the process of happening, they notice it because the friends to whom it's happening are apt to withdraw and stop being friends quite so much. What form of words do I use to explain and at the same time somehow gloss over the idea that someone's mum and dad are now happy to kill each other and that this will have a lowering effect on their son's frame of mind? I don't want to increase the level of anxiety by saying, truthfully, that people of my generation are perverse, selfish and destructive. I don't want to give the impression that my son's friends are the offspring of a bunch of shits. But they know perfectly well that married people do not present each other with garlands every morning and say, like Brutus in *Julius Caesar*, 'You are my true and honourable wife/As dear to me as the ruddy drops/That visit my sad heart.' I want to give the impression that a messy, rancid divorce is the most natural thing in the world; but not so natural that it is going to happen in his family.

Awkward, when Susie and I are going at each other, not to hint at it, though. And when we're merely going about our business in our usual way, I have to stop myself short sometimes and ask myself, *Should I make more of a show of affection to keep the boys happy?* Or should I show them that you can go around being bitchy and discontented but still, underneath it all, hold the fondest feelings? This was never a problem when they were small. We could fight like savages, assuming that the kids were just too tiny to pick up the vibes. Although come to think of it, they probably did pick up the vibes, and may now be chronically damaged by Susie's trying to take out my brains with a plum, or me smashing my sandwich on the floor. And if they didn't pick up the vibes before, they will definitely pick them up now.

Why am I not an expert at parenting by now? I *must* be. This is a good ten years down the line. I must have acquired a body of knowledge that would pass as expertise. But because children are always ahead of you in the arms race, always contriving new ways to throw you off your line, you can never really use what experience has taught you. With some practice, my nappy-changing technique would still be one of the finest. But I don't change nappies any more. I also know what kills a kids' party (my involvement) and what makes it go (The Animal Men). I can spot a half-decent nursery school. I'm clear on toys for five-year-olds. And none of it is any use to me now. And because parents go through parenthood making decisions on their own (unless meddlesome grandparents get involved, or know-all siblings) without asking around their friends whenever they want to buy a sweatshirt or sit in front of the TV, parents like me don't get interrogated very often for advice. In fact, fathers almost never get interrogated for advice, unless it's for the kind of advice that fathers can only give to other fathers. This is the dodgy, delinquent sort of advice that involves getting out of things or doing complicated and demanding things in a slipshod and disengaged manner. Avoiding most of school sports days (always travel separately) or cooking for other children (make sure there's never anything they might want to eat; they'll get the message and won't come back). Mothers ask each other for advice all the time. Or at least, they don't always ask for advice as such: they talk about problems and dilemmas in a way that encourages the sharing of information and experiences. They elicit advice without necessarily requesting it. I've even seen Susie do this. But fathers don't – partly because they don't want to be tarred with the brush of fussing, perpetually anxious motherhood; partly because most fathers have only got the most arbitrary and random pieces of advice to give, advice which may well be wholly useless.

And yet, I know I'm acquiring some small residue of knowledge. I know this, not because I offer much information, but because I find myself looking at the antics of children smaller than my own, and at the antics of their parents and thinking to myself, *Ah well, I could have told you so*. Or, *He's going to start screaming in a minute. Yep, there he goes*. Or even, *That child is clever/stupid/gifted musically/emotionally disturbed*. These insights flash irregularly across my consciousness and I know them to be true. I am a walking bag of instant hindsights, of *Told you so*'s, of unhelpful recognitions from my own past. Not long ago, I brilliantly diagnosed a case of psychosomatic stomach cramps in a friend's daughter. None the less painful for being psychologically induced (a stress complaint),

I wasn't going to come over all senselessly bracing and dismissive. So I offered this opinion, but it was a waste of knowledge. It wasn't my child, and you can never offer an opinion about someone else's kid. And I was offering it to the mother, and mothers know that the opinions of fathers in sensitive matters of health and welfare (no matter that the father was an engaged, involved me) are just so much crap. So I clammed up.

The pedestrian-minded will point out that even if I can't use my wisdom now, I will be able to use it when I become a grandfather. This is a neatly inclusive approach to life's possibilities, but again, I don't see it happening. My parents have never offered me a word of advice, partly out of tact; partly because they have always claimed that the world when I was young was so different from the world in which my children are young that any tips and tricks would be irrelevant or misleading. Fair enough. That may be what happens when the generations breed at a fairly leisurely rate. Different, I suppose, if you're from a fast-breeder family, and only twenty-two years have elapsed between motherhood and grandmotherhood. The landscape won't have changed that significantly. All the same, grandparents who *do* offer the benefits of their wisdom seem to end up hated by the parents. And I can't see any realistic way of imposing my knowledge on my own children, as and when they do start families of their own, if they don't ask me first. Too awful to contemplate: me in a virtually knee-length cardigan, twill shirt, bushels of hair coming out of my nostrils and ears, lurching up to *my* kids and hectoring them about *their* kids. This is not the function of grandparents.

So what am I going to do with this huge and costly and pointless mass of wisdom and insight? Turn it into a book, of course.

It all comes back to the future. The thing that is hanging over us.

The teenage years. Actually, where we are now is what's known in marketing as the *tweens*. This is a pimply hinterland between the ages of about nine and twelve and has become a meaningful consumer sub-division because children of that age now are rich enough to have consumer preferences. One estimate recently put the total annual tween spend in the States at $50 billion. So this is where we are. But where we are is not where we are going to be in a couple of years. So we look to the real teenagers, the hard core, to fuel our dreads and our fantasies. And they look repulsive, in a way which I am certain I did not. I looked hairy, spotty (God! The spots!), grimy and self-absorbed. I had the kind of lank curtains of hair that tend to slump forward and catch in your teeth; there were often handy bits of food there that I could chew on during the day. I also had festering jeans, scurfy pullovers and the sort of sullen introspection that I sometimes catch on the face of one or other of my boys and which I know will drive me to the lip of insanity, just as it must have done to my parents. What I wasn't, was large, threatening or pissed (at least, very rarely). Which is what all teenagers now appear to me, as I hobble through middle-age.

That they look so repulsive is mainly a function of my sensibilities. I can tell I am getting old because I see all young people as threatening. In this, I am showing no more than the usual symptoms. Old people always find young people threatening and hideous. The historian Sir Arthur Bryant wrote in 1954 about 'the drifting youth of the welfare state,' as they then were. These scumbags became 'the inevitable prey of the gang-leader or at best, grow up to lead, despite all the material opportunities of our age, inert, stunted and purposeless lives.' Even the BMA had a go, arguing (in a 1961 paper entitled *The Adolescent*) that 'the adolescent can take on an alarming aspect: he has learned no definite moral standards from his parents, is contemptuous of the law, easily bored . . . He is vulnerable to the influence of TV programmes of a deplorably low standard . . .' All I can do is nod and mutter a footling agreement. And when youth aren't the object of the horrified fascination of the BMA and Sir Arthur Bryant, they're the object of the horrified fascination of cheesy middle-aged film-makers: *Rebel Without A Cause* (Nicholas Ray, 1955); *Badlands* (Terrence Malick, 1973); *Quadrophenia* (Franc Roddam, 1979) and *Kids* (Larry Clark, 1995).

There is a seeping climate of hysteria out there and I am happy to be a part of it. Teenagers are wastrels and vandals, tippling, puking, fighting and breaking off car aerials. This is what they do. I know this because even I tried to do this when I was a teenager. Less of the fighting, more of the drunkenness, and the nearest I generally got to vandalism was an anarcho/conceptualist gesture I used to make around Finchley when I was about fifteen. I used to find the home of one of the wealthier inhabitants, take an old crisp packet (so I couldn't be traced) and write DIE CAPITALIST EXPLOITER on it in Biro and post it through the letterbox. Then run like the wind. Instead of the revolution, of course, we got Margaret Thatcher, but it's no use telling my boys that. They'll do graffiti and drugs and sex and will be transformed from the faultless creatures they are now into youth-custody jobs.

Unless they go the other way. This is the *really* baffling thing about teenagers. Parents of teenagers invariably roll their eyes and start trembling when they stop to recall their depravities. *Just you wait* is all they say to us. But at the same time, I have come across a number of genuinely likeable, charming teenagers – clearly teenagers, horrible to look at, dog-like, greasy, thin, preening, but still charming. There was the boy who kissed his dad on the cheek. There are baby-sitters who are still at school but who can be nicer at sixteen than I am now. And there was an occasion when a couple we knew celebrated a wedding anniversary. They had a year or so up on us, and had three kids, mid- to late-teens, real trouble-maker stuff. They certainly looked the part – cropped hair, nose studs, knock-off athletic gear – but, unbelievably, *they put on a show to amuse their parents*. I mean, one played the piano while another (a daughter) sang a song. And the third got up and delivered a witty and beguiling speech about his parents and the fact they'd been together so long. I was incredulous. In fact, I wasn't the only one who was incredulous. The room was full of parents, all with their mouths hanging open or with their eyes twinkling with liquid approval. We applauded for about ten minutes non-stop when it was all over, scarcely able to believe what we had seen. Come to think of it, this wasn't the first time the children had distinguished themselves. I can remember them coming round to our house some years earlier and playing with our children (who were only small and dirty and banal at the time) generously, unassumingly: building things out of Duplo that I could never have imagined. Keeping them rapt. It was unnerving.

And rather than console me with the notion that teenagers might be other than leering delinquents, this makes me wonder: how on earth will my boys ever become these smiling, engaged nonpareils? What have I done to make it possible? Anything? Or have I so organised things so far that they can only become sullen and asocial?

A series of pictures taken just over ten years ago. Alistair hasn't quite reached his first birthday. It's hard – it's virtually impossible – to believe that it's him: pudgy, round-faced, blond-haired, dwarfish, a prototype of what he will become. A baby, mysteriously lodged in among our semi-randomly-ordered collection of photo-essays of children and adults. In one shot, he's with a similarly-aged friend. We called this other child Globule at the time. One of those random furtive cruelties parents find so easy: Globule used to sit on the floor a lot with his mouth open and a bead of spit dangling from his chin. In the photo, they're both in a park, somewhere I don't recognise: must have been one of Susie's afternoons. Globule's grinning stupidly and poking his tongue out, the cretin. Alistair, on the other hand, is looking curiously at the camera, his mouth set in a thoughtful, appraising pucker. Evidently thinking, learning. That's my boy.

Another series of pictures, five or six years on. We are at an airfield in Hampshire. I have been sent there by a newspaper to go up with an aerobatic squadron of Tiger Moth aircraft. These are little pre-War biplanes – open cockpits, struts, wires, a sort of big car engine turning the propellor. You can see that the sky is black with an approaching thunderstorm. We duly fly into this: *Might get a bit bumpy*, shouts the pilot of my plane above the din as we lurch through the sky. It is appallingly cold and horrible. I spend most of the flight with my gloves pressed over my mouth so as not to vomit in the pilot's classic machine. No one on the ground can spot this, of course, so they wander off to the nearby army museum to look at tanks. But before that, the boys – the *boys*, a pair now – pose with me in the background, standing on the runway, trying not to crap in my strides. Alistair now looks like a real kid, the mop of brownish hair, the face longer, evidently shouting some sort of important instruction to Susie behind the camera. He's wearing a sweatshirt that Tim only stopped wearing last year. And of course, there is Tim beside him – past the toddler stage, but still amazingly younger than he is now. His cheeks are rounder, his eyes bigger and browner. He used to turn his eyes on people, like chocolatey foglamps, to win their favours. If it was a woman whose attention he was trying to grab, she would nine times out of ten fall for it and fawn over him. Tim has always had this knack, still has it. He has always been unnaturally good, when motivated, at charming grandparents, friends, the parents of friends, schoolteachers, strangers in hotels. We used to listen, and still do, with amazement to stories of Tim's allure. Not that we can't see it – he can easily charm *us*, any time – but that we almost never get it. He woos the outside world and then comes home and treats us like ordure. Which is his prerogative. We are his parents, after all.

And now, we come almost up to date – pictures taken last year, on the American trip. They're standing in front of a huge black stretch limo outside the Ritz Hotel, San Francisco (we went inside to look at the toilets, trusting that our English accents would account for our well-bred shabbiness). They're both great big strapping boys. They both wear enormous shoes, sweatshirts you could lose a pig in, jungly haircuts. They both pose for the camera now, instead of shouting impulsively at the cameraman or looking in the opposite direction, distracted by a passing moment. They know that this is a small, semi-formal moment in life and that they must act in a particular way. Not that they always do act in the way required: quite often, they do the opposite of what the rest of society wants. But at least they now know that there is a context and it expects a certain kind of behaviour. They both put on rather correct smiles, and Alistair places his hand fraternally on Tim's shoulder, instead of playfully trying to choke the life out of him. They are getting older.

But they're still in that hallowed state of being able to grow *up* without actually growing *old*. They've been ageing – if you want to put it that way – since the moment of conception. But it doesn't appear that way. Instead, they've been growing up, maturing, and will carry on doing so until – when? Some time in their twenties, when they peak, and have all the intellectual powers and physical attributes of maturity, but are still incontrovertibly *young*. Only after that will they start to age. And what about the parents, meanwhile?

What about the discrepancy between those two pictures of me pre-kids and post-kids? Is there an account of this, somewhere in the background of these other pictures? Because we are in the background now. Whereas once there was only us to photograph, plus our friends and relations, now there are only our kids to photograph, plus *their* friends and relations. So Susie and I are much more like walk-ons, or like Rosencrantz and Guildenstern, speaking parts but relegated to the odd line here and there.

So how *did* it happen? How did I get from fresh-faced *ingénu* to rat-faced tyrant? At what point did I become both porky and haggard? Why am I looking so shattered, even though – so far – my kids have been, taking the broad view, wonderful? Are my boys twin Dorian Grays, absorbing my energies and youthfulness and leaving me as the loathsome wreck in the attic? Or would I have looked like this even if I hadn't had children? Would I have looked even older and wreckier?

Well, I'll tell you: I'm not going to try and answer. I'm not going to ask any more questions even. Apart from all the emotions, experiences, love, fury, happiness, bankruptcy and exhaustion they bring, not the least of my boys' gifts is that they put an end to speculation. They live in the here-and-now, *right* now. And they will not put up with soul-searching when there is food to be eaten or friends who need to be visited or important stuff to go and buy. They make you live absolutely in the present. And that is the best.

Now you can order superb titles directly from Abacus

☐ Up North: Travels Beyond the Watford Gap	Charles Jennings	£6.99
☐ People Like Us: A Season Among the Upper Class	Charles Jennings	£6.99
☐ Greenwich: The Place Where Days Begin and End	Charles Jennings	£10.00
☐ The Big Picture	Douglas Kennedy	£5.99
☐ Frost on my Moustache	Tim Moore	£6.99

──────────────── ⟨ABACUS⟩ ────────────────

Please allow for postage and packing: **Free UK delivery**.
Europe; add 25% of retail price; Rest of World; 45% of retail price.

To order any of the above or any other Abacus titles, please call our credit
card orderline or fill in this coupon and send/fax it to:

Abacus, 250 Western Avenue, London, W3 6XZ, UK.
Fax 0181 324 5678   Telephone 0181 324 5517

☐ I enclose a UK bank cheque made payable to Abacus for £...........

☐ Please charge £........... to my Access, Visa, Delta, Switch Card No.

Expiry date ☐☐☐☐ Switch Issue No. ☐☐

Name (Block Letters please) _____

Address _____

_____

_____

Post/zip code: _____ Telephone _____

Signature _____

Please allow 28 days for delivery within the UK. Offer subject to price and availability.

Please do not send any further mailings from companies carefully selected by Abacus   ☐